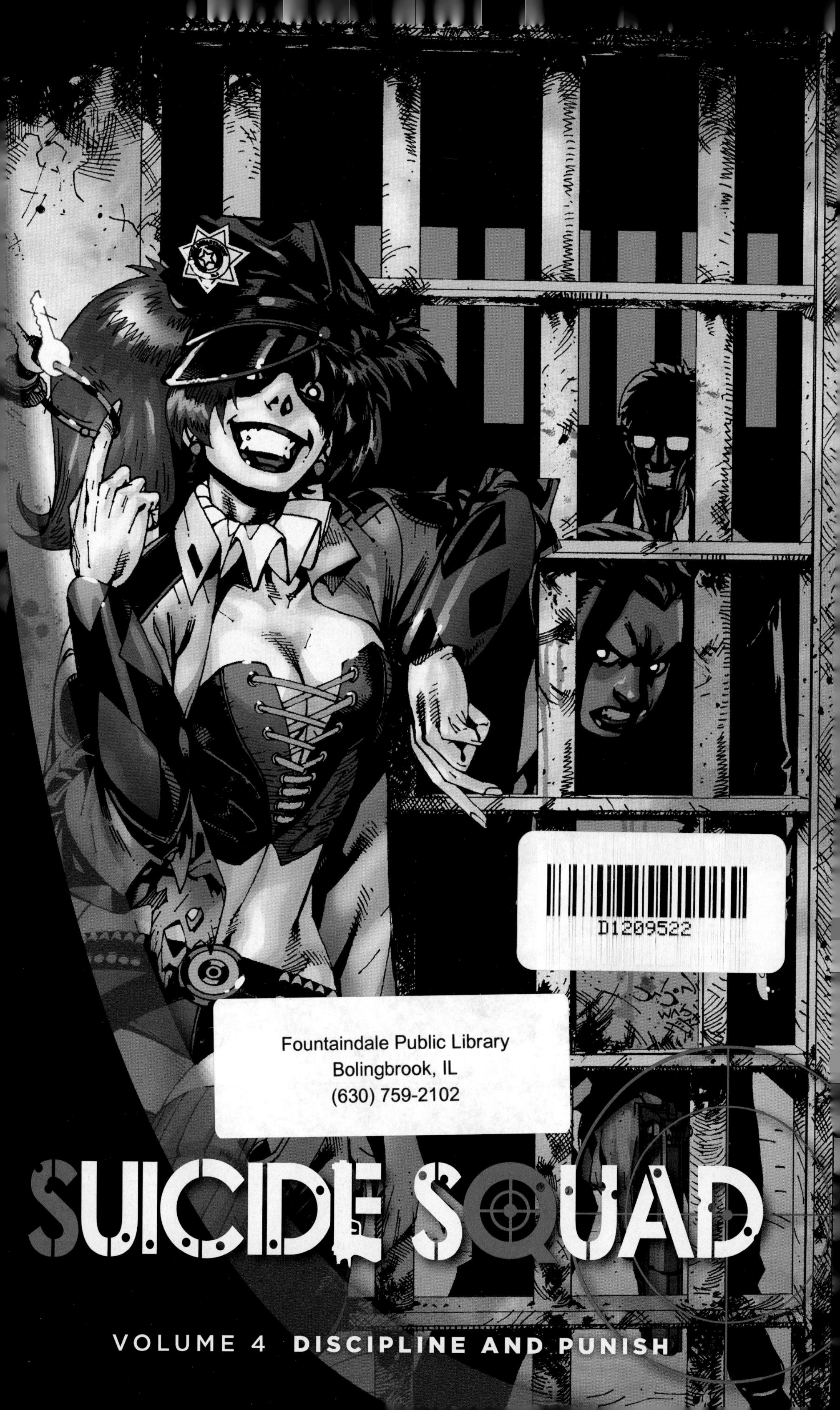

SUICIDE SQUAD

VOLUME 4 **DISCIPLINE AND PUNISH**

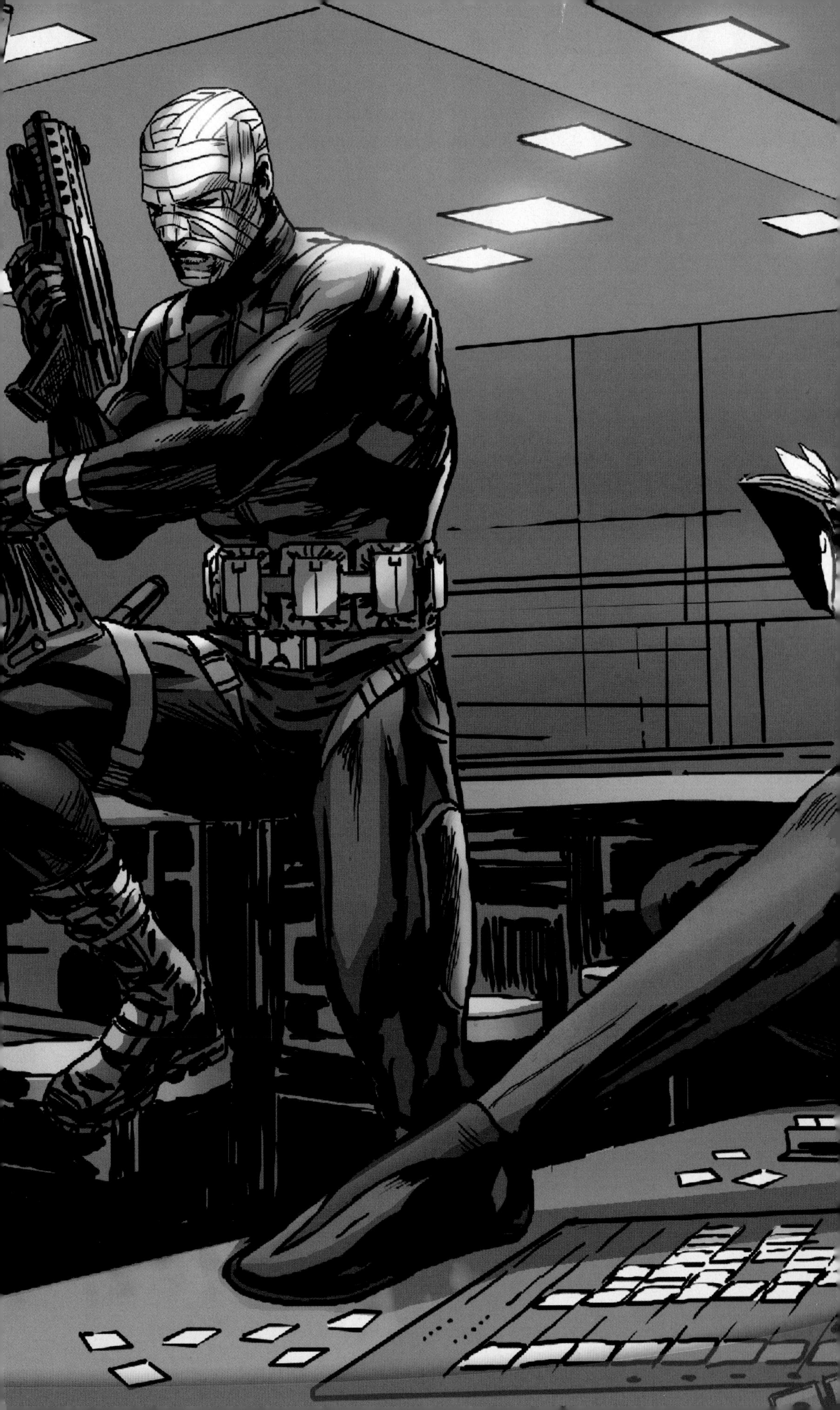

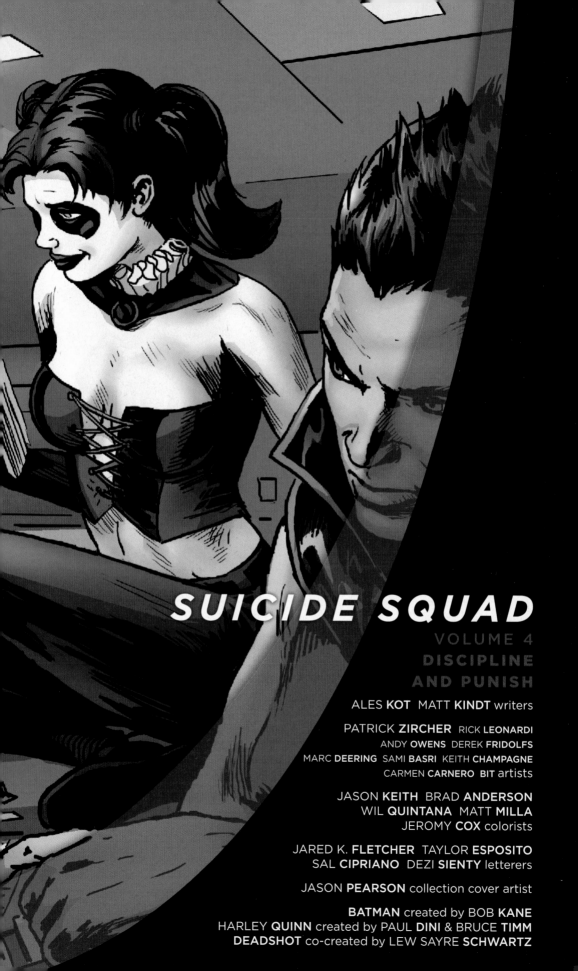

SUICIDE SQUAD

VOLUME 4
DISCIPLINE
AND PUNISH

ALES **KOT** MATT **KINDT** writers

PATRICK **ZIRCHER** RICK **LEONARDI**
ANDY **OWENS** DEREK **FRIDOLFS**
MARC **DEERING** SAMI **BASRI** KEITH **CHAMPAGNE**
CARMEN **CARNERO** **BIT** artists

JASON **KEITH** BRAD **ANDERSON**
WIL **QUINTANA** MATT **MILLA**
JEROMY **COX** colorists

JARED K. **FLETCHER** TAYLOR **ESPOSITO**
SAL **CIPRIANO** DEZI **SIENTY** letterers

JASON **PEARSON** collection cover artist

BATMAN created by BOB **KANE**
HARLEY **QUINN** created by PAUL **DINI** & BRUCE **TIMM**
DEADSHOT co-created by LEW SAYRE **SCHWARTZ**

BRIAN CUNNINGHAM WIL MOSS Editors – Original Series HARVEY RICHARDS Associate Editor – Original Series
ROWENA YOW Editor ROBBIN BROSTERMAN Design Director – Books
ROBBIE BIEDERMAN Publication Design

BOB HARRAS Senior VP – Editor-in-Chief, DC Comics

DIANE NELSON President DAN DIDIO and JIM LEE Co-Publishers
GEOFF JOHNS Chief Creative Officer
JOHN ROOD Executive VP – Sales, Marketing and Business Development
AMY GENKINS Senior VP – Business and Legal Affairs NAIRI GARDINER Senior VP – Finance
JEFF BOISON VP – Publishing Planning MARK CHIARELLO VP – Art Direction and Design
JOHN CUNNINGHAM VP – Marketing TERRI CUNNINGHAM VP – Editorial Administration
ALISON GILL Senior VP – Manufacturing and Operations HANK KANALZ Senior VP – Vertigo and Integrated Publishing
JAY KOGAN VP – Business and Legal Affairs, Publishing JACK MAHAN VP – Business Affairs, Talent
NICK NAPOLITANO VP – Manufacturing Administration SUE POHJA VP – Book Sales
COURTNEY SIMMONS Senior VP – Publicity BOB WAYNE Senior VP – Sales

SUICIDE SQUAD VOLUME 4: DISCIPLINE AND PUNISH

DC Comics, 1700 Broadway, New York, NY 10019
A Warner Bros. Entertainment Company.
Printed by RR Donnelley, Salem, VA, USA. 3/28/14. First Printing.

ISBN: 978-1-4012-4701-0

Library of Congress Cataloging-in-Publication Data

Kot, Ales, 1986- author.
Suicide Squad. Volume 4, Discipline and Punish / Ales Kot ; illustrated by Patrick Zircher.
pages cm. — (The New 52!)
ISBN 978-1-4012-4701-0 (paperback)
1. Graphic novels. I. Zircher, Patrick, illustrator. II. Title. III. Title: Discipline and Punish.
PN6728.S825K68 2014
741.5'973—dc23
                                          2014000328

SUSTAINABLE   Certified Chain of Custody
FORESTRY   At Least 20% Certified Forest Content
INITIATIVE   www.sfiprogram.org
               SFI-01042
               APPLIES TO TEXT STOCK ONLY

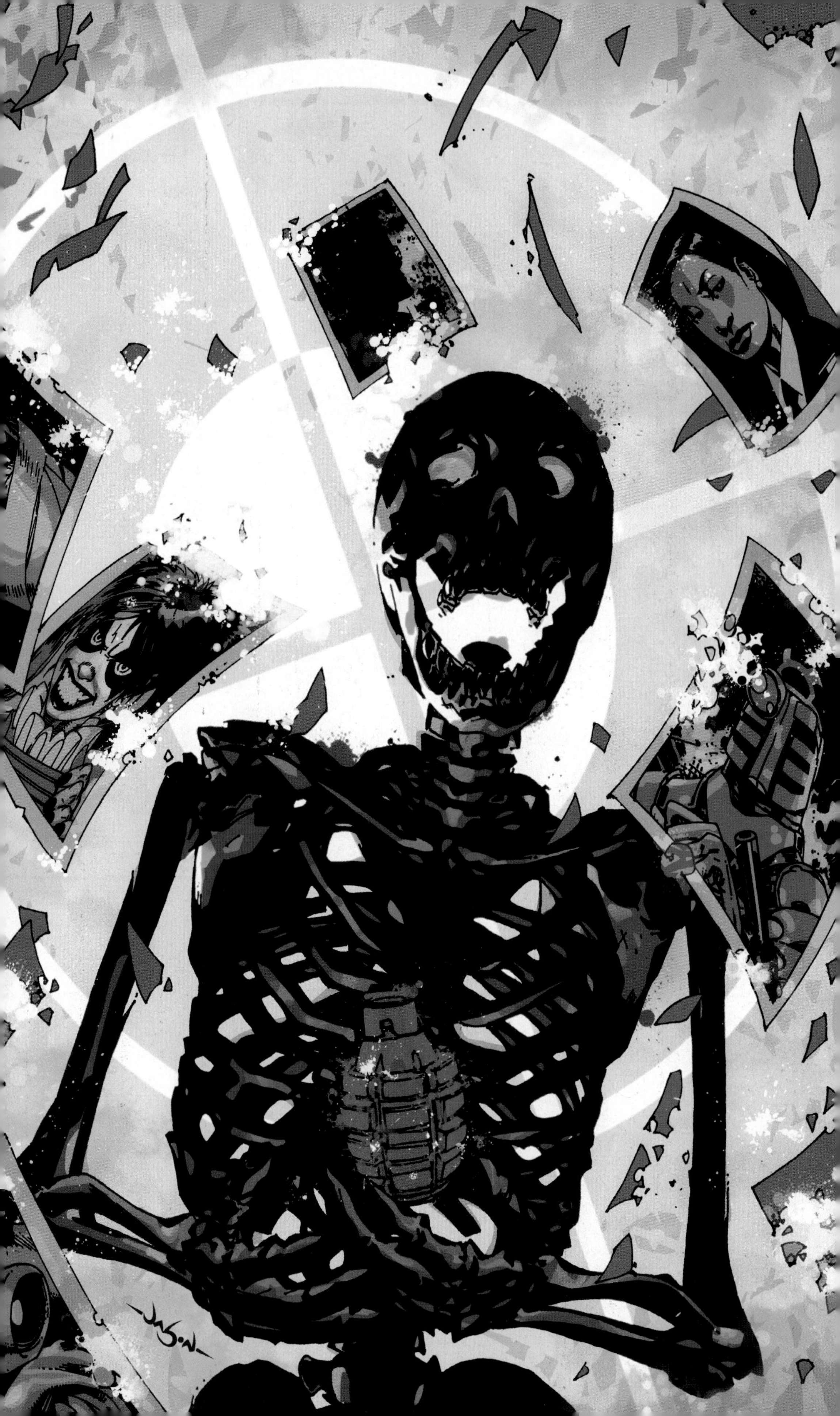

DISCIPLINE AND PUNISH: PART ONE

ALES KOT writer **PATRICK ZIRCHER** artist cover by **JASON PEARSON**

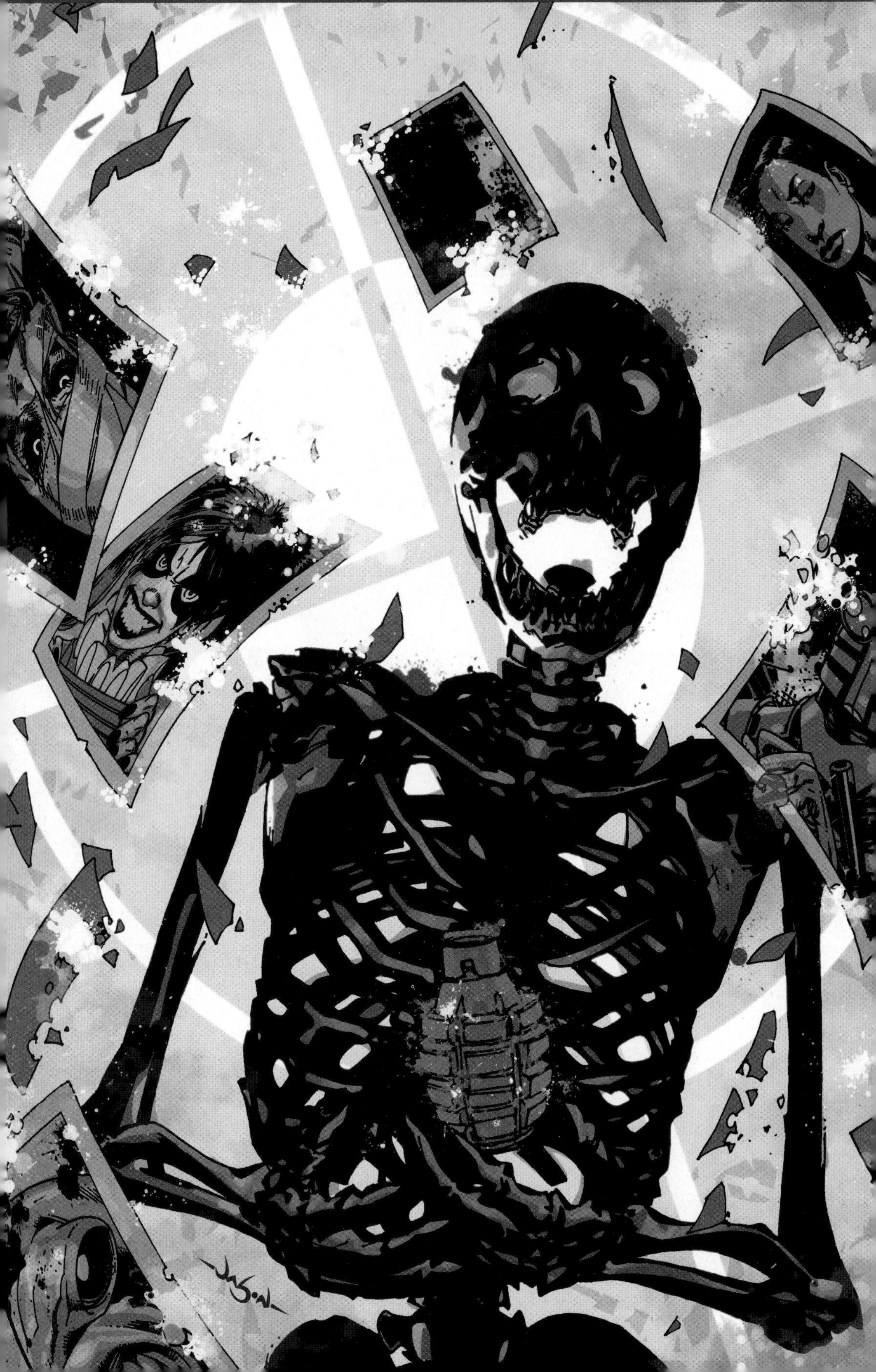

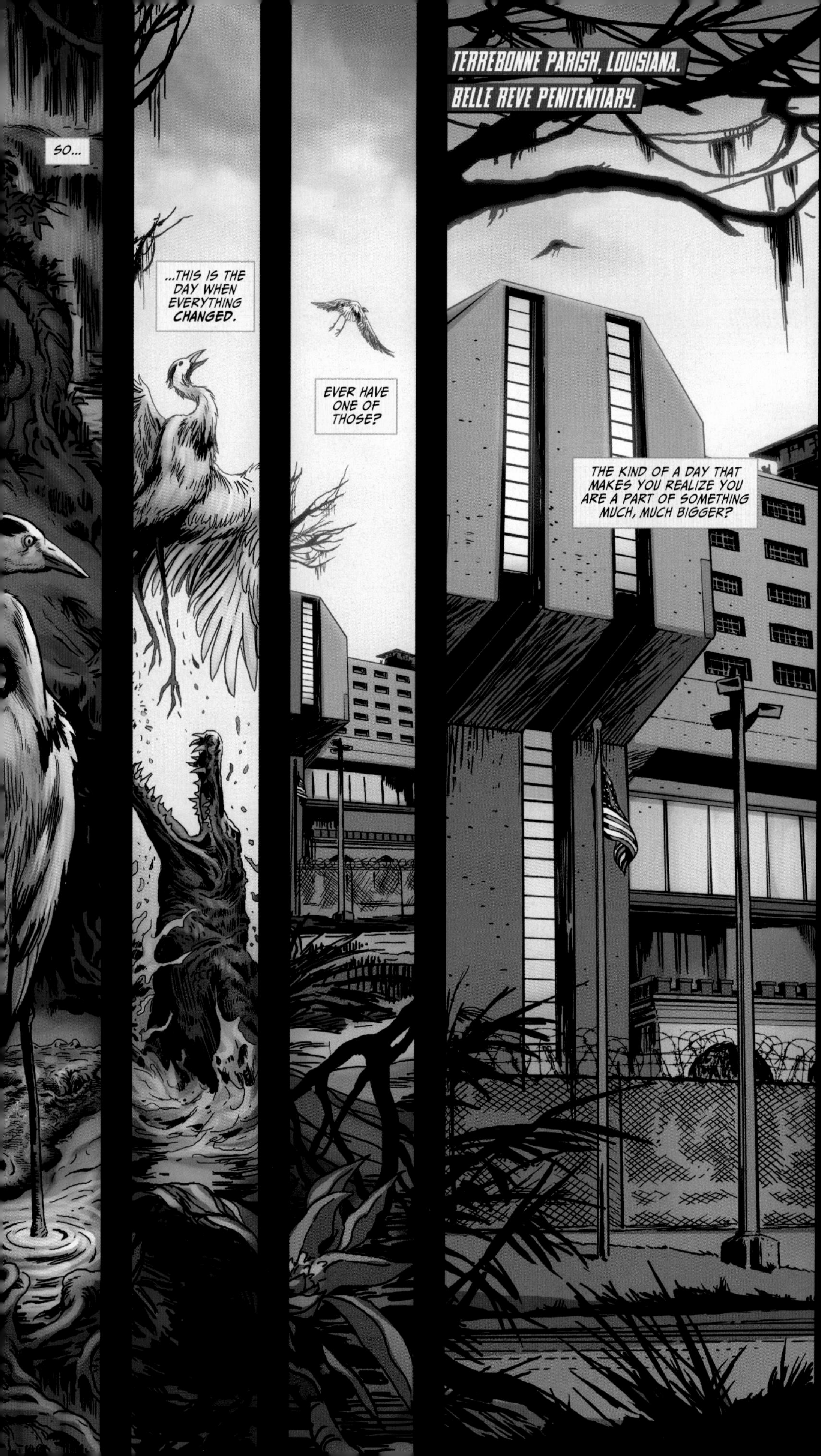
TERREBONNE PARISH, LOUISIANA.
BELLE REVE PENITENTIARY.
SO...
...THIS IS THE DAY WHEN EVERYTHING CHANGED.
EVER HAVE ONE OF THOSE?
THE KIND OF A DAY THAT MAKES YOU REALIZE YOU ARE A PART OF SOMETHING MUCH, MUCH BIGGER?

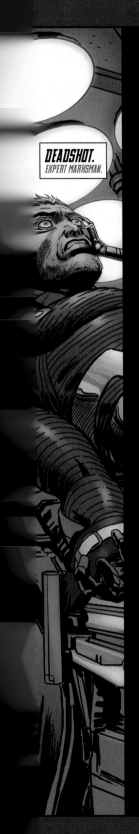

DEADSHOT.
EXPERT MARKSMAN.

VOLTAIC.
GENERATES ELECTRICAL ENERGY.

HARLEY QUINN.
PSYCHOANALYST. PSYCHO.

THE UNKNOWN SOLDIER.
NEWEST MEMBER OF THE TEAM.
AMANDA WALLER'S HOUND.

CLASSIFIED.

KING SHAR
RAW POWER.

DISCIPLINE AND PUNIS
PART ONE OF TI

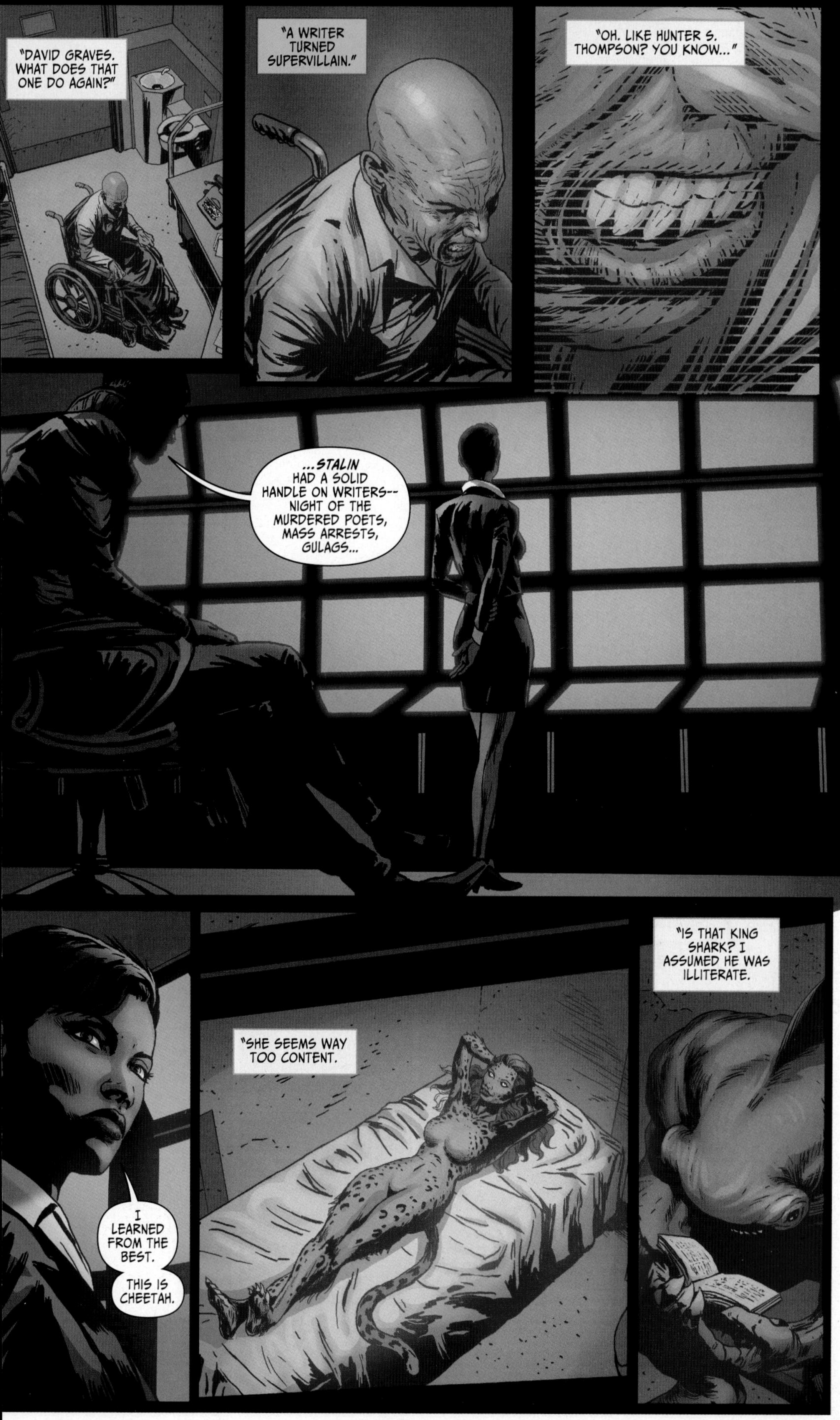
"DAVID GRAVES. WHAT DOES THAT ONE DO AGAIN?"
"A WRITER TURNED SUPERVILLAIN."
"OH. LIKE HUNTER S. THOMPSON? YOU KNOW..."
...STALIN HAD A SOLID HANDLE ON WRITERS-- NIGHT OF THE MURDERED POETS, MASS ARRESTS, GULAGS...
I LEARNED FROM THE BEST.
THIS IS CHEETAH.
"SHE SEEMS WAY TOO CONTENT.
"IS THAT KING SHARK? I ASSUMED HE WAS ILLITERATE.

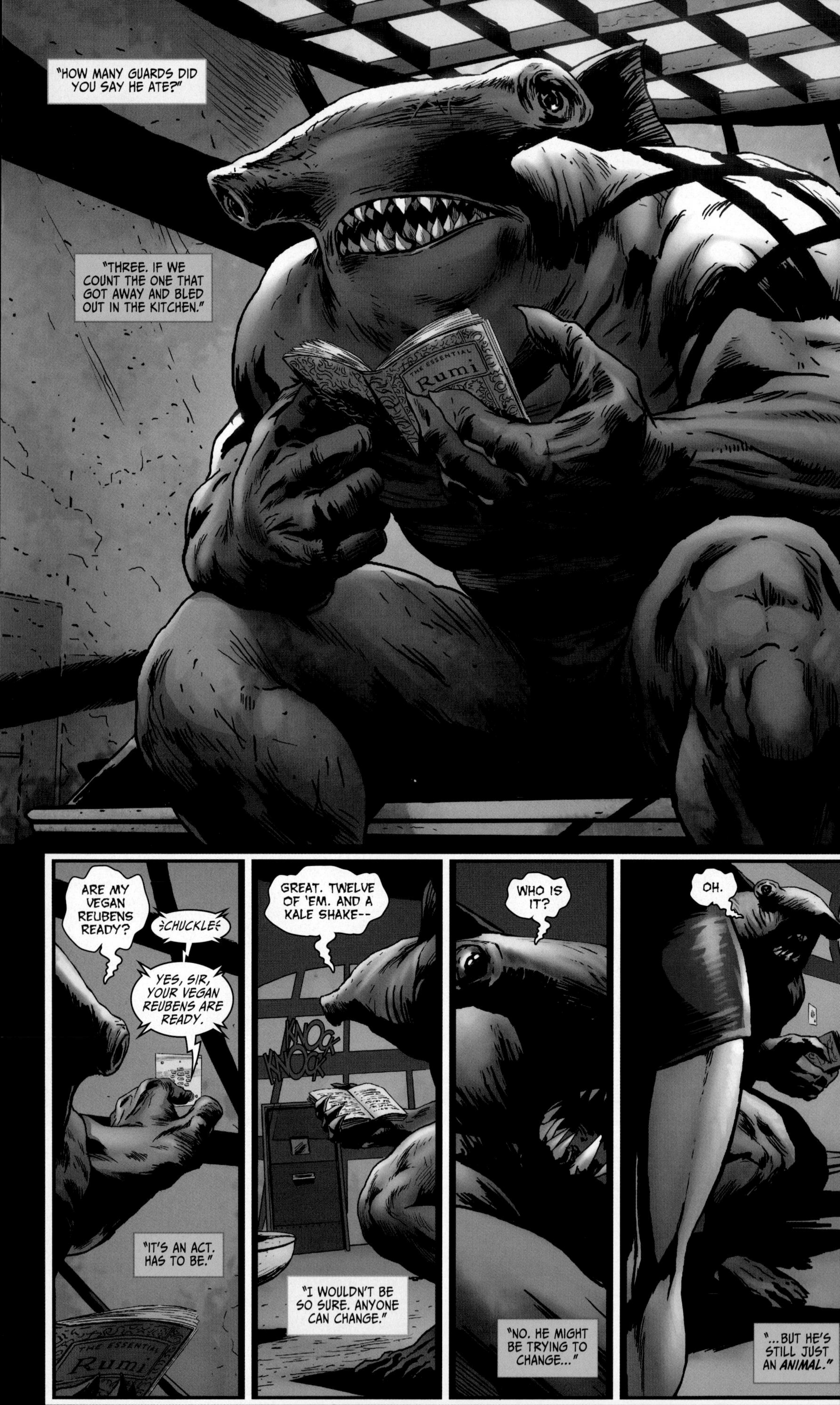
"HOW MANY GUARDS DID YOU SAY HE ATE?"
"THREE. IF WE COUNT THE ONE THAT GOT AWAY AND BLED OUT IN THE KITCHEN."
THE ESSENTIAL Rumi
ARE MY VEGAN REUBENS READY?
CHUCKLE
YES, SIR, YOUR VEGAN REUBENS ARE READY.
"IT'S AN ACT. HAS TO BE."
THE ESSENTIAL Rumi
GREAT. TWELVE OF 'EM. AND A KALE SHAKE--
KNOCK KNOCK
"I WOULDN'T BE SO SURE. ANYONE CAN CHANGE."
WHO IS IT?
"NO. HE MIGHT BE TRYING TO CHANGE..."
OH.
"...BUT HE'S STILL JUST AN ANIMAL."

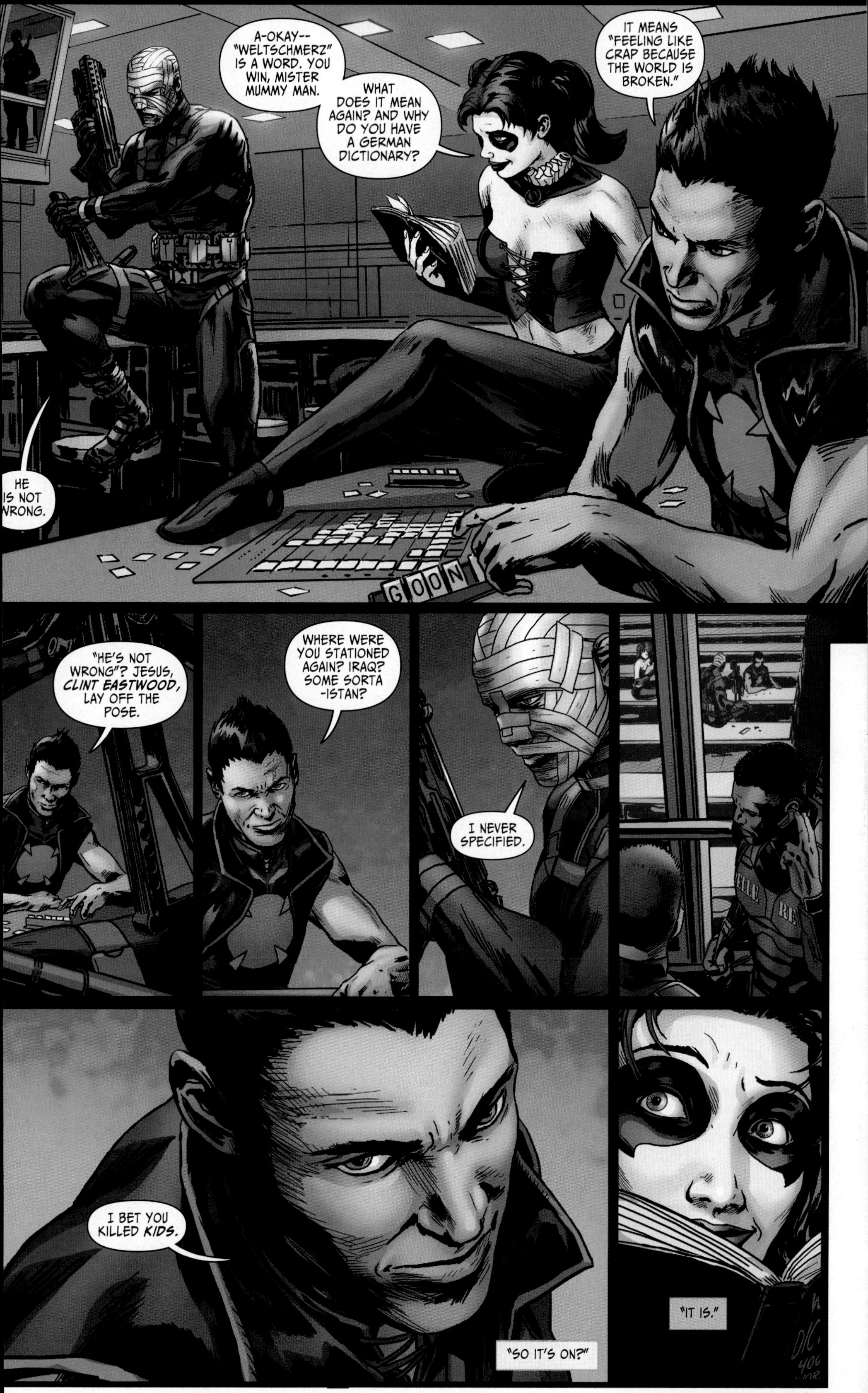
A-OKAY-- "WELTSCHMERZ" IS A WORD. YOU WIN, MISTER MUMMY MAN.
WHAT DOES IT MEAN AGAIN? AND WHY DO YOU HAVE A GERMAN DICTIONARY?
IT MEANS "FEELING LIKE CRAP BECAUSE THE WORLD IS BROKEN."
HE IS NOT WRONG.
GOON
"HE'S NOT WRONG"? JESUS, CLINT EASTWOOD, LAY OFF THE POSE.
WHERE WERE YOU STATIONED AGAIN? IRAQ? SOME SORTA -ISTAN?
I NEVER SPECIFIED.
I BET YOU KILLED KIDS.
"SO IT'S ON?"
"IT IS."

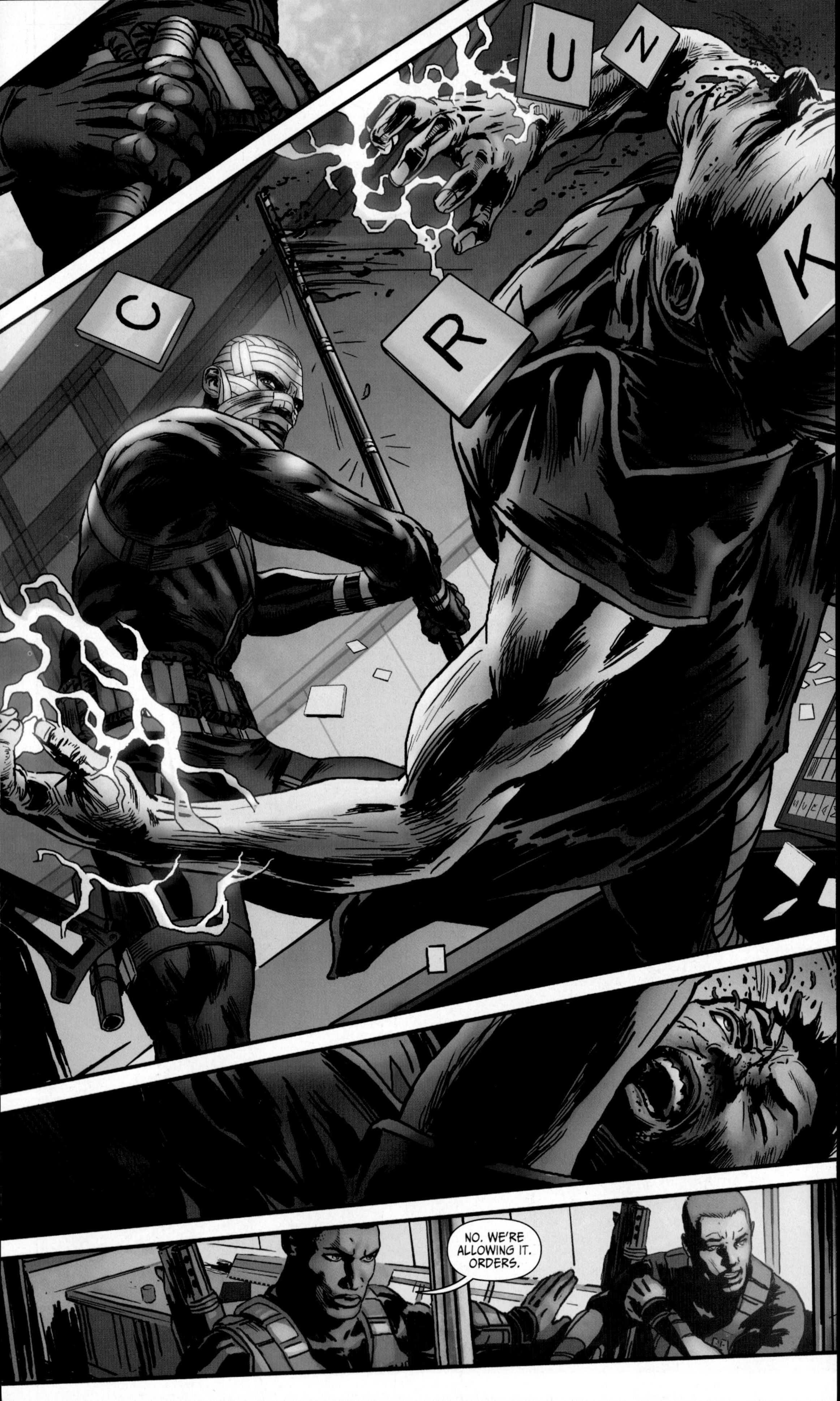

CRUNK
NO. WE'RE ALLOWING IT. ORDERS.

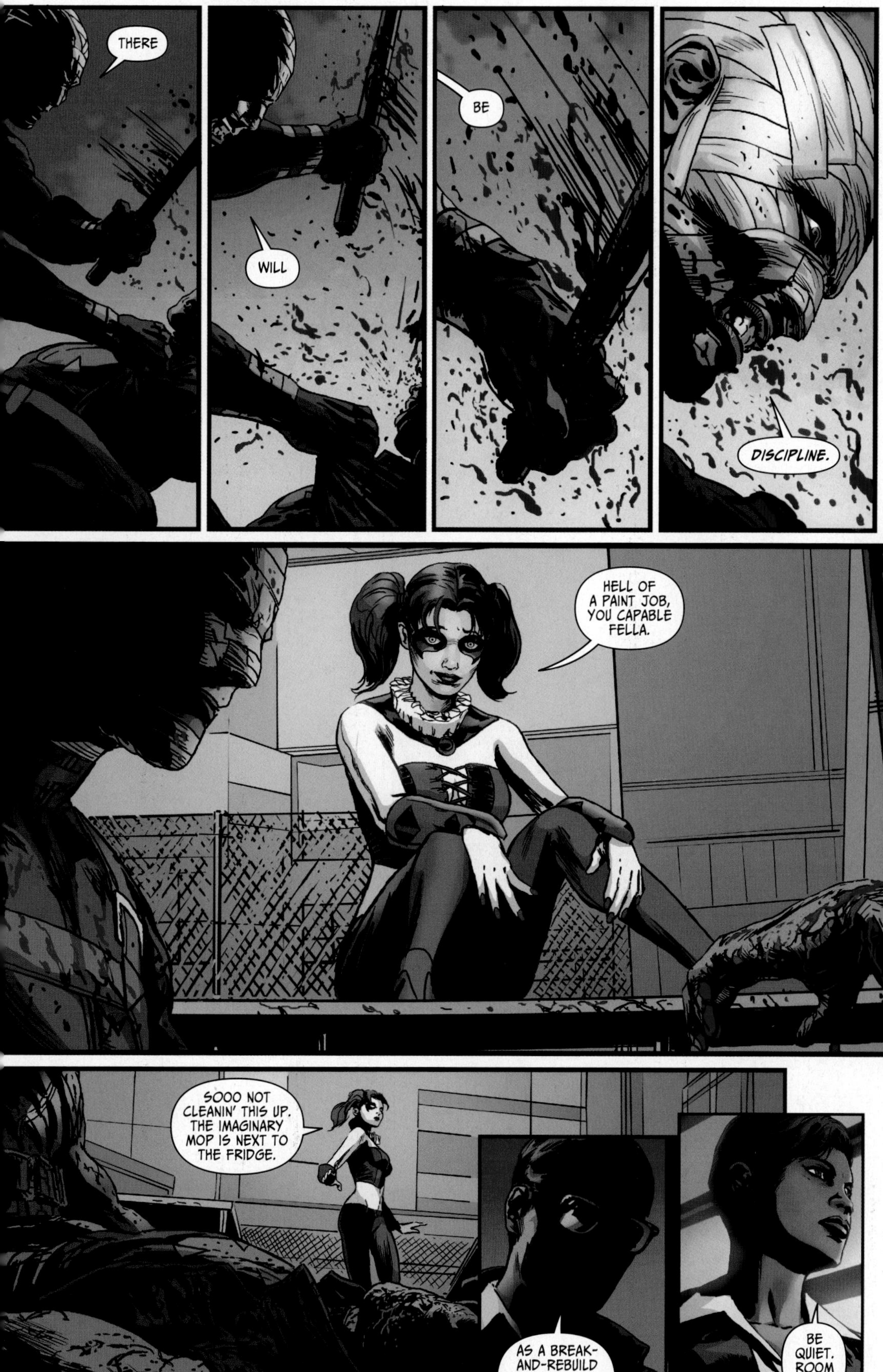
THERE
WILL
BE
DISCIPLINE.
HELL OF A PAINT JOB, YOU CAPABLE FELLA.
SOOO NOT CLEANIN' THIS UP. THE IMAGINARY MOP IS NEXT TO THE FRIDGE.
AS A BREAK-AND-REBUILD EXPERIENCE, THIS IS REALLY DEVIOUS.
BE QUIET. ROOM FOUR.

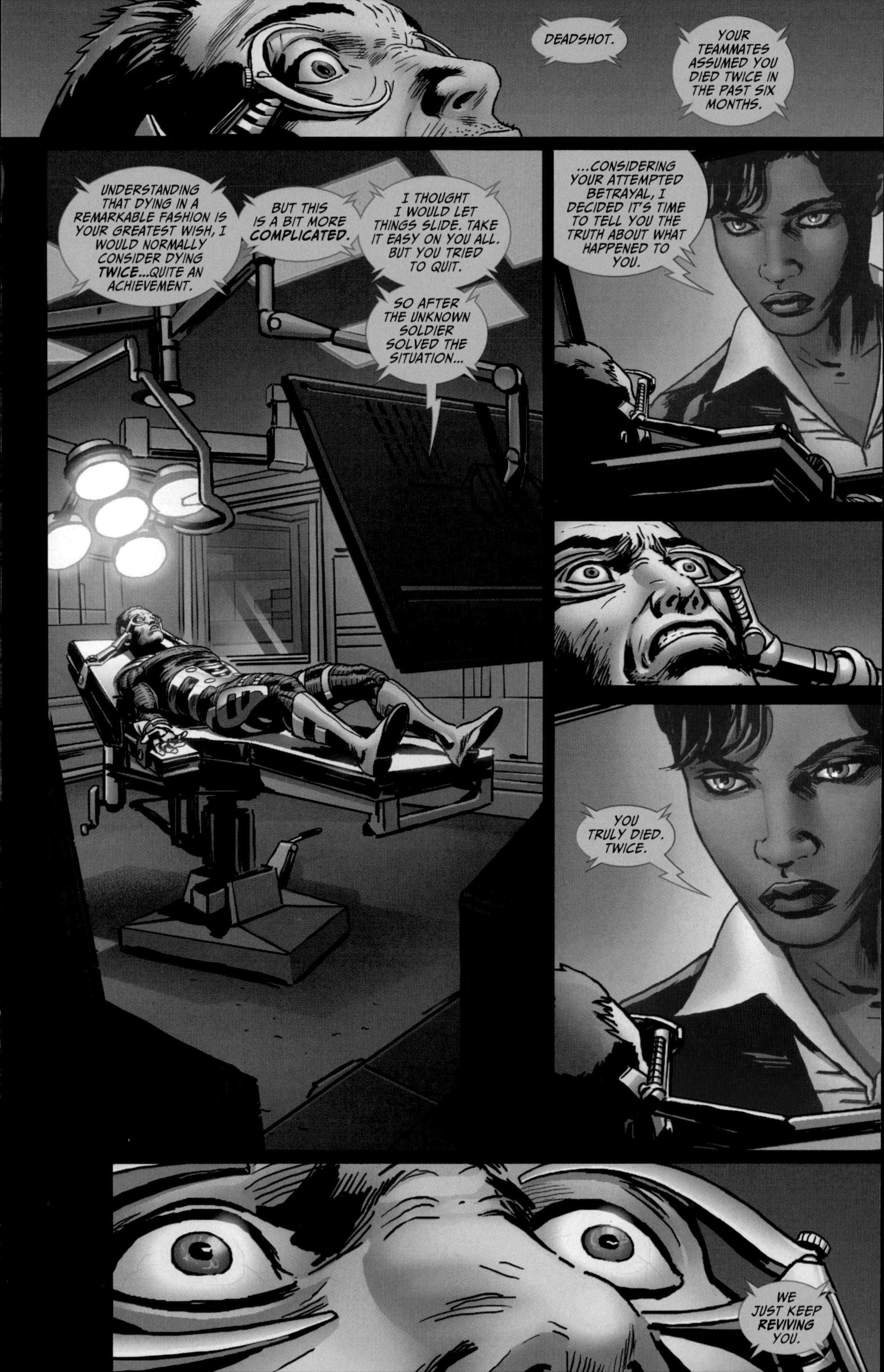
DEADSHOT.
YOUR TEAMMATES ASSUMED YOU DIED TWICE IN THE PAST SIX MONTHS.
UNDERSTANDING THAT DYING IN A REMARKABLE FASHION IS YOUR GREATEST WISH, I WOULD NORMALLY CONSIDER DYING TWICE...QUITE AN ACHIEVEMENT.
BUT THIS IS A BIT MORE COMPLICATED.
I THOUGHT I WOULD LET THINGS SLIDE. TAKE IT EASY ON YOU ALL. BUT YOU TRIED TO QUIT.
SO AFTER THE UNKNOWN SOLDIER SOLVED THE SITUATION...
...CONSIDERING YOUR ATTEMPTED BETRAYAL, I DECIDED IT'S TIME TO TELL YOU THE TRUTH ABOUT WHAT HAPPENED TO YOU.
YOU TRULY DIED. TWICE.
WE JUST KEEP REVIVING YOU.

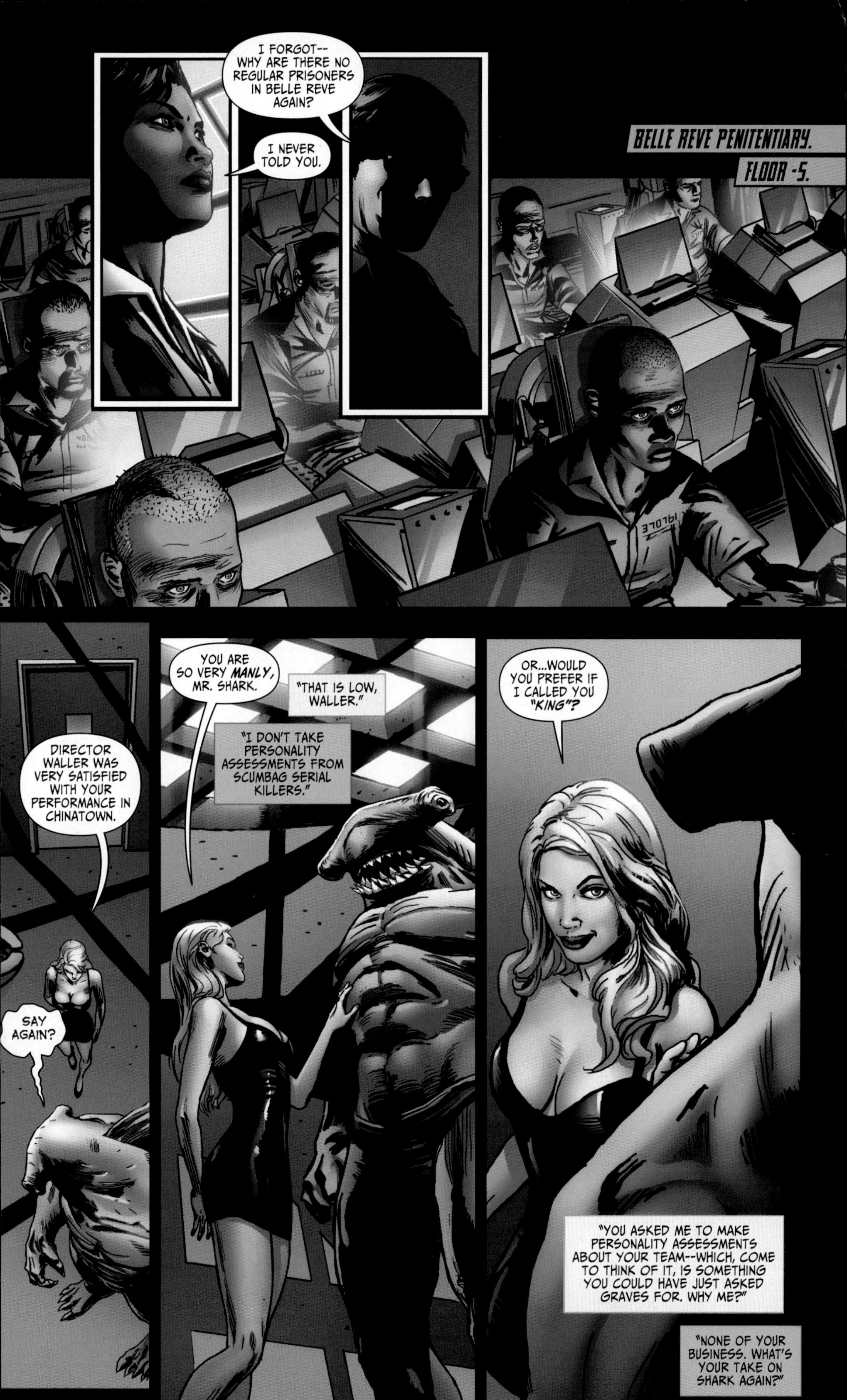
I FORGOT-- WHY ARE THERE NO REGULAR PRISONERS IN BELLE REVE AGAIN?
I NEVER TOLD YOU.
BELLE REVE PENITENTIARY.
FLOOR -5.
DIRECTOR WALLER WAS VERY SATISFIED WITH YOUR PERFORMANCE IN CHINATOWN.
SAY AGAIN?
YOU ARE SO VERY MANLY, MR. SHARK.
"THAT IS LOW, WALLER."
"I DON'T TAKE PERSONALITY ASSESSMENTS FROM SCUMBAG SERIAL KILLERS."
OR...WOULD YOU PREFER IF I CALLED YOU "KING"?
"YOU ASKED ME TO MAKE PERSONALITY ASSESSMENTS ABOUT YOUR TEAM--WHICH, COME TO THINK OF IT, IS SOMETHING YOU COULD HAVE JUST ASKED GRAVES FOR. WHY ME?"
"NONE OF YOUR BUSINESS. WHAT'S YOUR TAKE ON SHARK AGAIN?"

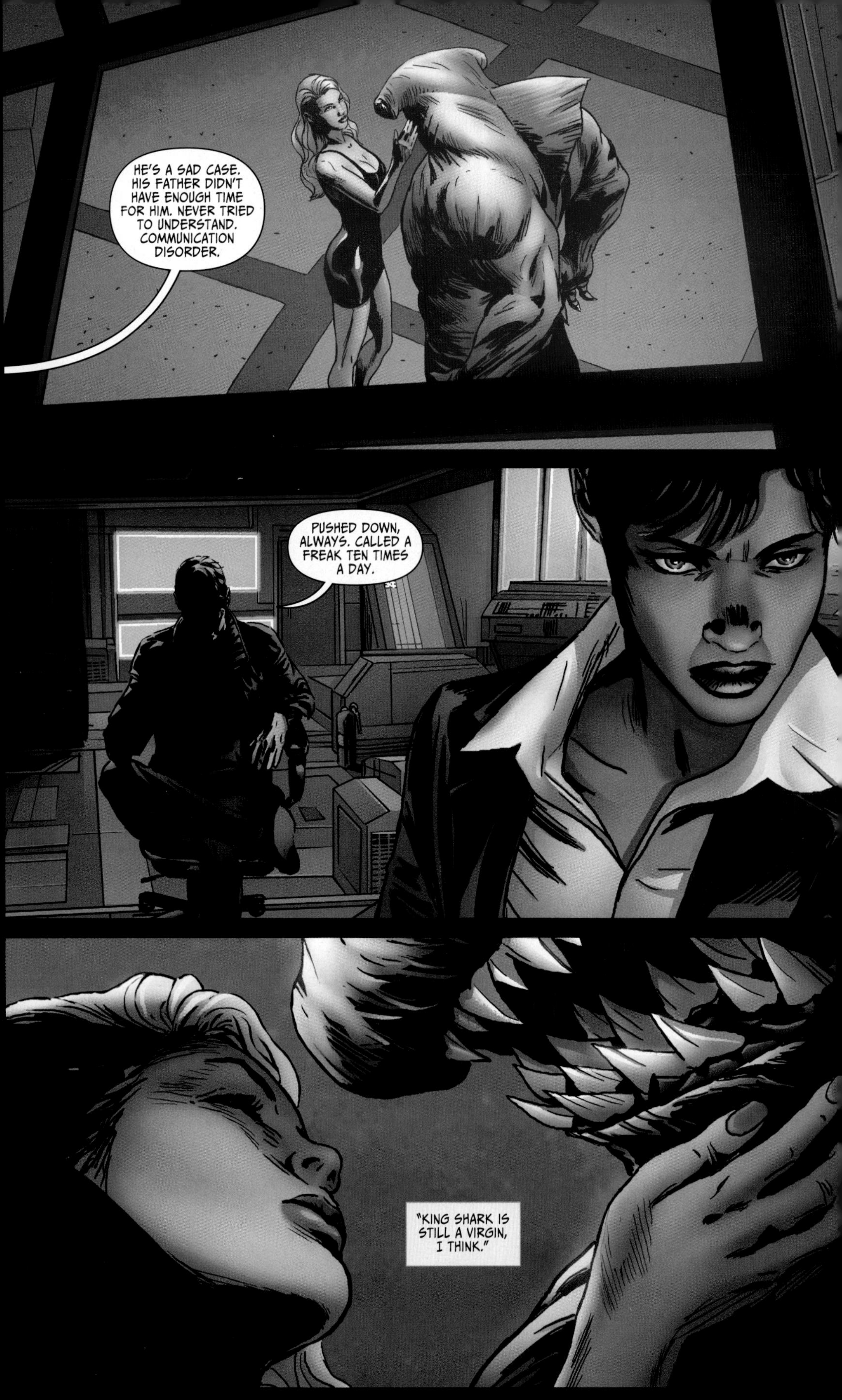
HE'S A SAD CASE. HIS FATHER DIDN'T HAVE ENOUGH TIME FOR HIM. NEVER TRIED TO UNDERSTAND. COMMUNICATION DISORDER.
PUSHED DOWN, ALWAYS. CALLED A FREAK TEN TIMES A DAY.
"KING SHARK IS STILL A VIRGIN, I THINK."

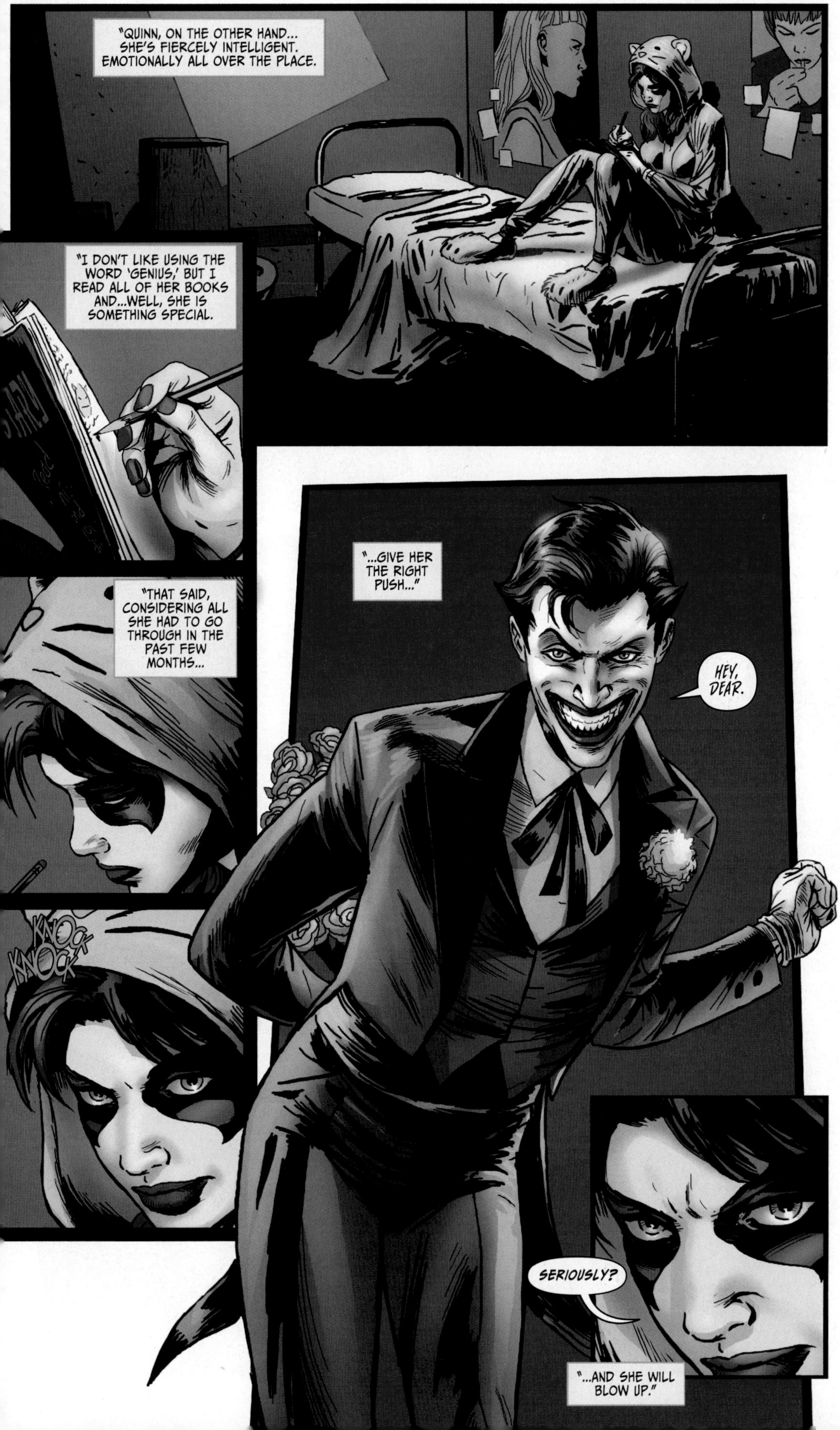
"QUINN, ON THE OTHER HAND... SHE'S FIERCELY INTELLIGENT. EMOTIONALLY ALL OVER THE PLACE.
"I DON'T LIKE USING THE WORD 'GENIUS,' BUT I READ ALL OF HER BOOKS AND...WELL, SHE IS SOMETHING SPECIAL.
"THAT SAID, CONSIDERING ALL SHE HAD TO GO THROUGH IN THE PAST FEW MONTHS...
KNOCK KNOCK
"...GIVE HER THE RIGHT PUSH..."
HEY, DEAR.
SERIOUSLY?
"...AND SHE WILL BLOW UP."

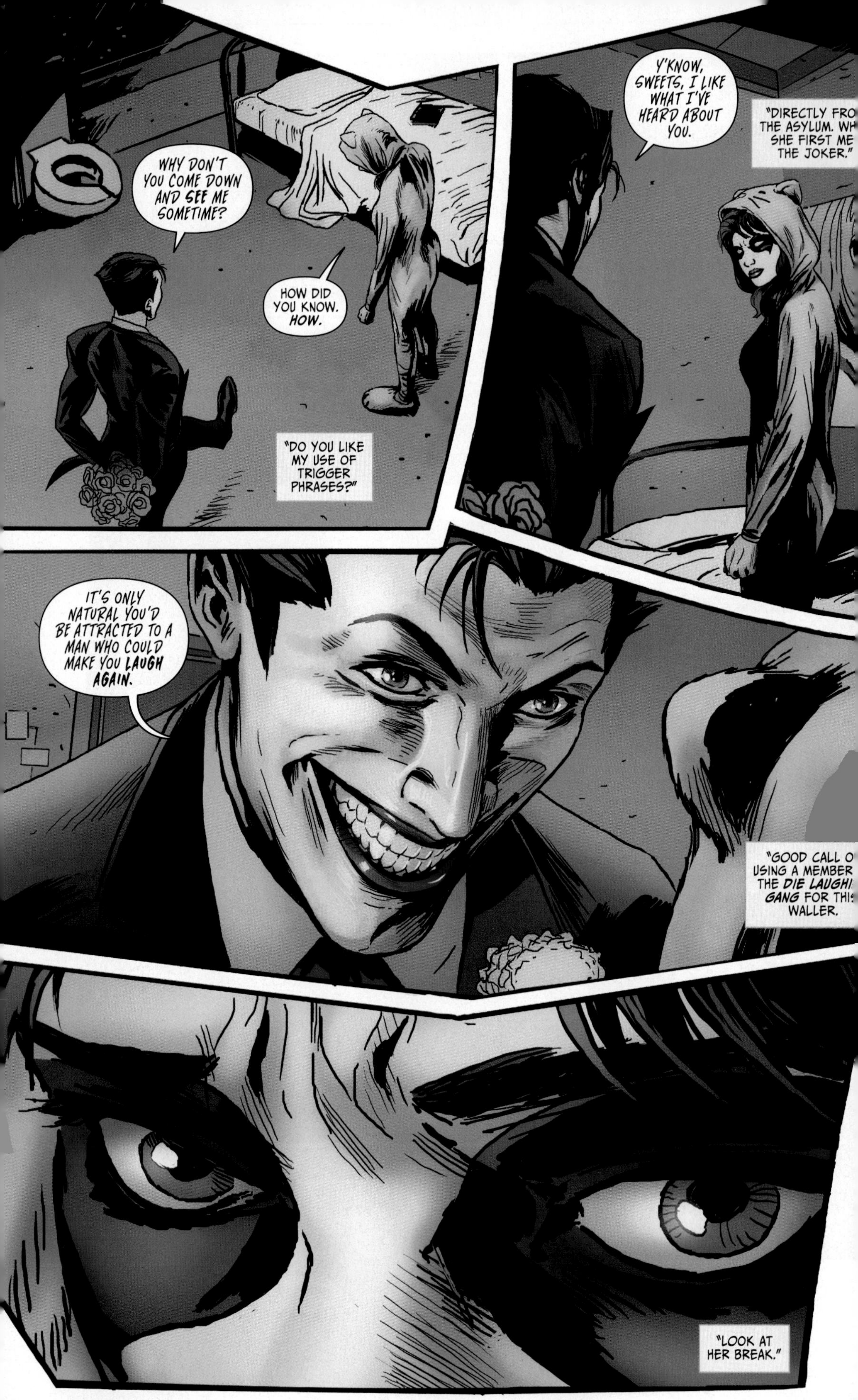
WHY DON'T YOU COME DOWN AND SEE ME SOMETIME?
HOW DID YOU KNOW. HOW.
"DO YOU LIKE MY USE OF TRIGGER PHRASES?"
Y'KNOW, SWEETS, I LIKE WHAT I'VE HEARD ABOUT YOU.
"DIRECTLY FRO THE ASYLUM. WH SHE FIRST ME THE JOKER."
IT'S ONLY NATURAL YOU'D BE ATTRACTED TO A MAN WHO COULD MAKE YOU LAUGH AGAIN.
"GOOD CALL O USING A MEMBER THE DIE LAUGHI GANG FOR THIS WALLER.
"LOOK AT HER BREAK."

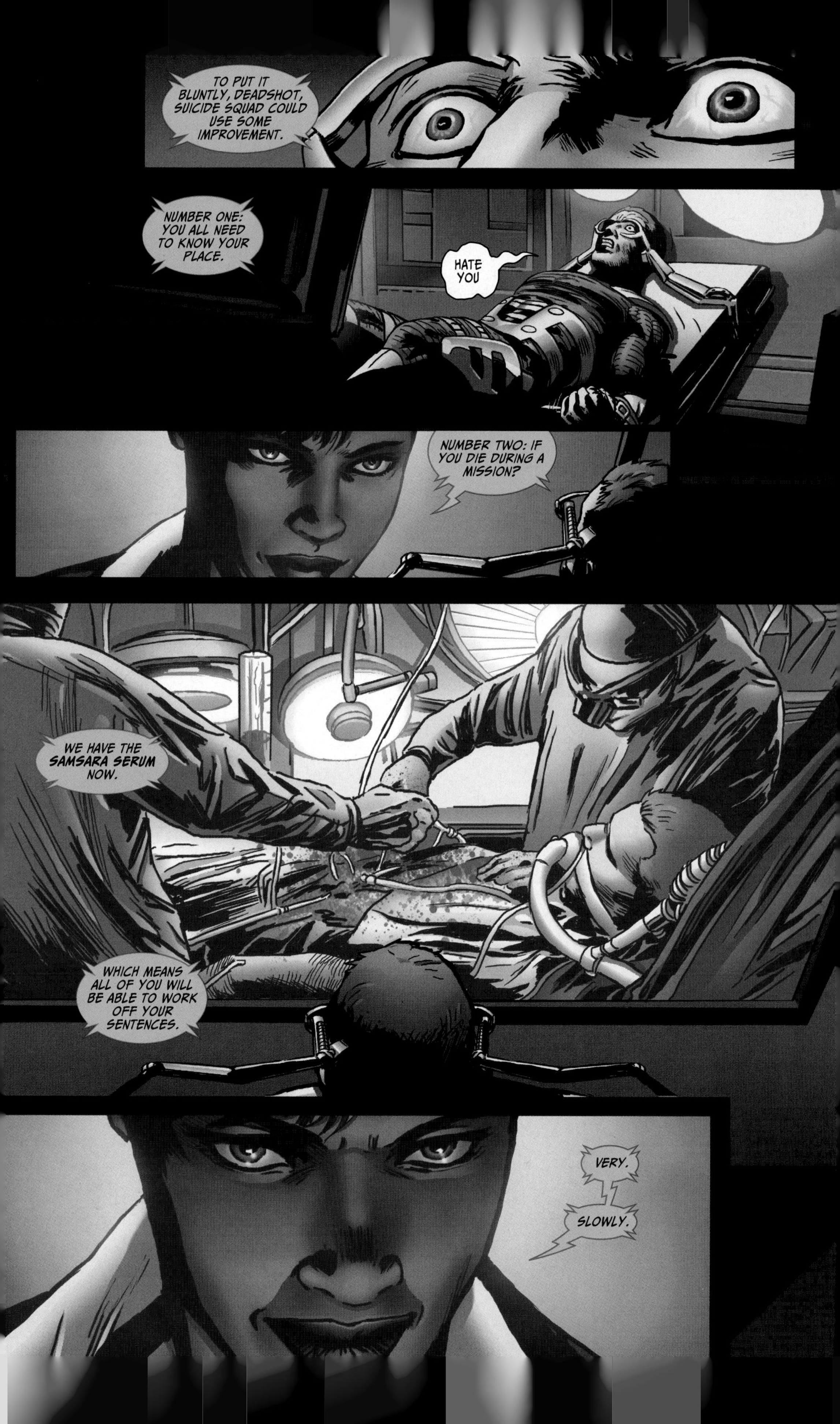
TO PUT IT BLUNTLY, DEADSHOT, SUICIDE SQUAD COULD USE SOME IMPROVEMENT.
NUMBER ONE: YOU ALL NEED TO KNOW YOUR PLACE.
HATE YOU
NUMBER TWO: IF YOU DIE DURING A MISSION?
WE HAVE THE SAMSARA SERUM NOW.
WHICH MEANS ALL OF YOU WILL BE ABLE TO WORK OFF YOUR SENTENCES.
VERY.
SLOWLY.

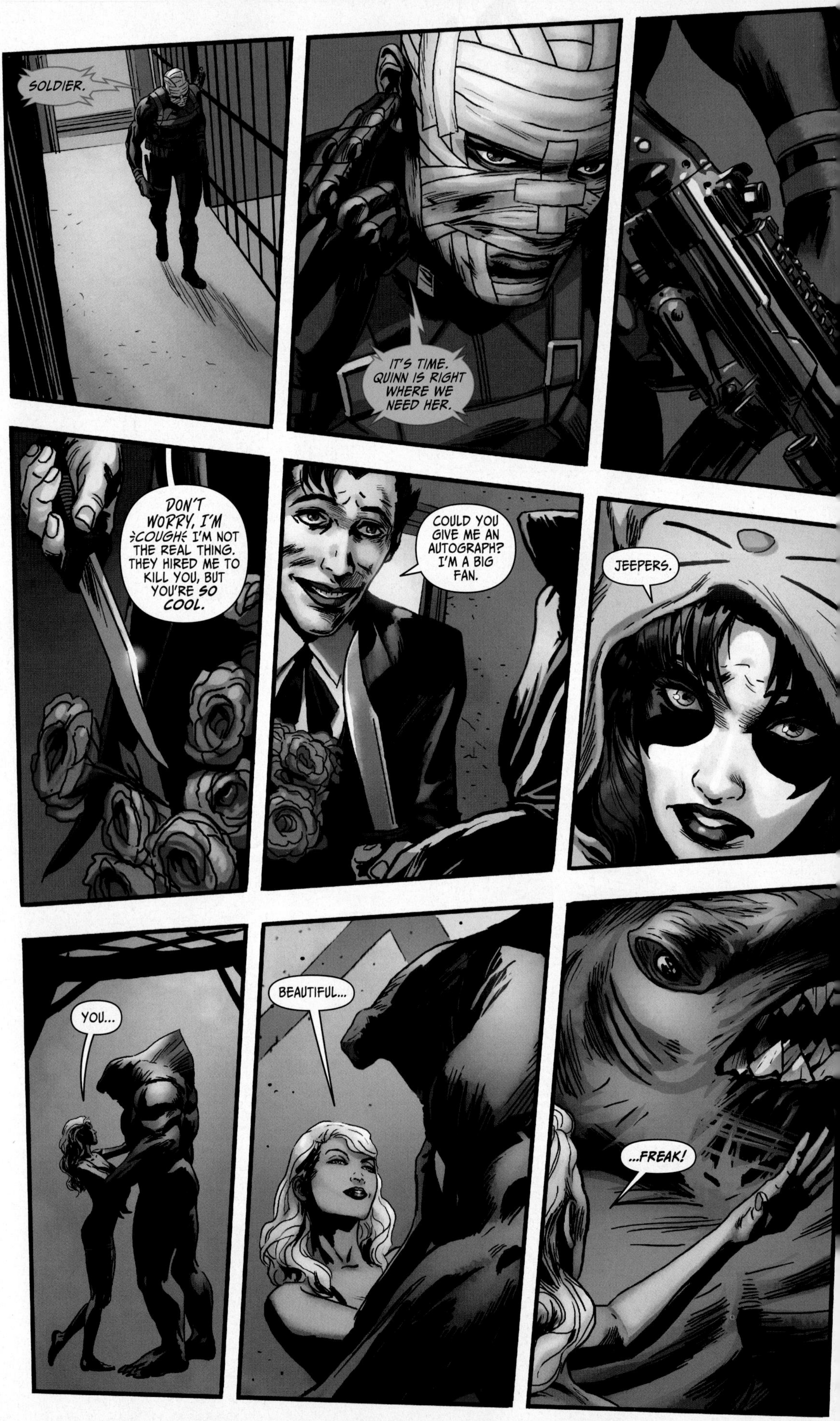
SOLDIER.
IT'S TIME. QUINN IS RIGHT WHERE WE NEED HER.
DON'T WORRY, I'M *COUGH* I'M NOT THE REAL THING. THEY HIRED ME TO KILL YOU, BUT YOU'RE SO COOL.
COULD YOU GIVE ME AN AUTOGRAPH? I'M A BIG FAN.
JEEPERS.
YOU...
BEAUTIFUL...
...FREAK!

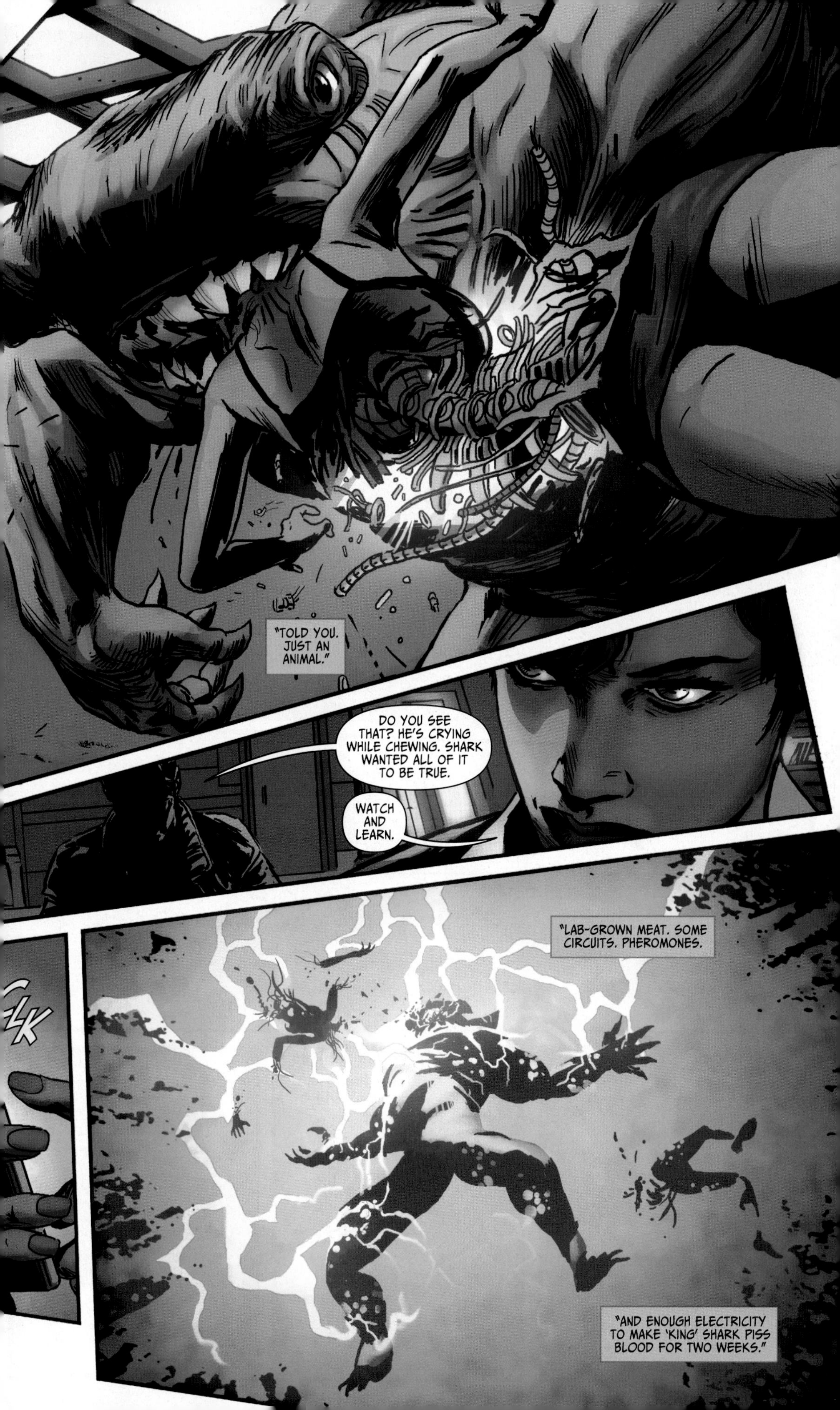
"TOLD YOU. JUST AN ANIMAL."
DO YOU SEE THAT? HE'S CRYING WHILE CHEWING. SHARK WANTED ALL OF IT TO BE TRUE.
WATCH AND LEARN.
"LAB-GROWN MEAT. SOME CIRCUITS. PHEROMONES.
"AND ENOUGH ELECTRICITY TO MAKE 'KING' SHARK PISS BLOOD FOR TWO WEEKS."

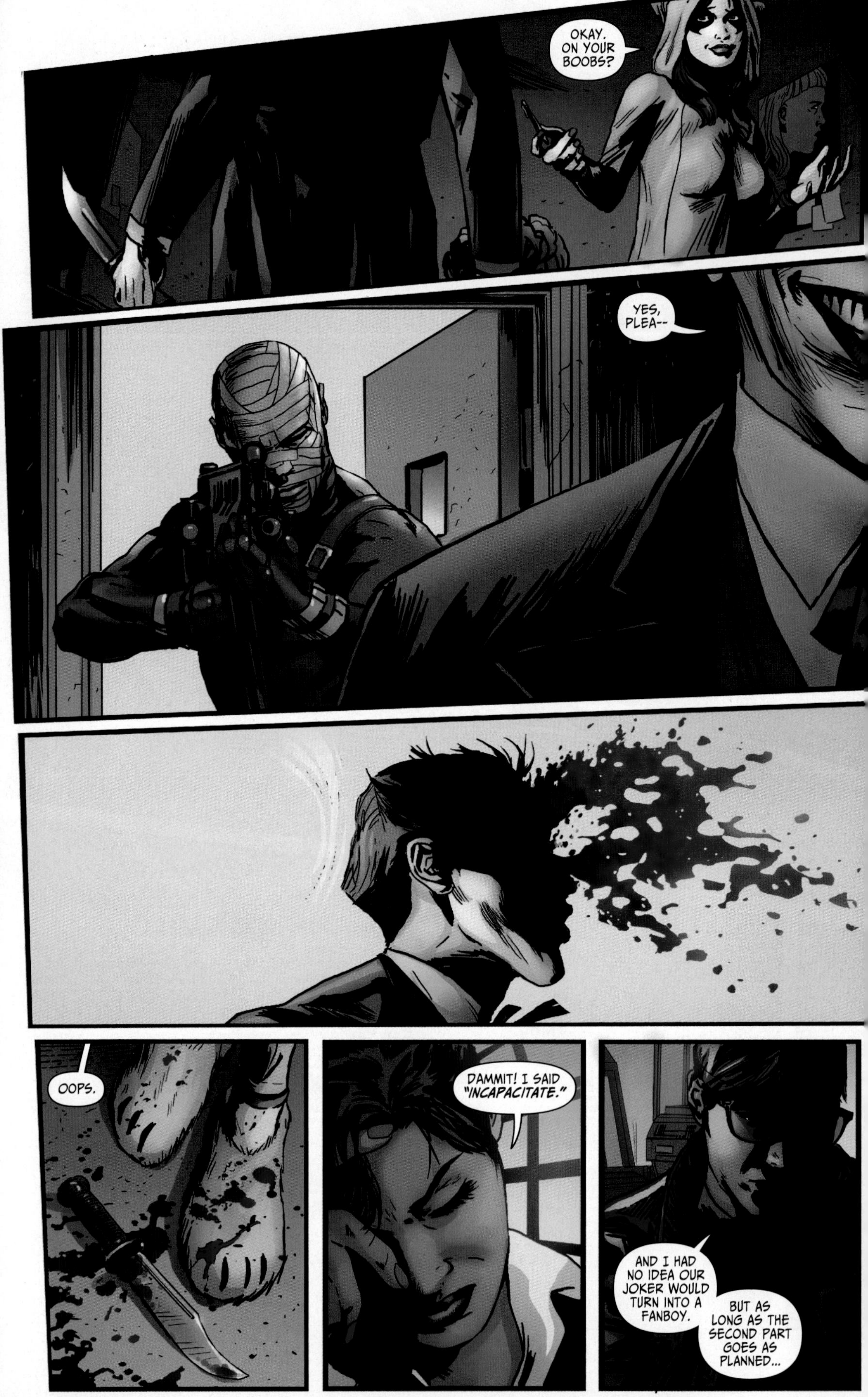
OKAY. ON YOUR BOOBS?
YES, PLEA--
OOPS.
DAMMIT! I SAID "INCAPACITATE."
AND I HAD NO IDEA OUR JOKER WOULD TURN INTO A FANBOY.
BUT AS LONG AS THE SECOND PART GOES AS PLANNED...

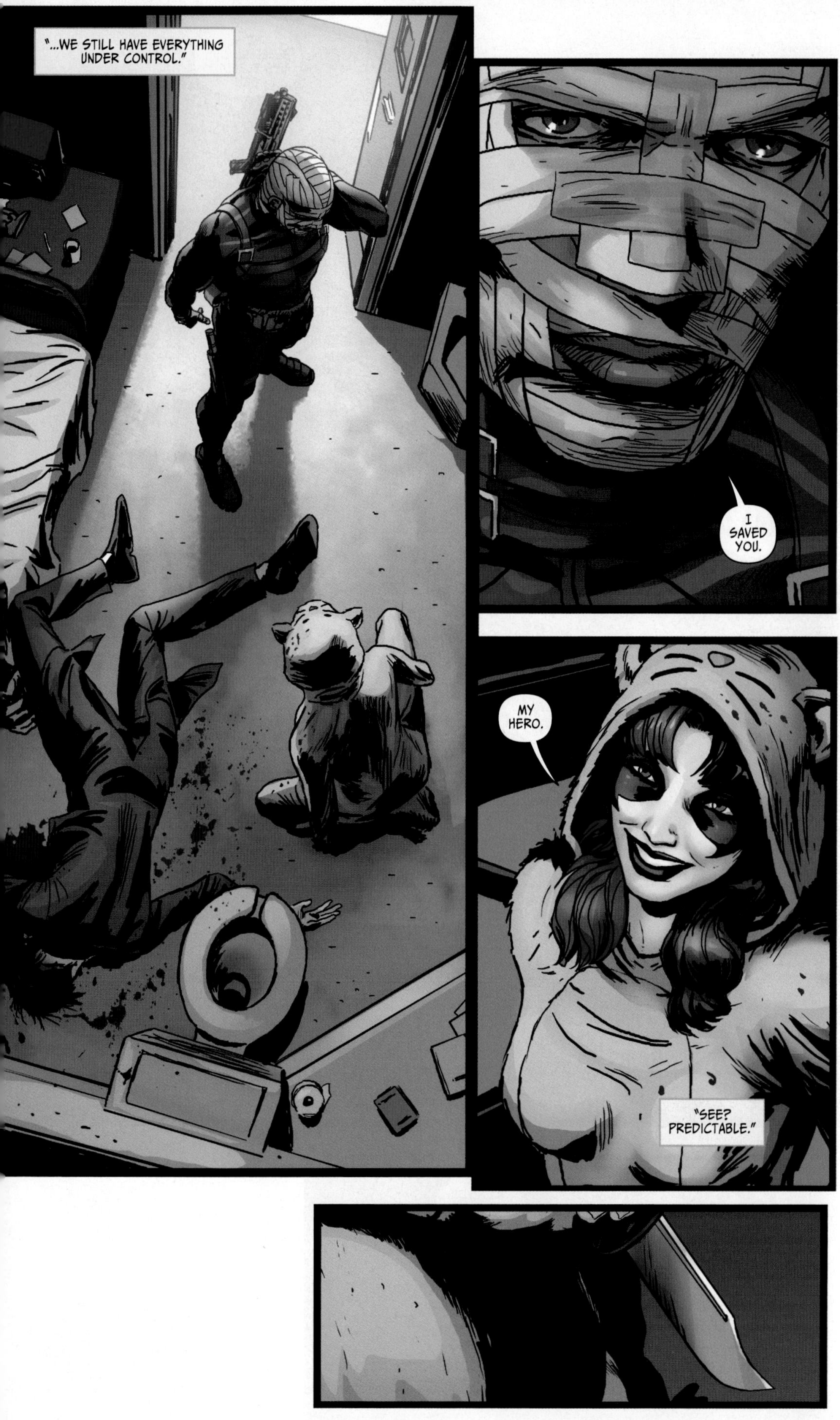
"...WE STILL HAVE EVERYTHING UNDER CONTROL."
I SAVED YOU.
MY HERO.
"SEE? PREDICTABLE."

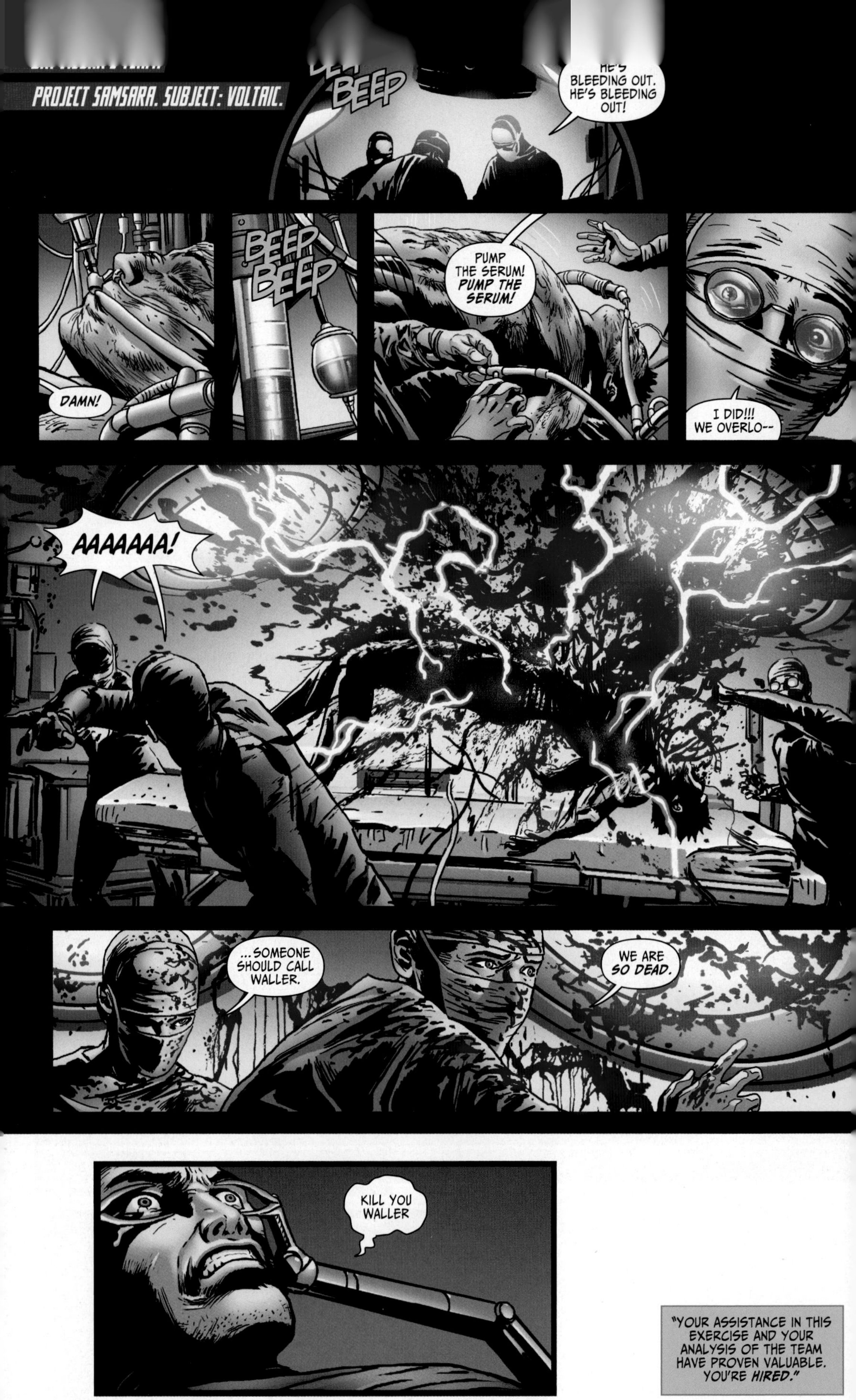

PROJECT SAMSARA. SUBJECT: VOLTAIC.
BEEP
HE'S BLEEDING OUT. HE'S BLEEDING OUT!
DAMN!
BEEP BEEP
PUMP THE SERUM! *PUMP THE SERUM!*
I DID!!! WE OVERLO--
AAAAAAA!
...SOMEONE SHOULD CALL WALLER.
WE ARE *SO DEAD.*
KILL YOU WALLER
"YOUR ASSISTANCE IN THIS EXERCISE AND YOUR ANALYSIS OF THE TEAM HAVE PROVEN VALUABLE. YOU'RE *HIRED.*"

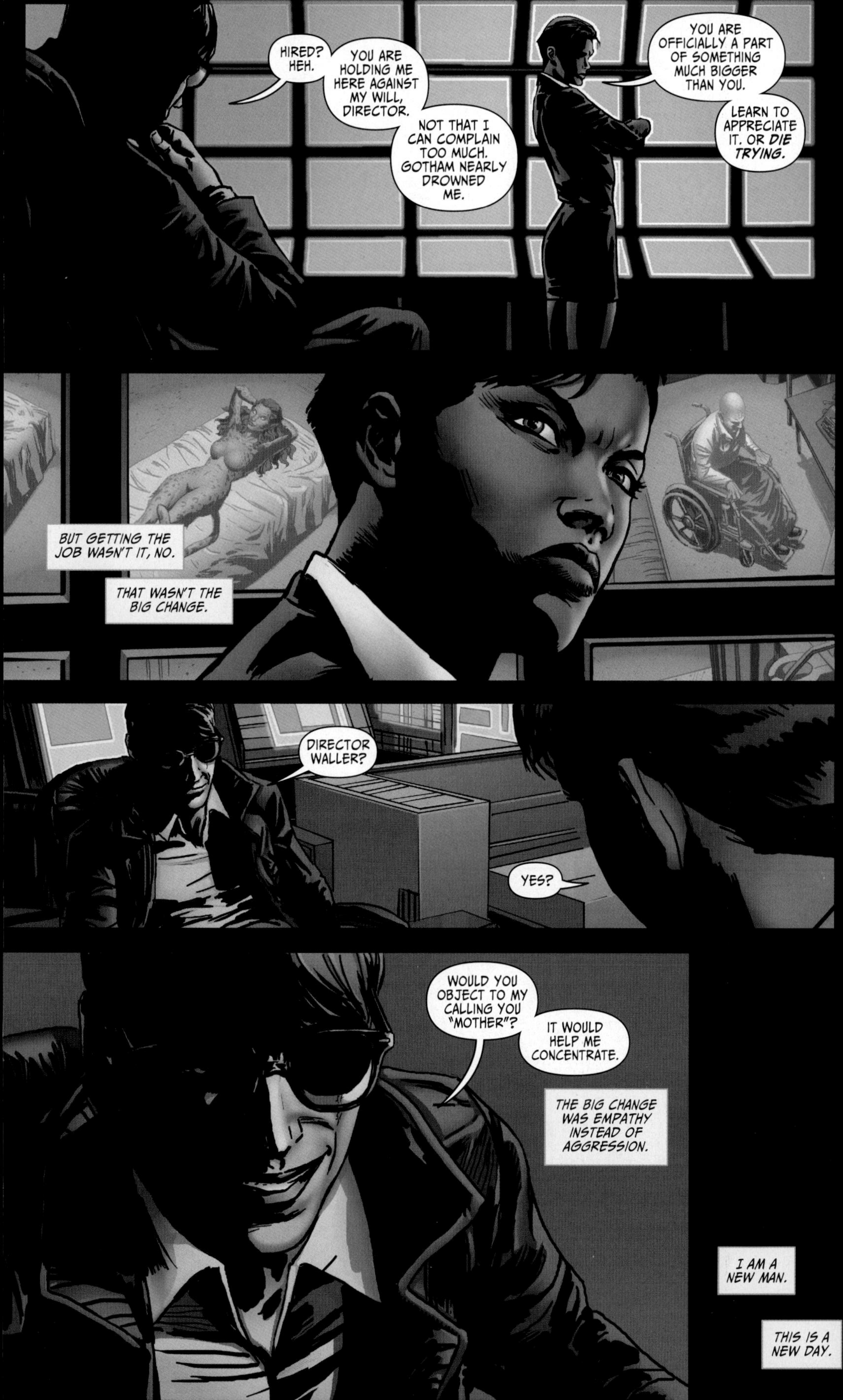
HIRED? HEH.
YOU ARE HOLDING ME HERE AGAINST MY WILL, DIRECTOR.
NOT THAT I CAN COMPLAIN TOO MUCH. GOTHAM NEARLY DROWNED ME.
YOU ARE OFFICIALLY A PART OF SOMETHING MUCH BIGGER THAN YOU.
LEARN TO APPRECIATE IT. OR DIE TRYING.
BUT GETTING THE JOB WASN'T IT, NO.
THAT WASN'T THE BIG CHANGE.
DIRECTOR WALLER?
YES?
WOULD YOU OBJECT TO MY CALLING YOU "MOTHER"?
IT WOULD HELP ME CONCENTRATE.
THE BIG CHANGE WAS EMPATHY INSTEAD OF AGGRESSION.
I AM A NEW MAN.
THIS IS A NEW DAY.

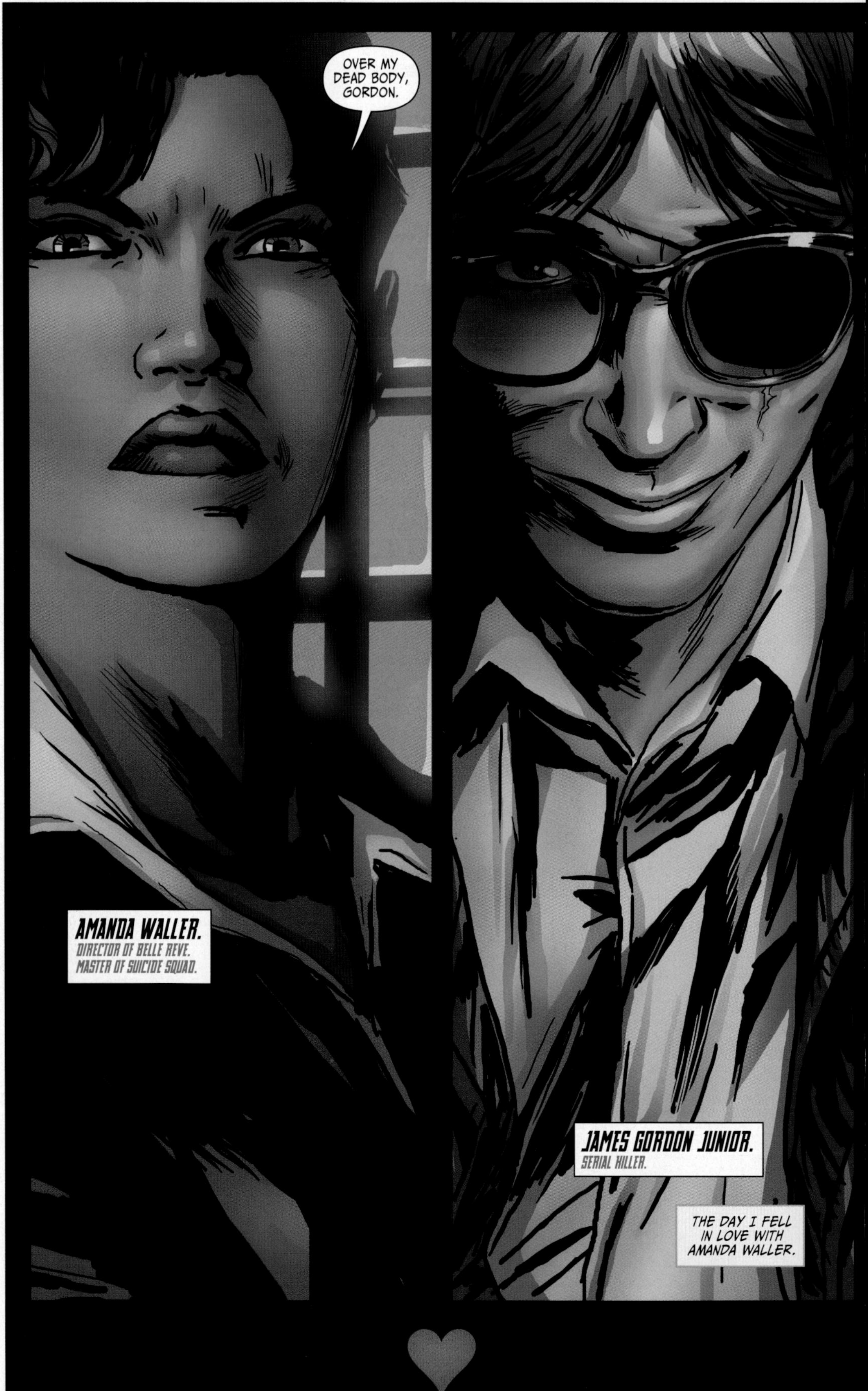
OVER MY DEAD BODY, GORDON.
AMANDA WALLER.
DIRECTOR OF BELLE REVE.
MASTER OF SUICIDE SQUAD.
JAMES GORDON JUNIOR.
SERIAL KILLER.
THE DAY I FELL IN LOVE WITH AMANDA WALLER.

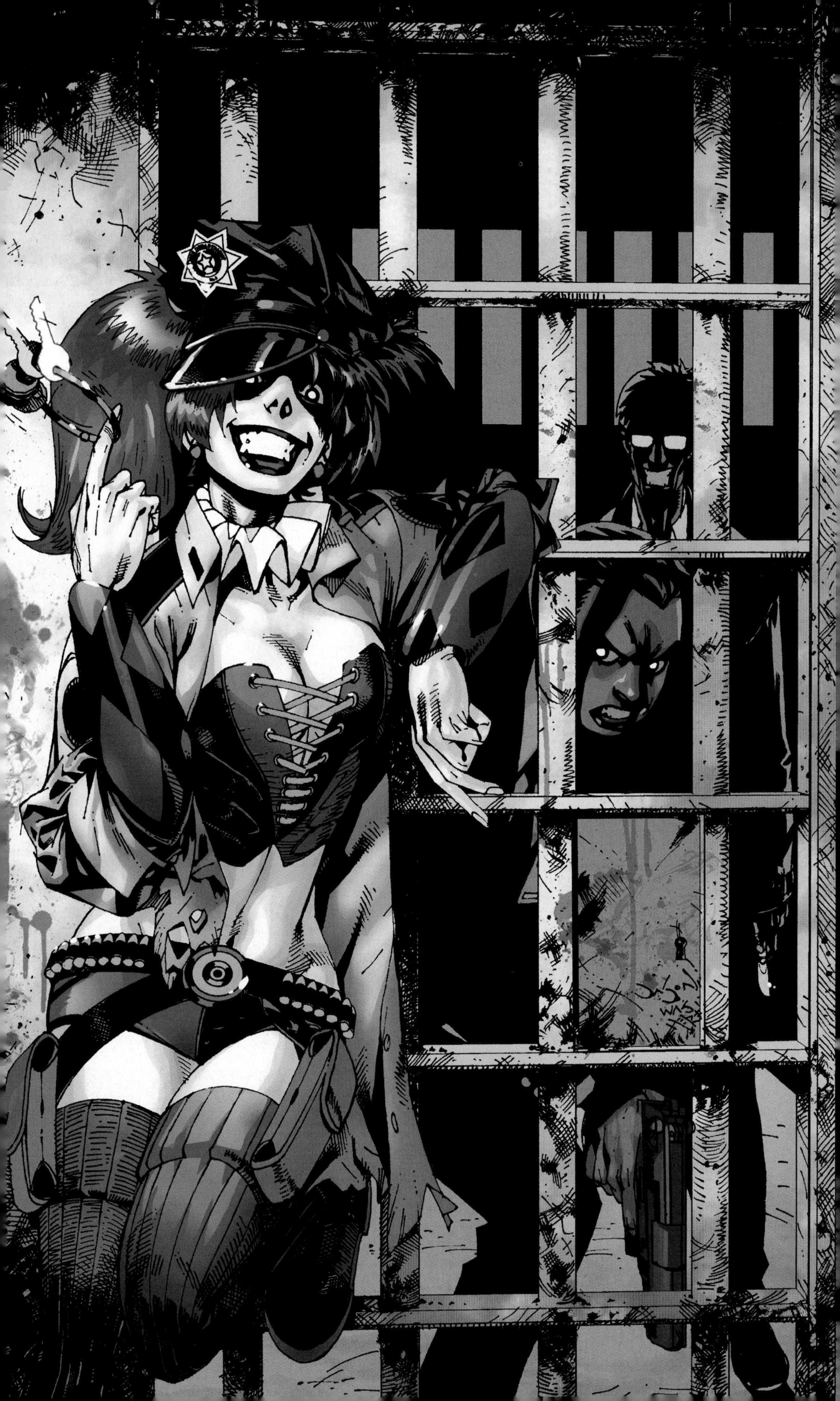

DISCIPLINE AND PUNISH: PART TWO

ALES KOT writer **PATRICK ZIRCHER** artist cover by **JASON PEARSON**

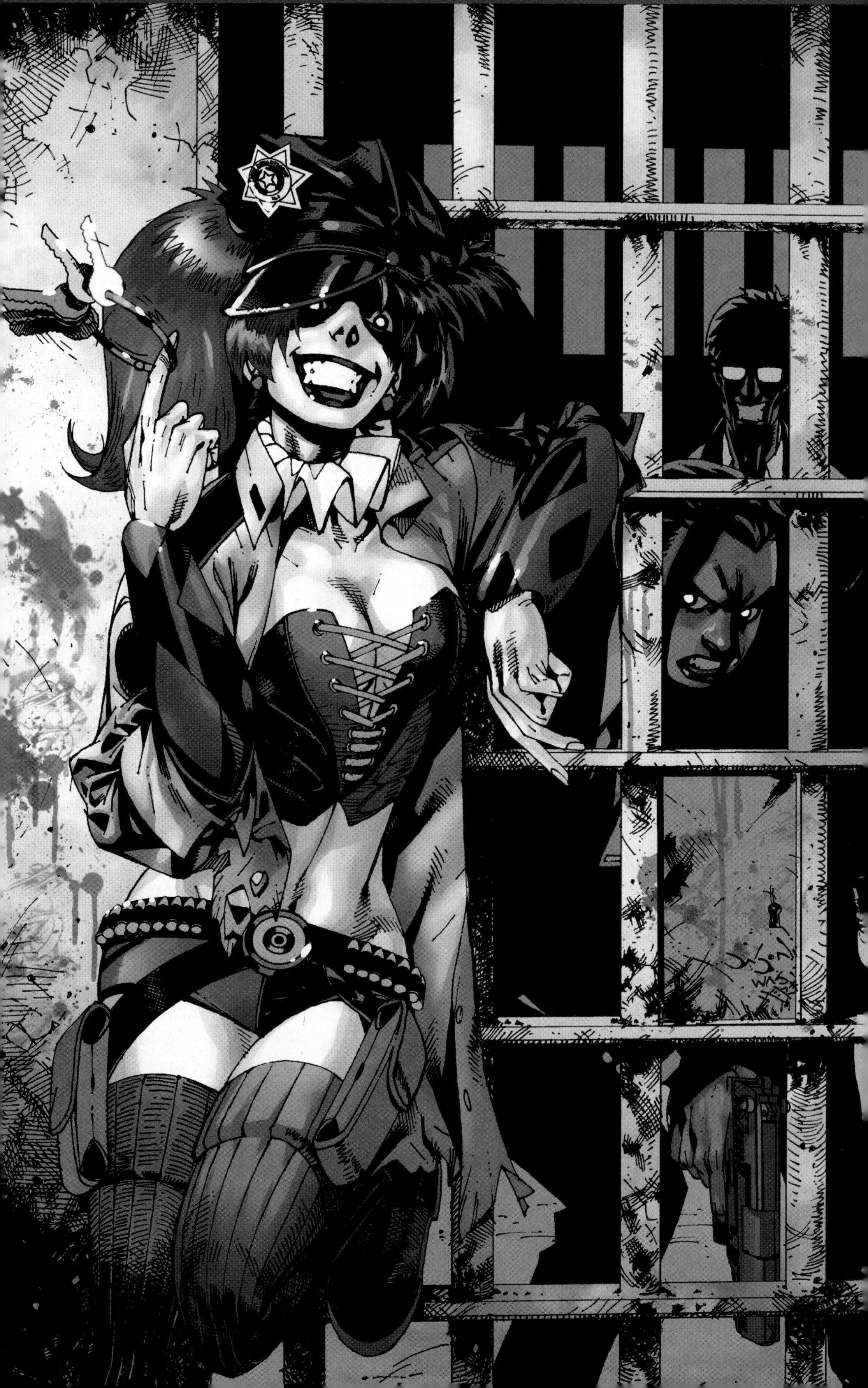

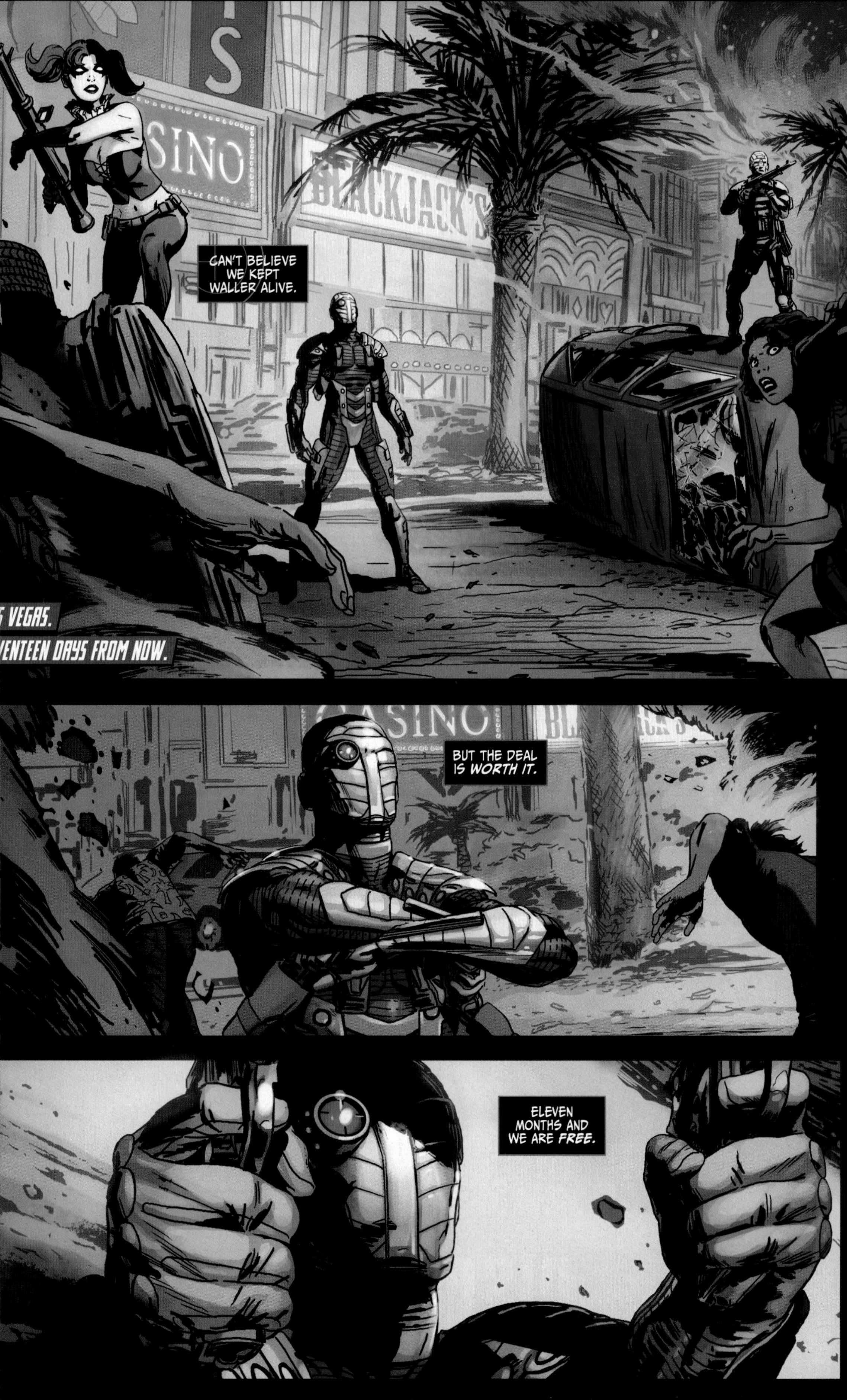

CAN'T BELIEVE WE KEPT WALLER ALIVE.
S VEGAS.
VENTEEN DAYS FROM NOW.
BUT THE DEAL IS WORTH IT.
ELEVEN MONTHS AND WE ARE FREE.

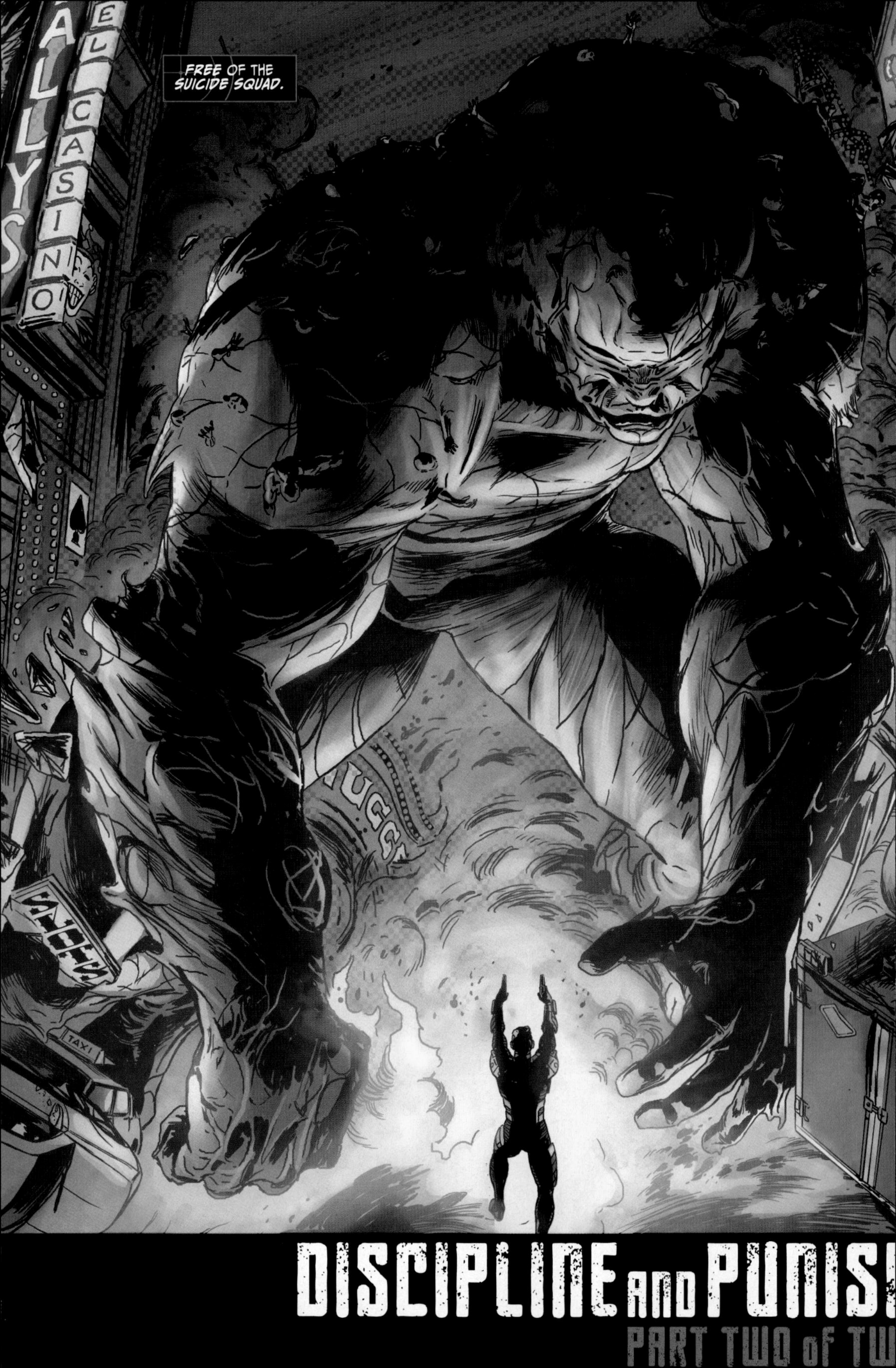
FREE OF THE SUICIDE SQUAD.
CASINO
TAXI

DISCIPLINE AND PUNIS

PART TWO OF TW

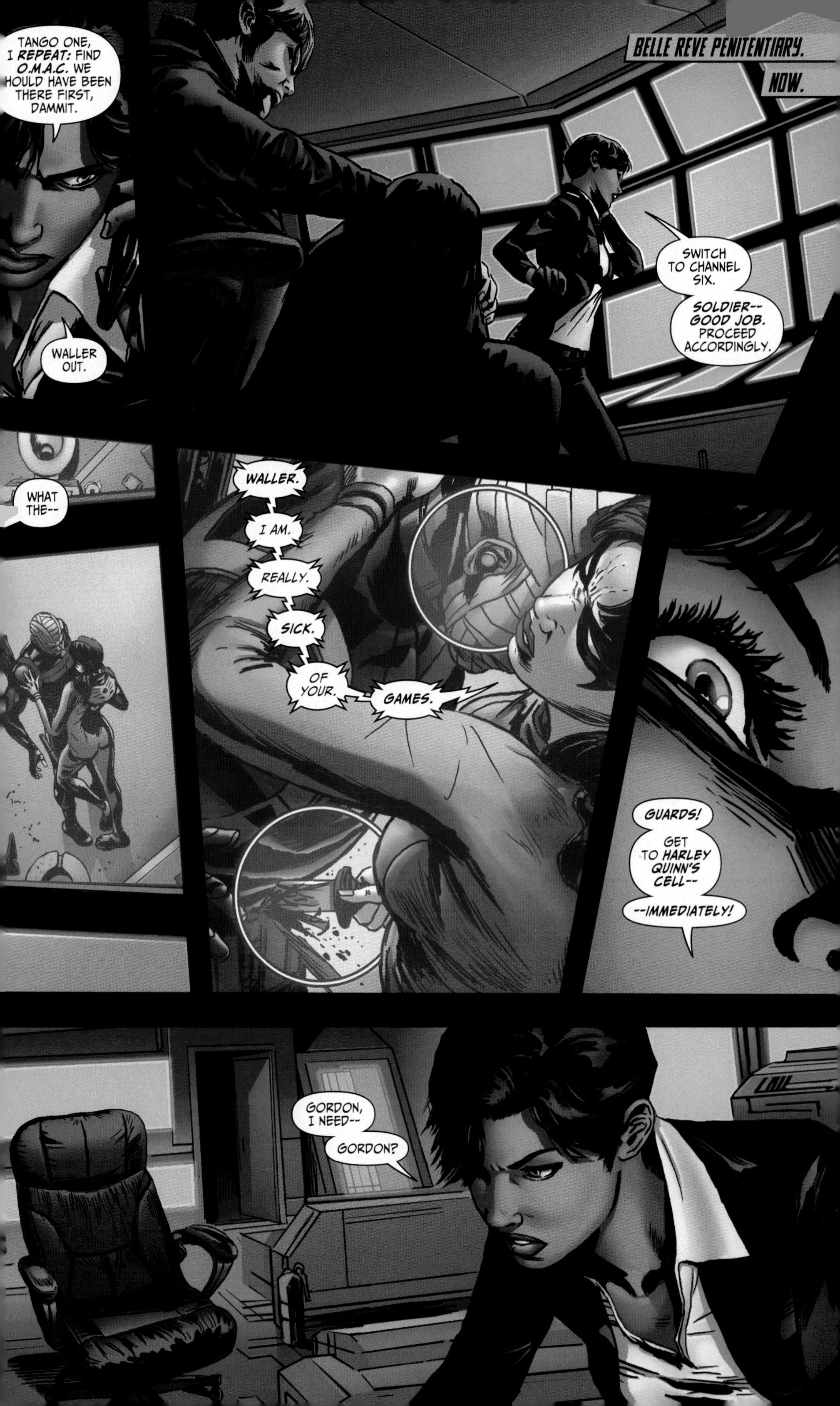
BELLE REVE PENITENTIARY.
NOW.
TANGO ONE, I REPEAT: FIND O.M.A.C. WE HOULD HAVE BEEN THERE FIRST, DAMMIT.
WALLER OUT.
SWITCH TO CHANNEL SIX.
SOLDIER-- GOOD JOB. PROCEED ACCORDINGLY.
WHAT THE--
WALLER.
I AM.
REALLY.
SICK.
OF YOUR.
GAMES.
GUARDS!
GET TO HARLEY QUINN'S CELL--
--IMMEDIATELY!
GORDON, I NEED--
GORDON?

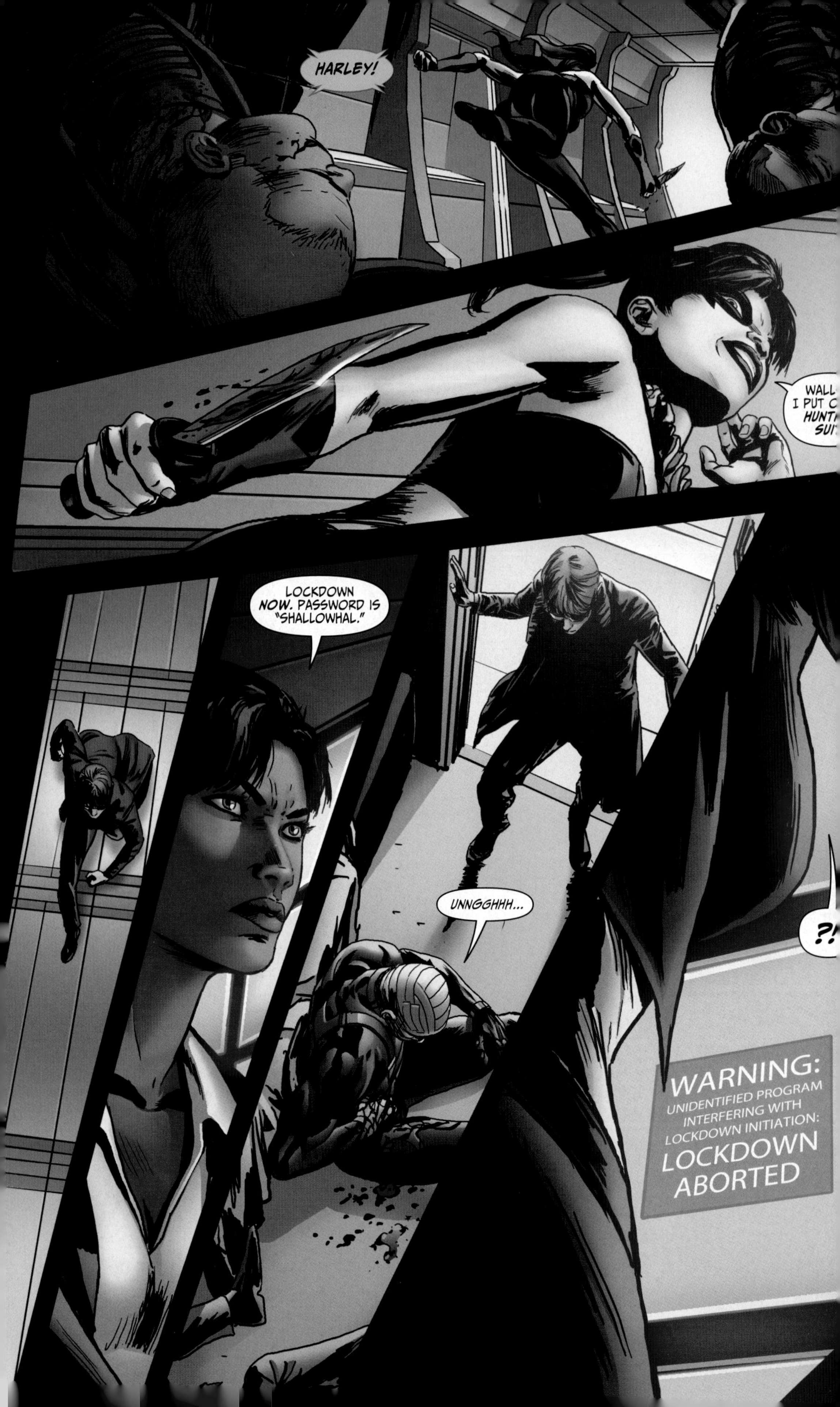
HARLEY!
LOCKDOWN NOW. PASSWORD IS "SHALLOWHAL."
UNNGGHHH...
?!
WARNING:
UNIDENTIFIED PROGRAM INTERFERING WITH LOCKDOWN INITIATION:
LOCKDOWN ABORTED

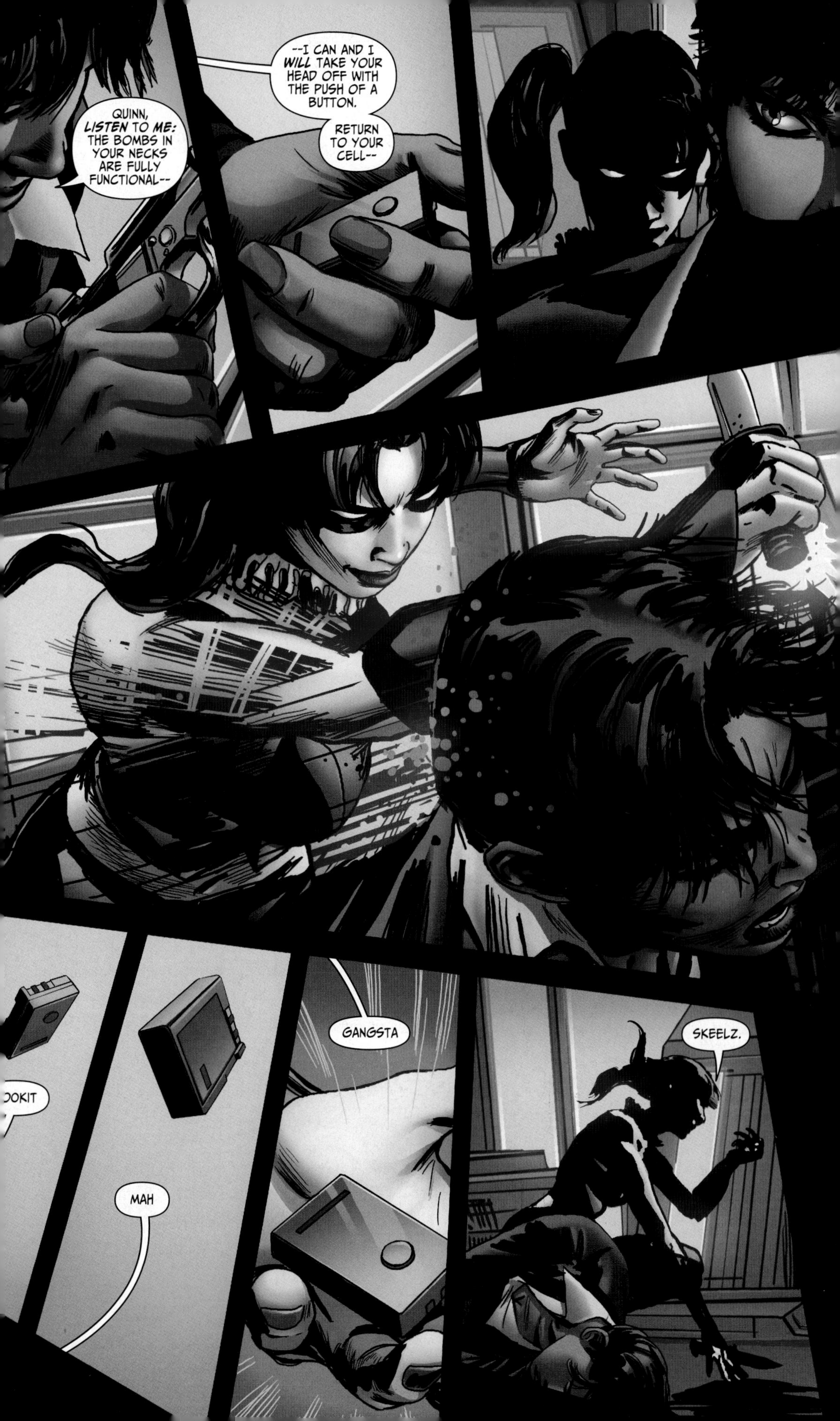
QUINN, LISTEN TO ME: THE BOMBS IN YOUR NECKS ARE FULLY FUNCTIONAL--
--I CAN AND I WILL TAKE YOUR HEAD OFF WITH THE PUSH OF A BUTTON.
RETURN TO YOUR CELL--
OOKIT
MAH
GANGSTA
SKEELZ.

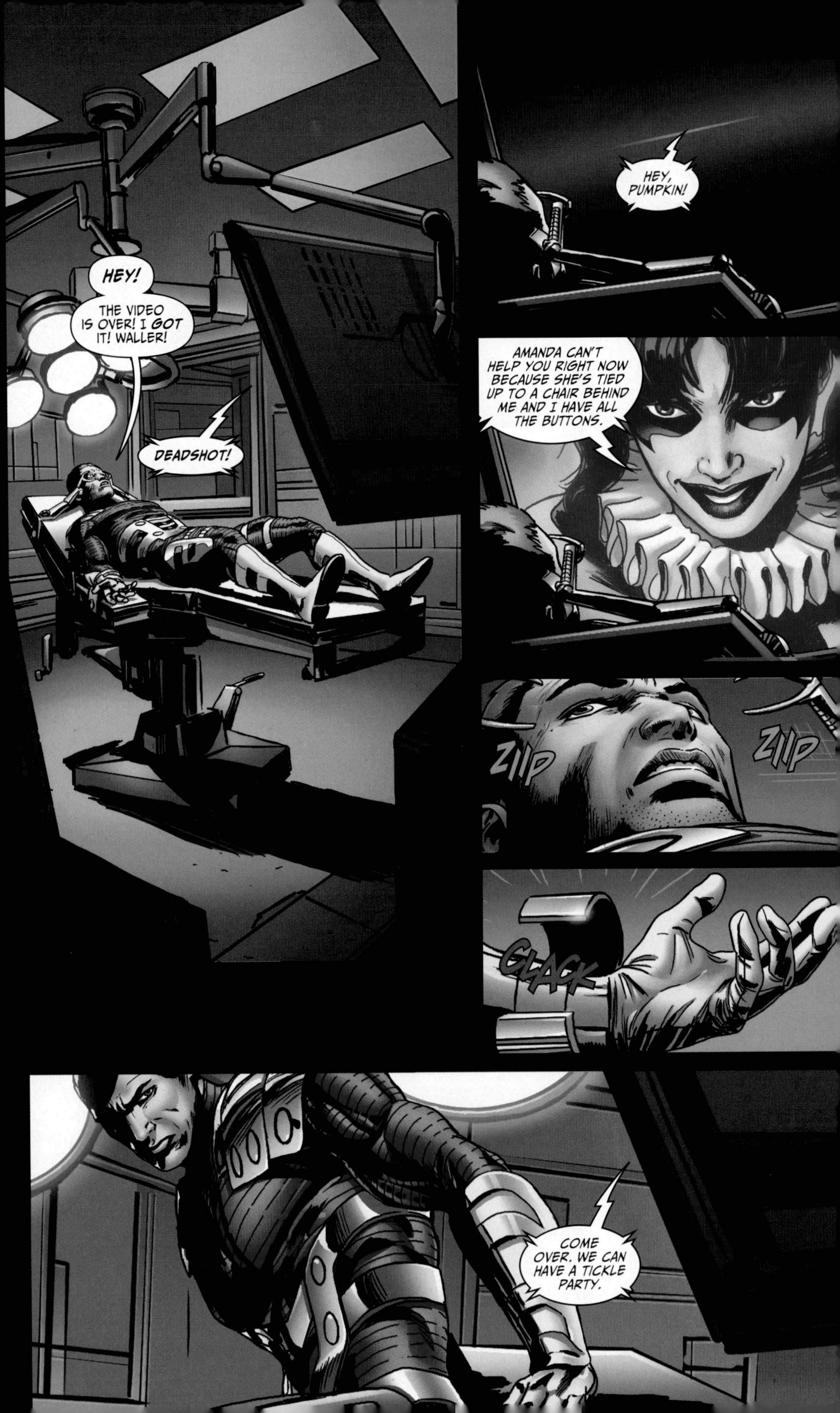
HEY!
THE VIDEO IS OVER! I GOT IT! WALLER!
DEADSHOT!
HEY, PUMPKIN!
AMANDA CAN'T HELP YOU RIGHT NOW BECAUSE SHE'S TIED UP TO A CHAIR BEHIND ME AND I HAVE ALL THE BUTTONS.
ZIP
ZIP
CLACK
COME OVER. WE CAN HAVE A TICKLE PARTY.

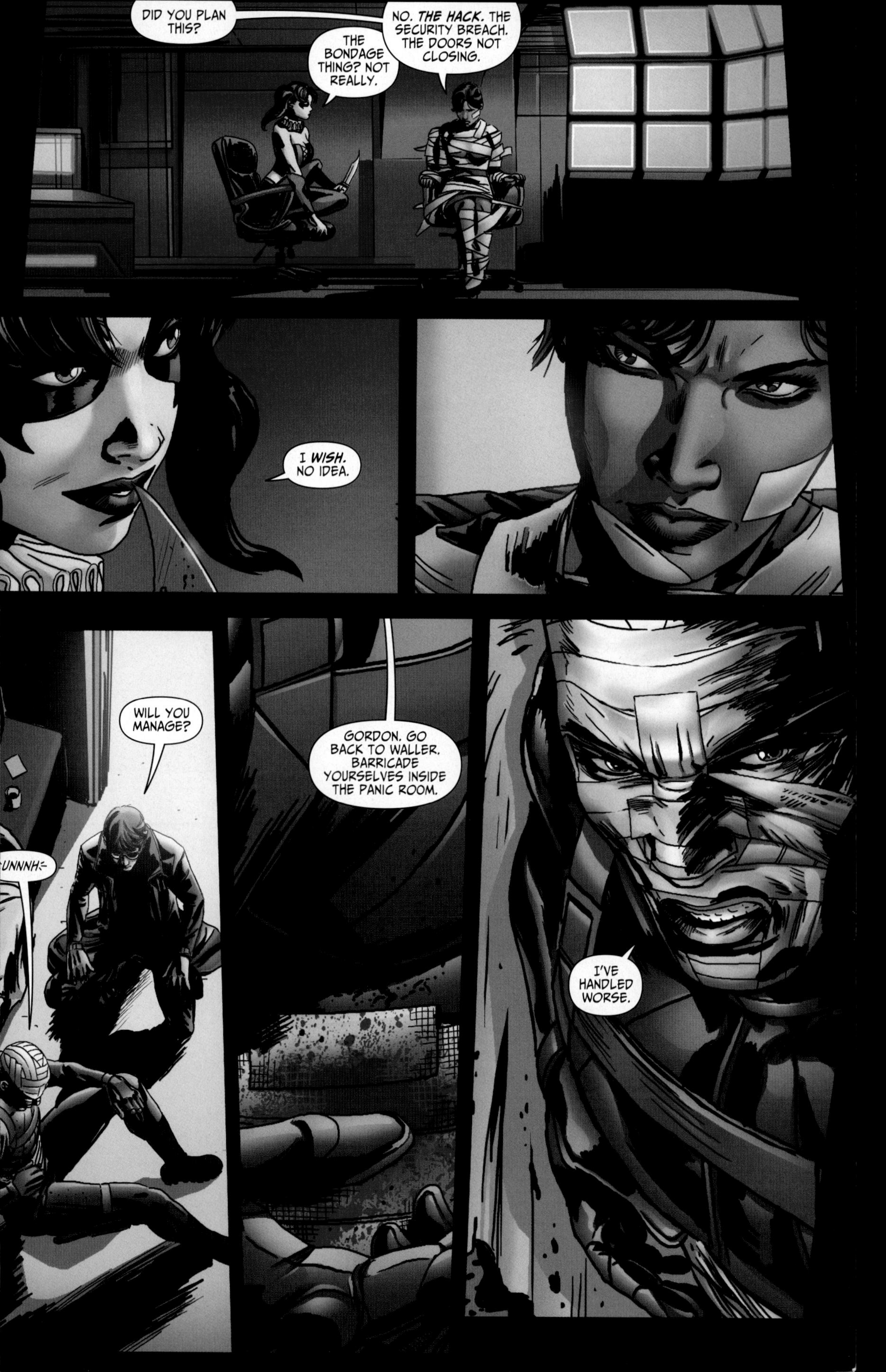
DID YOU PLAN THIS?
THE BONDAGE THING? NOT REALLY.
NO. THE HACK. THE SECURITY BREACH. THE DOORS NOT CLOSING.
I WISH. NO IDEA.
WILL YOU MANAGE?
UNNNH--
GORDON. GO BACK TO WALLER. BARRICADE YOURSELVES INSIDE THE PANIC ROOM.
I'VE HANDLED WORSE.

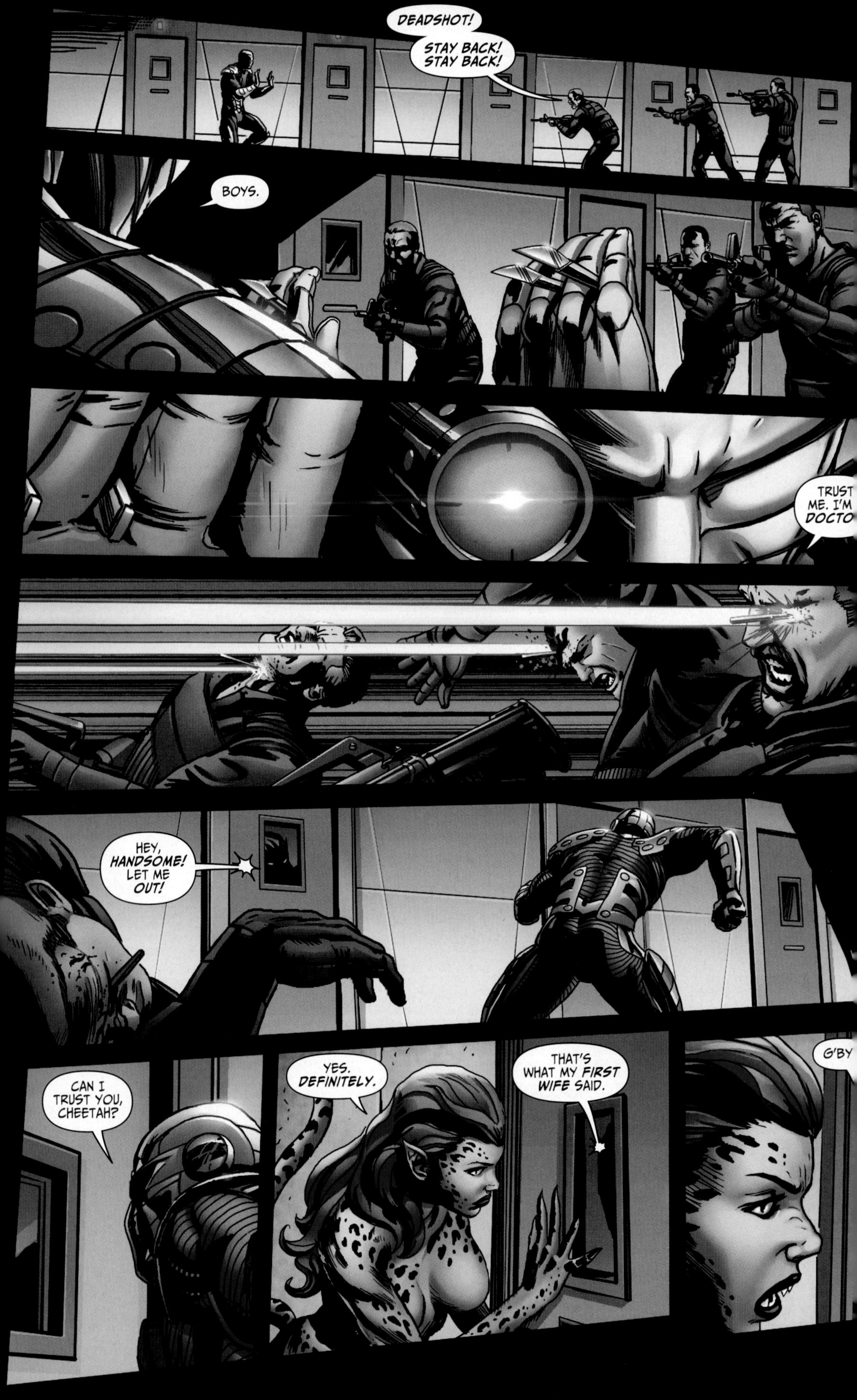

DEADSHOT!
STAY BACK! STAY BACK!
BOYS.
TRUST ME. I'M DOCTO
HEY, *HANDSOME!* LET ME *OUT!*
CAN I TRUST YOU, CHEETAH?
YES. *DEFINITELY.*
THAT'S WHAT MY *FIRST WIFE* SAID.
G'BY

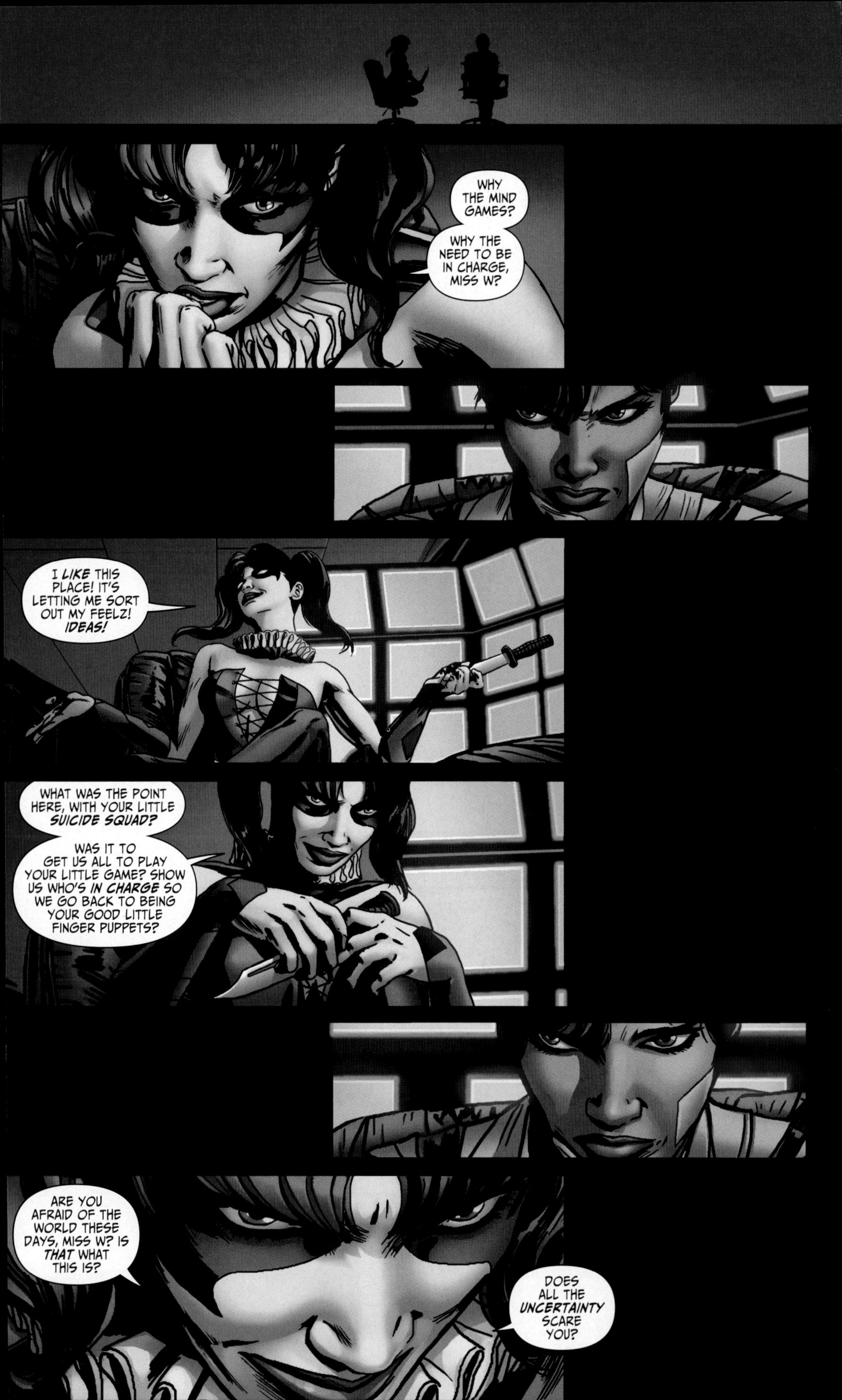
WHY THE MIND GAMES?
WHY THE NEED TO BE IN CHARGE, MISS W?
I *LIKE* THIS PLACE! IT'S LETTING ME SORT OUT MY FEELZ! *IDEAS!*
WHAT WAS THE POINT HERE, WITH YOUR LITTLE *SUICIDE SQUAD?*
WAS IT TO GET US ALL TO PLAY YOUR LITTLE GAME? SHOW US WHO'S *IN CHARGE* SO WE GO BACK TO BEING YOUR GOOD LITTLE FINGER PUPPETS?
ARE YOU AFRAID OF THE WORLD THESE DAYS, MISS W? IS *THAT* WHAT THIS IS?
DOES ALL THE *UNCERTAINTY* SCARE YOU?

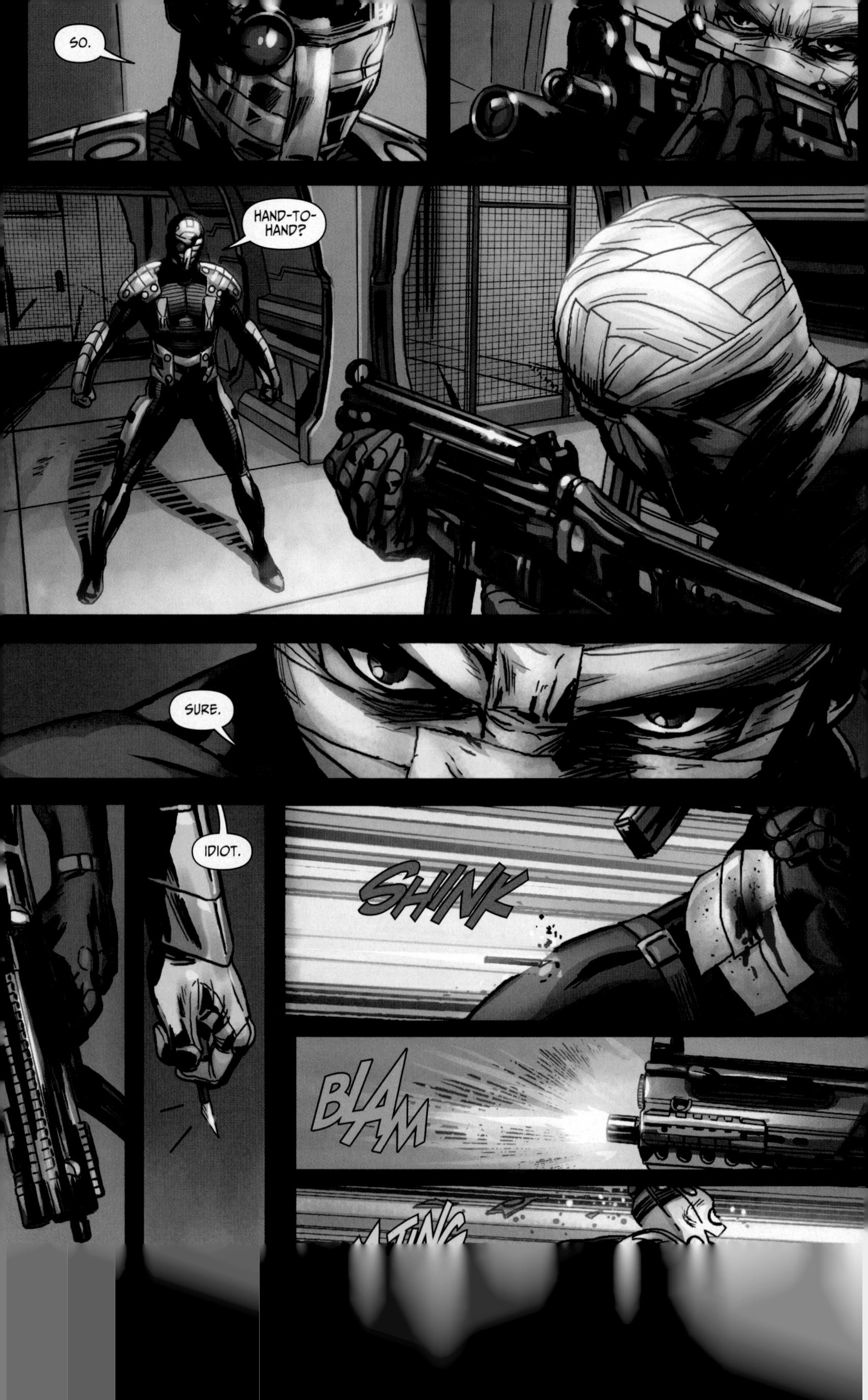
SO.
HAND-TO-HAND?
SURE.
IDIOT.
SHINK
BLAM

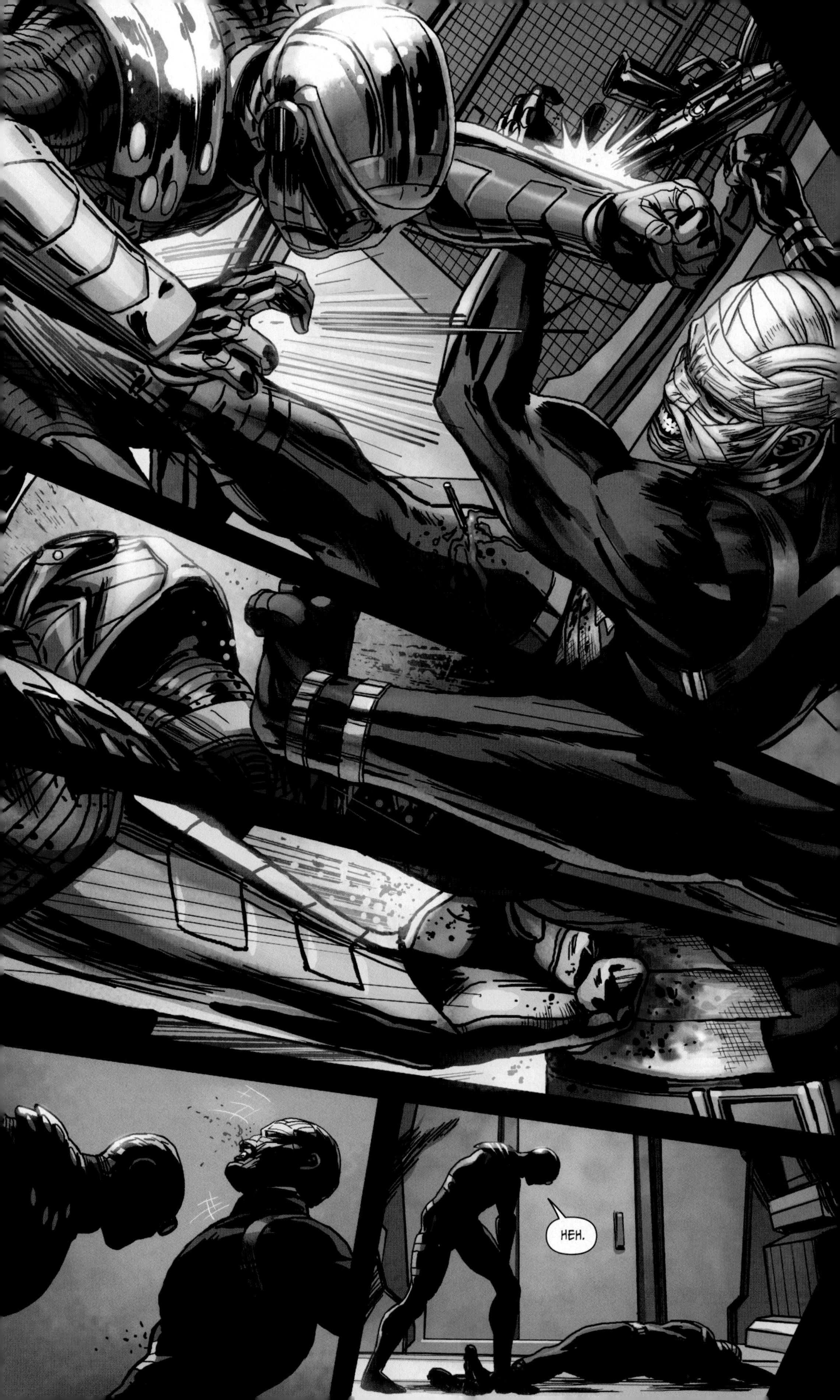
HEH.

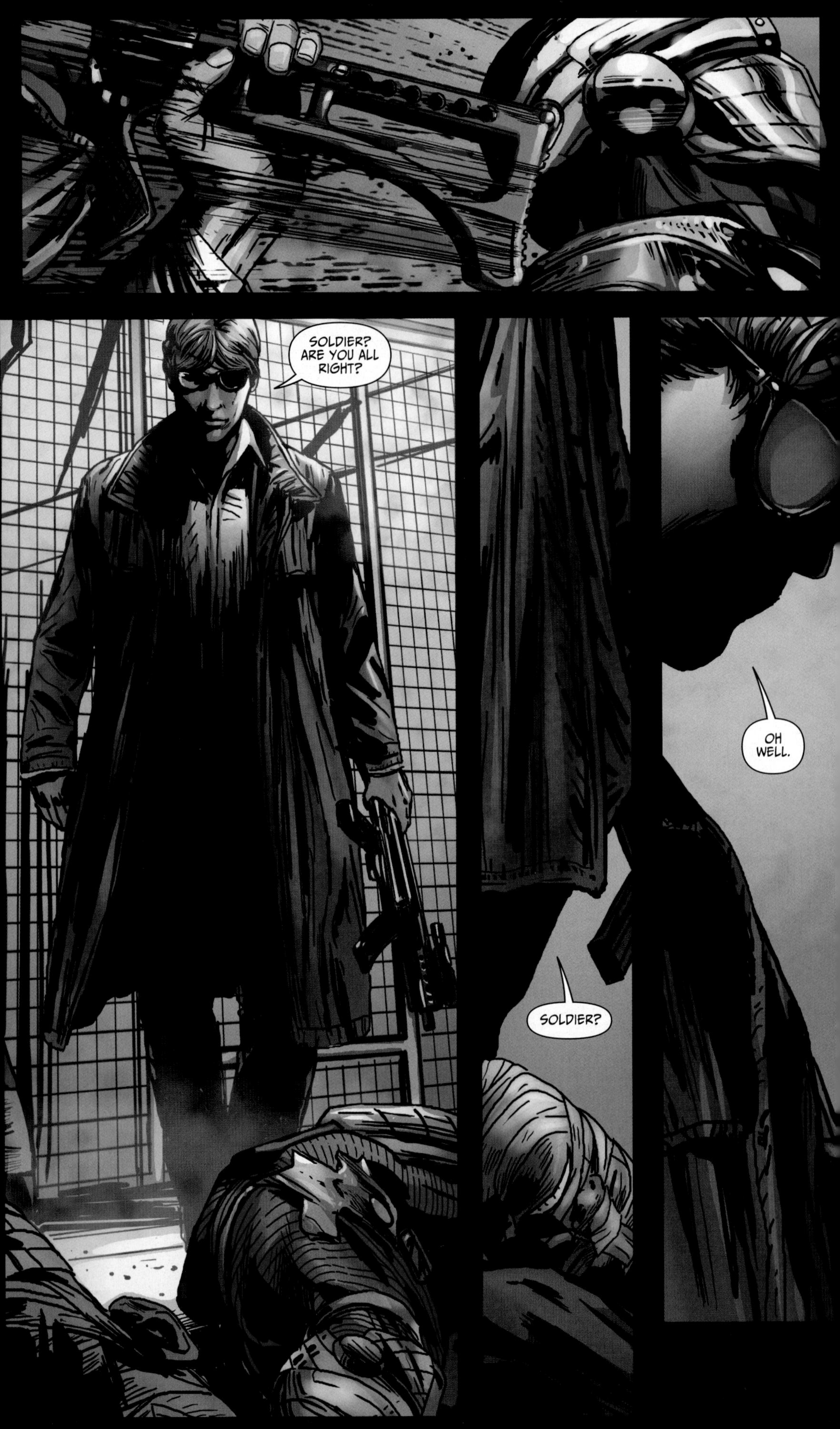
SOLDIER? ARE YOU ALL RIGHT?
SOLDIER?
OH WELL.

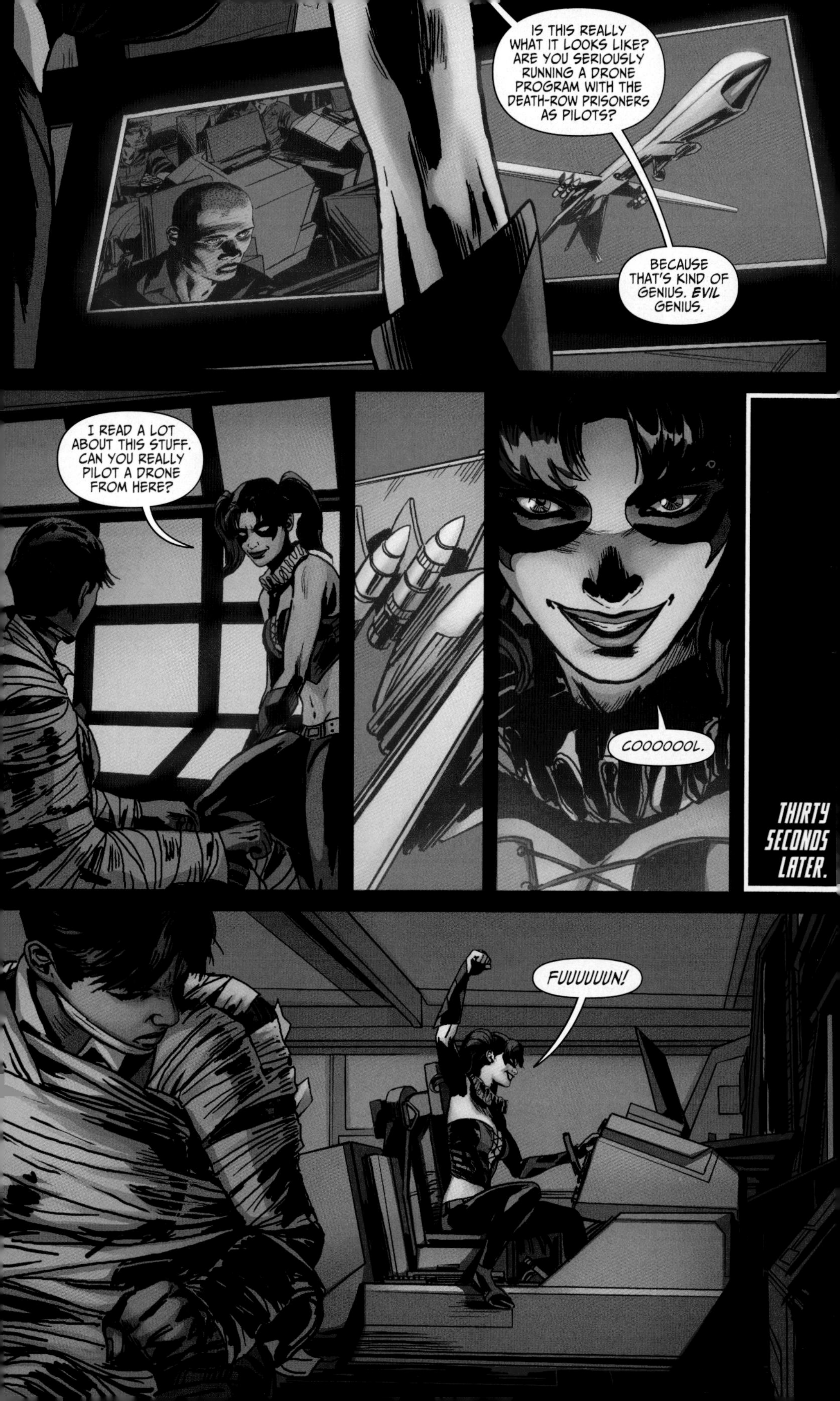
IS THIS REALLY WHAT IT LOOKS LIKE? ARE YOU SERIOUSLY RUNNING A DRONE PROGRAM WITH THE DEATH-ROW PRISONERS AS PILOTS?
BECAUSE THAT'S KIND OF GENIUS. EVIL GENIUS.
I READ A LOT ABOUT THIS STUFF. CAN YOU REALLY PILOT A DRONE FROM HERE?
COOOOOOL.
THIRTY SECONDS LATER.
FUUUUUUN!

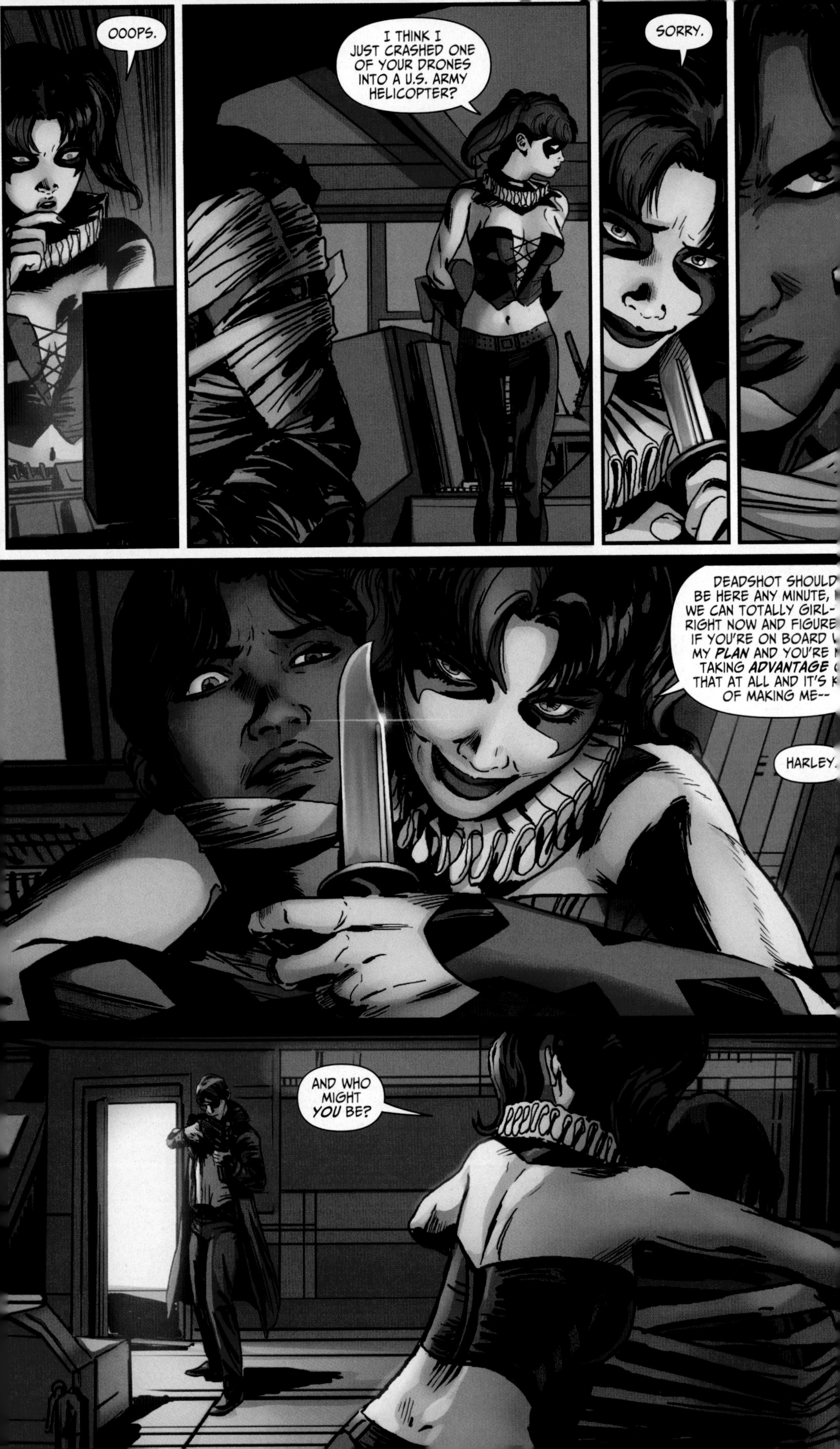
OOOPS.
I THINK I JUST CRASHED ONE OF YOUR DRONES INTO A U.S. ARMY HELICOPTER?
SORRY.
DEADSHOT SHOULD BE HERE ANY MINUTE, WE CAN TOTALLY GIRL- RIGHT NOW AND FIGURE IF YOU'RE ON BOARD MY PLAN AND YOU'RE TAKING ADVANTAGE THAT AT ALL AND IT'S OF MAKING ME--
HARLEY.
AND WHO MIGHT YOU BE?

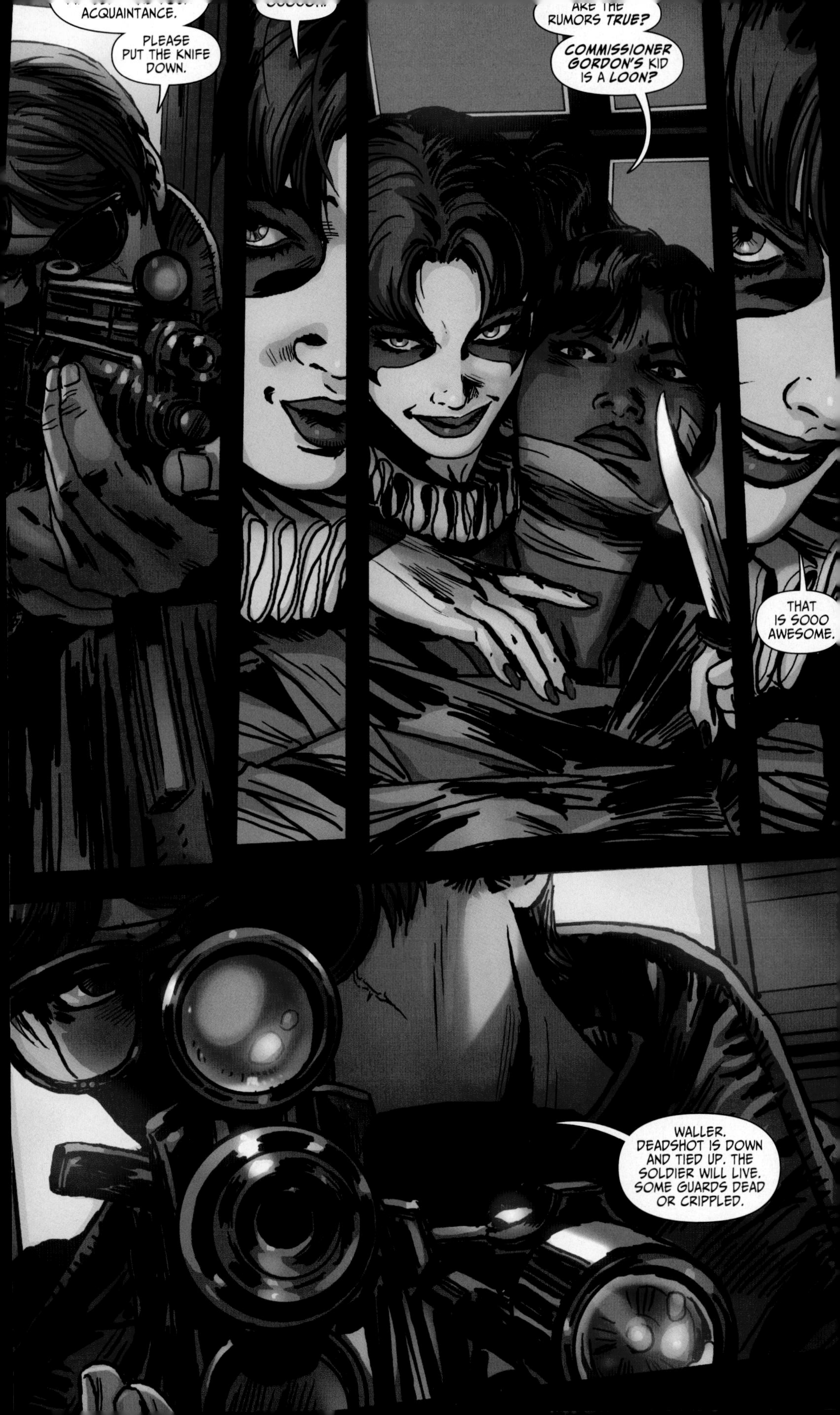
ACQUAINTANCE.
PLEASE PUT THE KNIFE DOWN.
ARE THE RUMORS TRUE?
COMMISSIONER GORDON'S KID IS A LOON?
THAT IS SOOO AWESOME.
WALLER. DEADSHOT IS DOWN AND TIED UP. THE SOLDIER WILL LIVE. SOME GUARDS DEAD OR CRIPPLED.

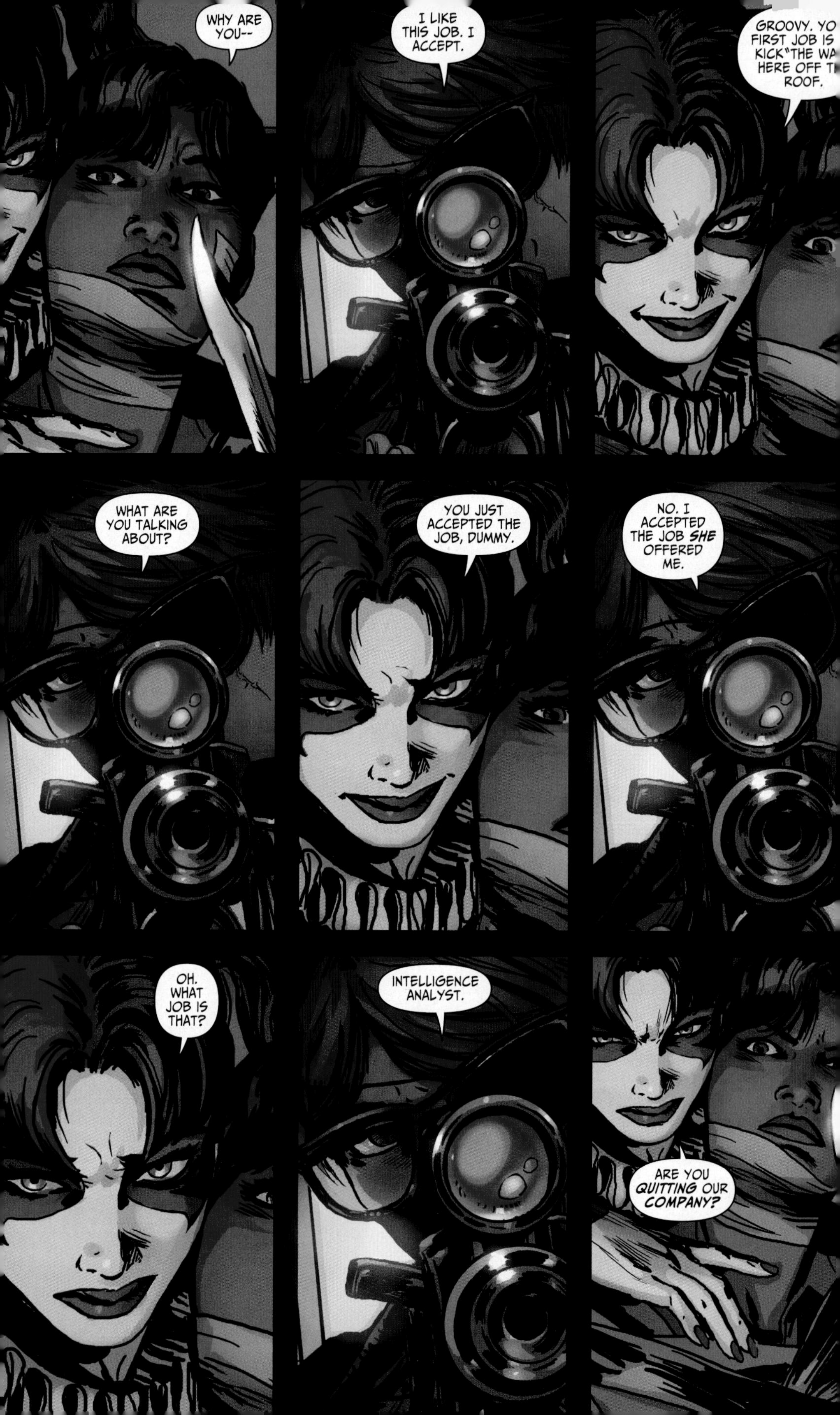
WHY ARE YOU--
I LIKE THIS JOB. I ACCEPT.
GROOVY. YO FIRST JOB IS KICK "THE WA HERE OFF T ROOF.
WHAT ARE YOU TALKING ABOUT?
YOU JUST ACCEPTED THE JOB, DUMMY.
NO. I ACCEPTED THE JOB SHE OFFERED ME.
OH. WHAT JOB IS THAT?
INTELLIGENCE ANALYST.
ARE YOU QUITTING OUR COMPANY?

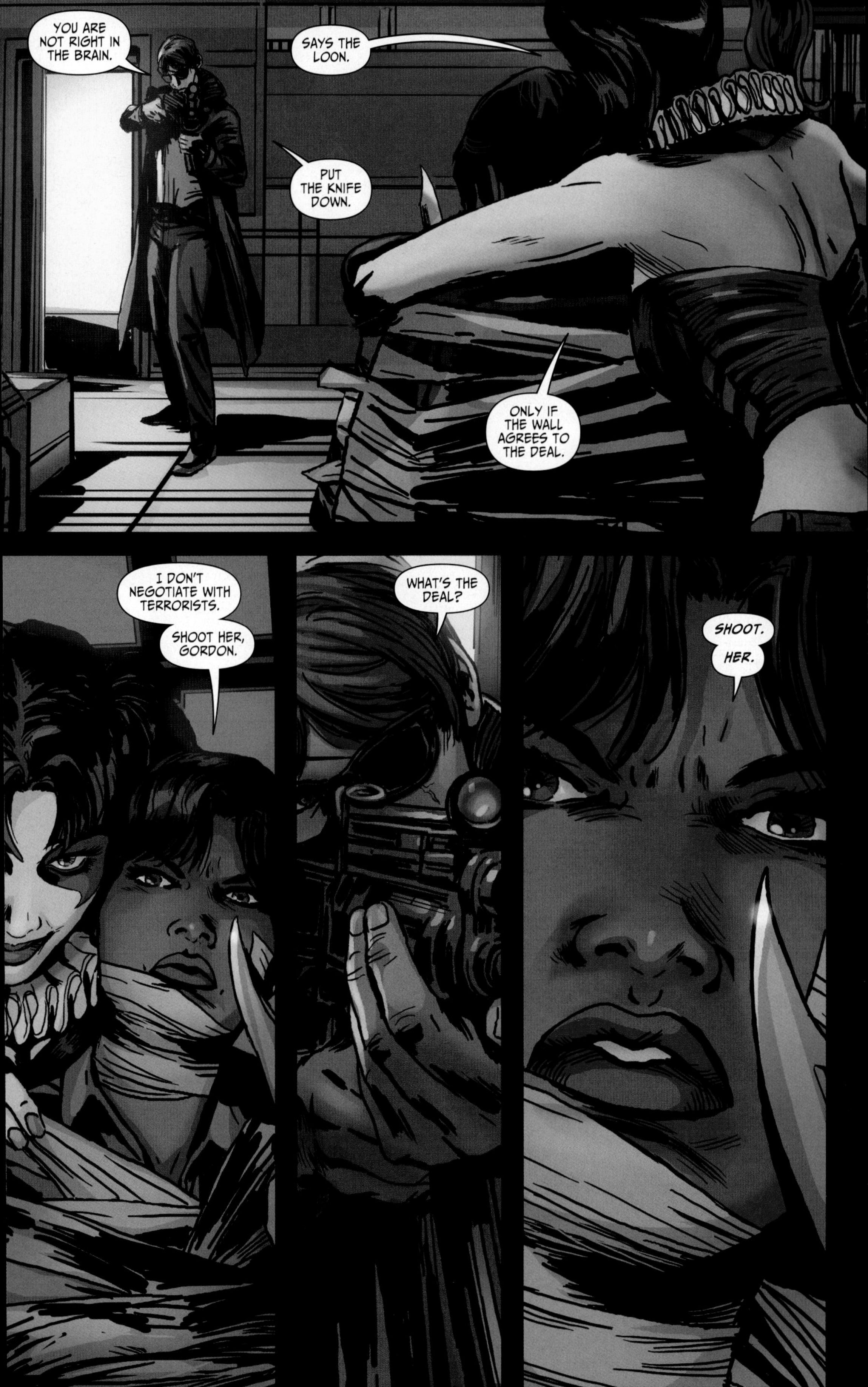
YOU ARE NOT RIGHT IN THE BRAIN.
SAYS THE LOON.
PUT THE KNIFE DOWN.
ONLY IF THE WALL AGREES TO THE DEAL.
I DON'T NEGOTIATE WITH TERRORISTS.
SHOOT HER, GORDON.
WHAT'S THE DEAL?
SHOOT.
HER.

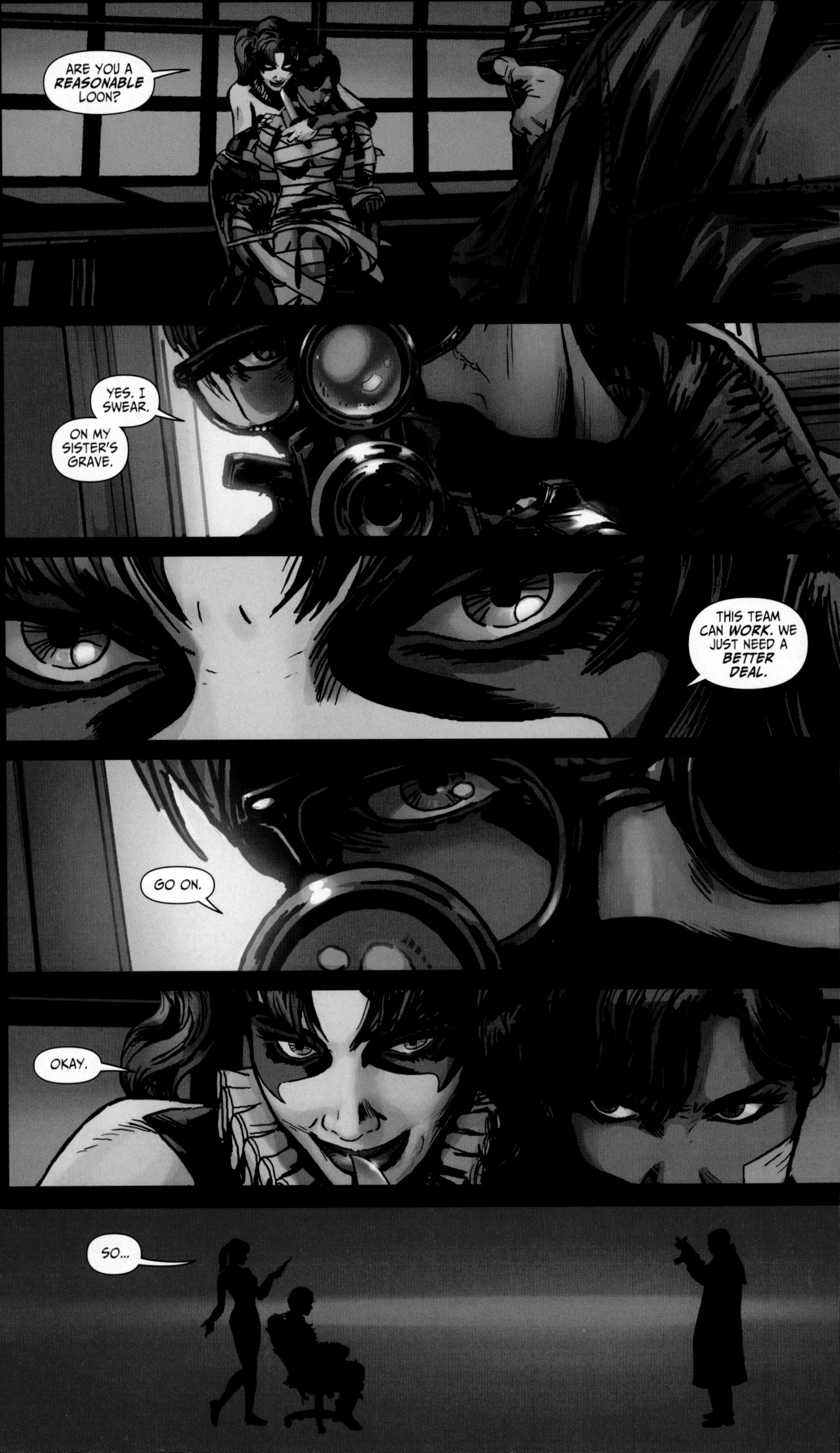
ARE YOU A REASONABLE LOON?
YES. I SWEAR.
ON MY SISTER'S GRAVE.
THIS TEAM CAN WORK. WE JUST NEED A BETTER DEAL.
GO ON.
OKAY.
SO...

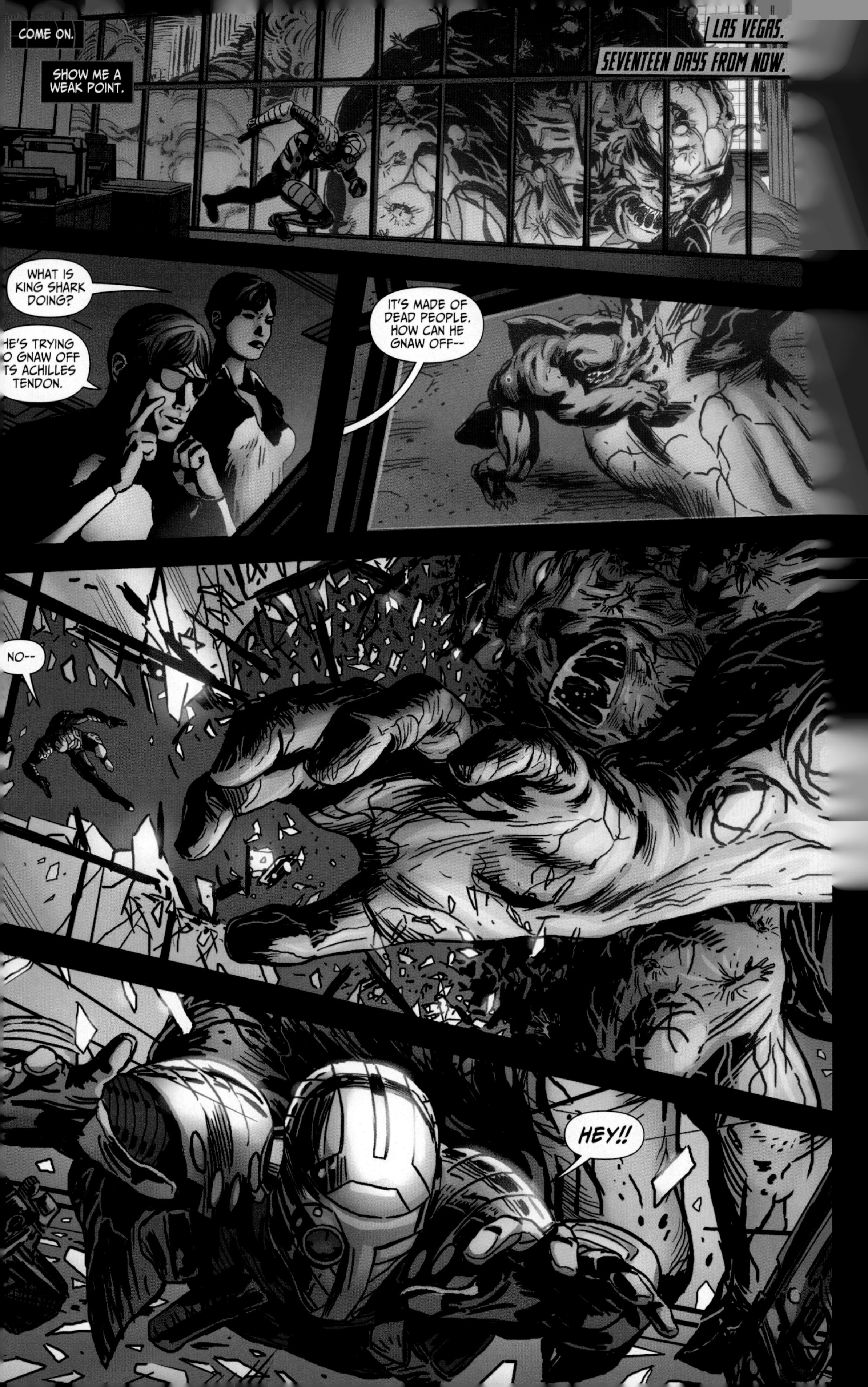
COME ON.
SHOW ME A WEAK POINT.
LAS VEGAS.
SEVENTEEN DAYS FROM NOW.
WHAT IS KING SHARK DOING?
HE'S TRYING TO GNAW OFF ITS ACHILLES TENDON.
IT'S MADE OF DEAD PEOPLE. HOW CAN HE GNAW OFF--
NO--
HEY!!

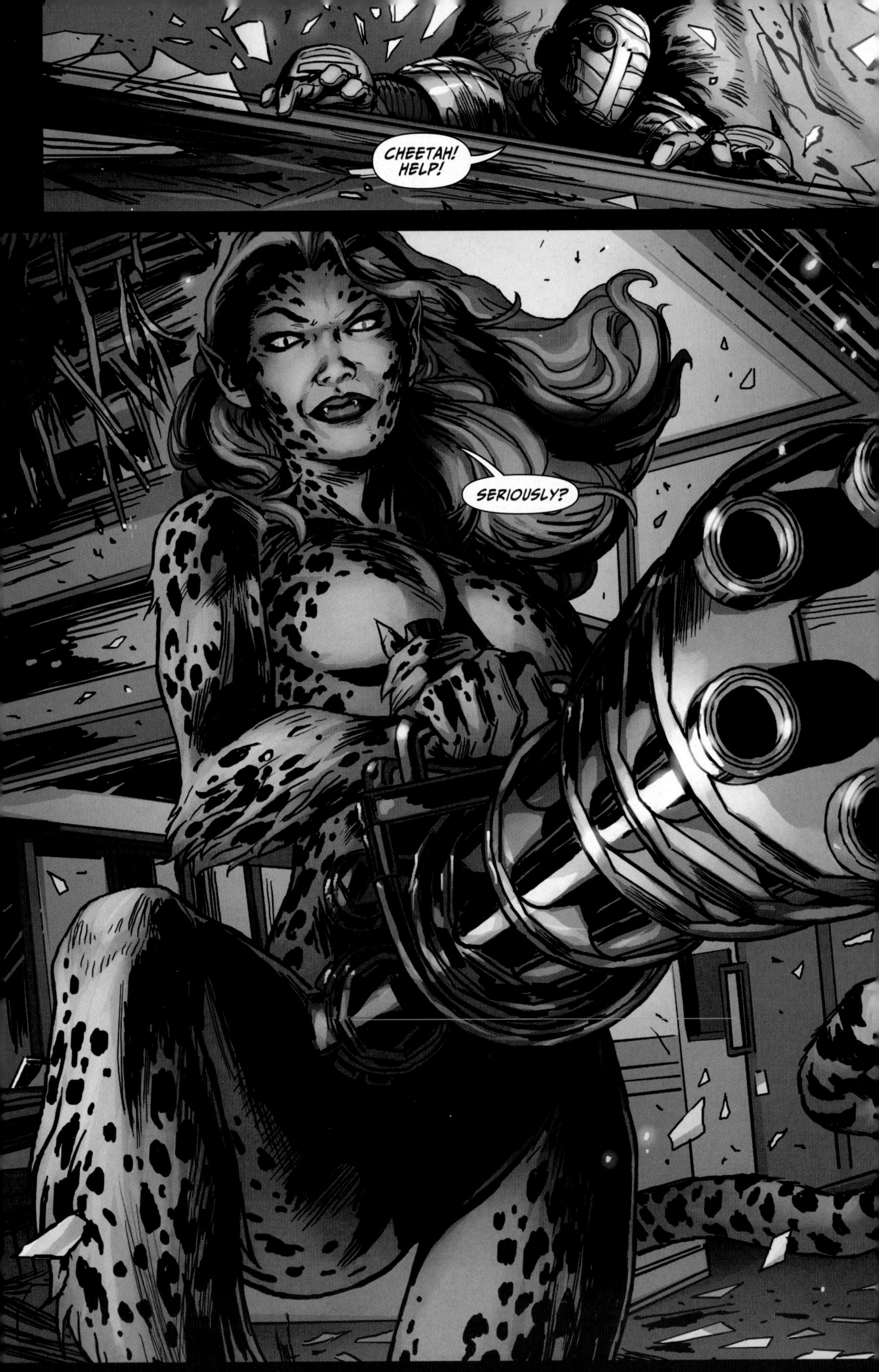
CHEETAH! HELP!
SERIOUSLY?

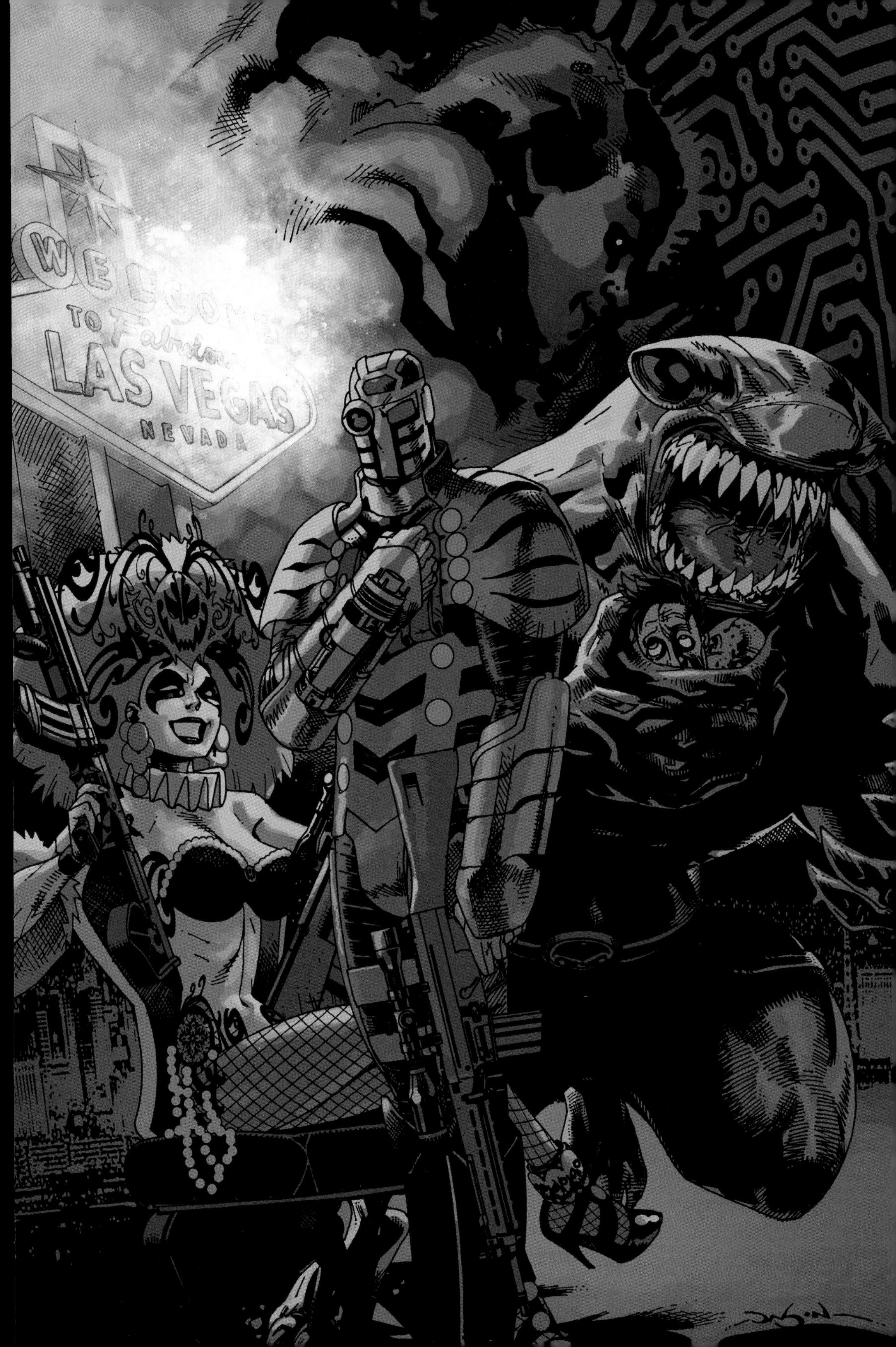
WELCOME
TO Fabulous
LAS VEGAS
NEVADA

LIGHT AT THE END OF THE TUNNEL

ALES KOT writer PATRICK ZIRCHER artist cover by JASON PEARSON

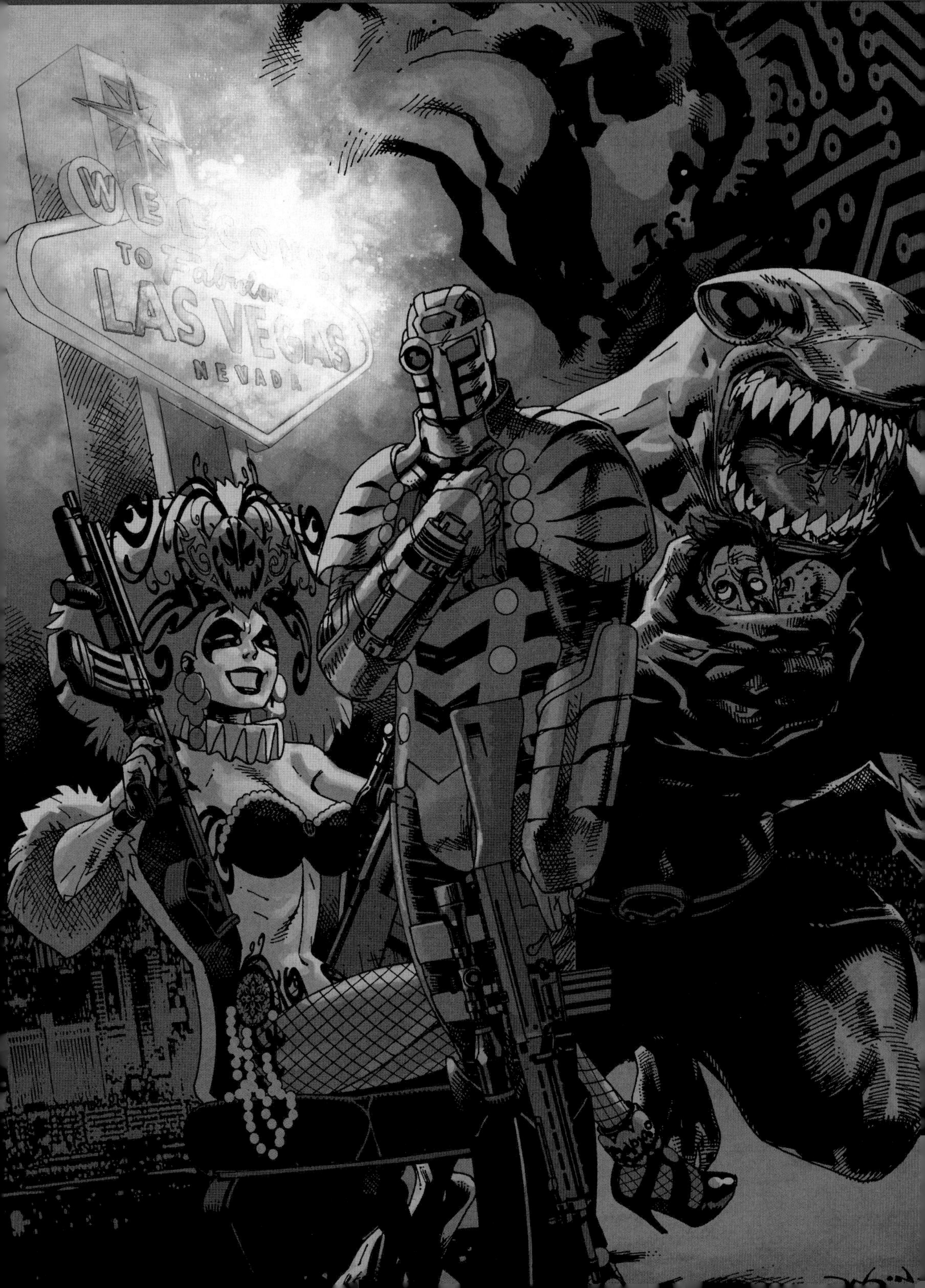
WELCOME
TO Fabulous
LAS VEGAS
NEVADA

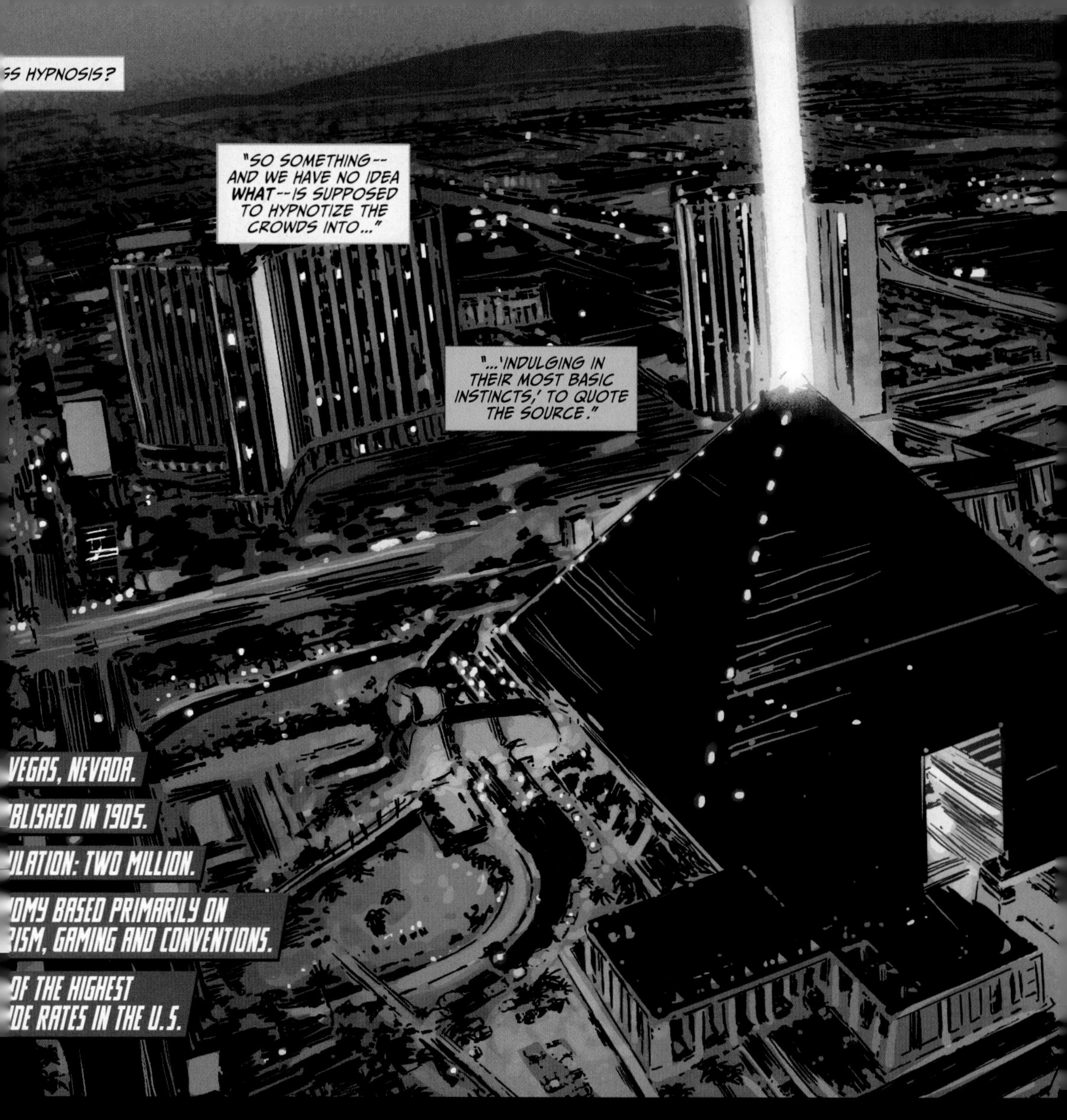

...GS HYPNOSIS?
"SO SOMETHING--AND WE HAVE NO IDEA WHAT--IS SUPPOSED TO HYPNOTIZE THE CROWDS INTO..."
"...'INDULGING IN THEIR MOST BASIC INSTINCTS,' TO QUOTE THE SOURCE."
...VEGAS, NEVADA.
...BLISHED IN 1905.
...ULATION: TWO MILLION.
...OMY BASED PRIMARILY ON
...RISM, GAMING AND CONVENTIONS.
...OF THE HIGHEST
...DE RATES IN THE U.S.

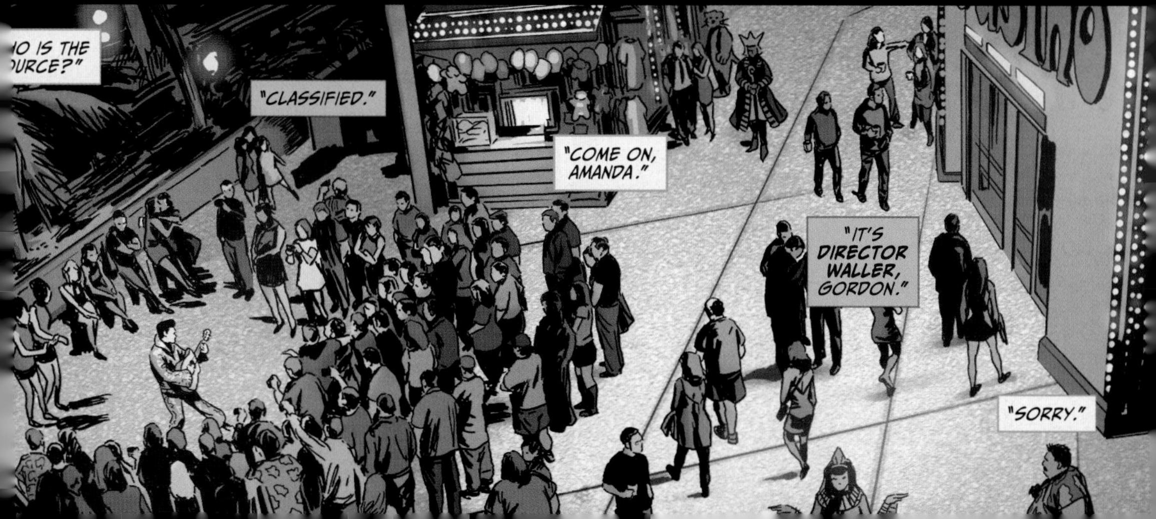

...HO IS THE
...OURCE?"
"CLASSIFIED."
"COME ON, AMANDA."
"IT'S DIRECTOR WALLER, GORDON."
"SORRY."

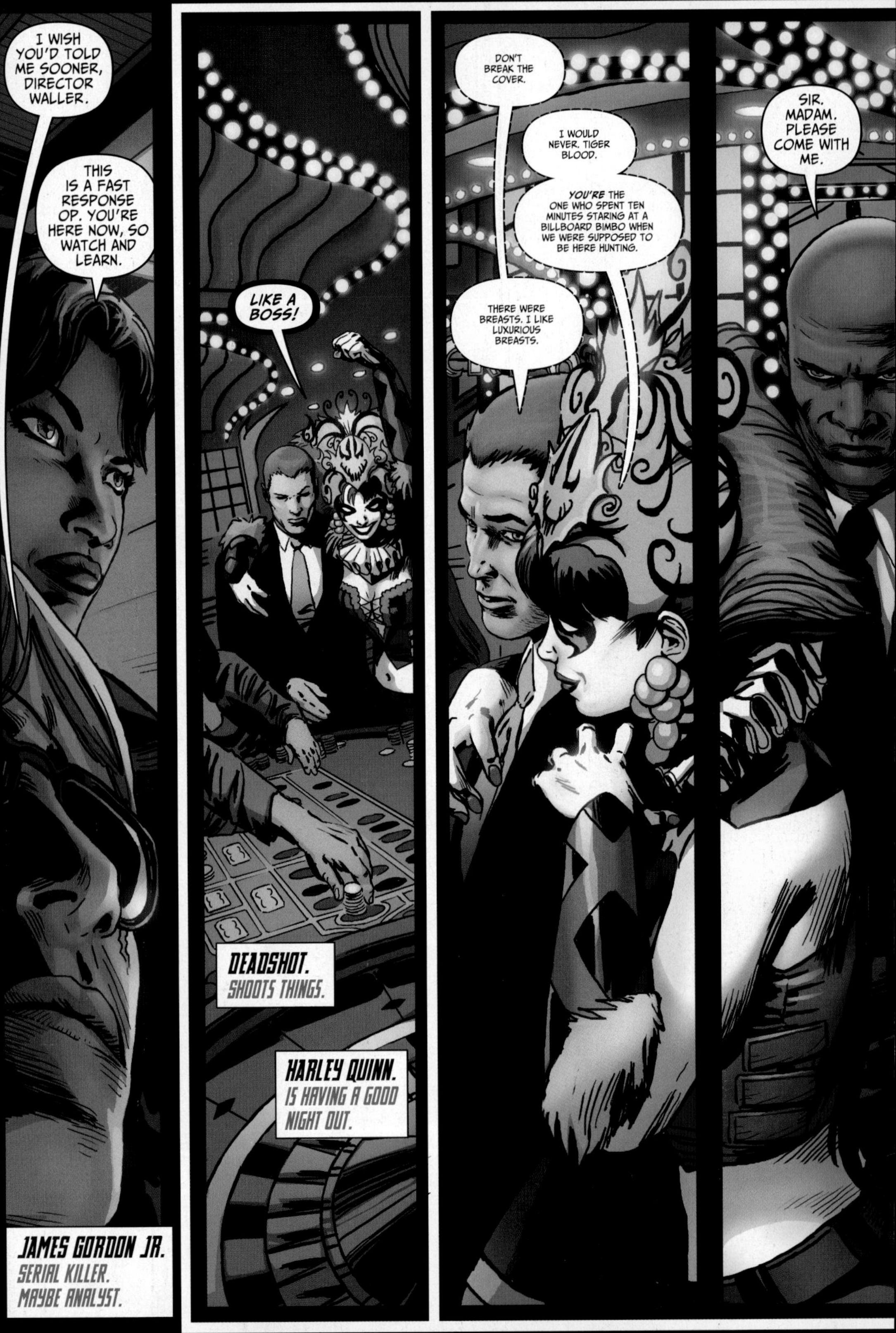
I WISH YOU'D TOLD ME SOONER, DIRECTOR WALLER.
THIS IS A FAST RESPONSE OP. YOU'RE HERE NOW, SO WATCH AND LEARN.
JAMES GORDON JR. SERIAL KILLER. MAYBE ANALYST.
LIKE A BOSS!
DEADSHOT. SHOOTS THINGS.
HARLEY QUINN. IS HAVING A GOOD NIGHT OUT.
DON'T BREAK THE COVER.
I WOULD NEVER, TIGER BLOOD.
YOU'RE THE ONE WHO SPENT TEN MINUTES STARING AT A BILLBOARD BIMBO WHEN WE WERE SUPPOSED TO BE HERE HUNTING.
THERE WERE BREASTS. I LIKE LUXURIOUS BREASTS.
SIR. MADAM. PLEASE COME WITH ME.

LIGHT AT THE END OF THE TUNNEL

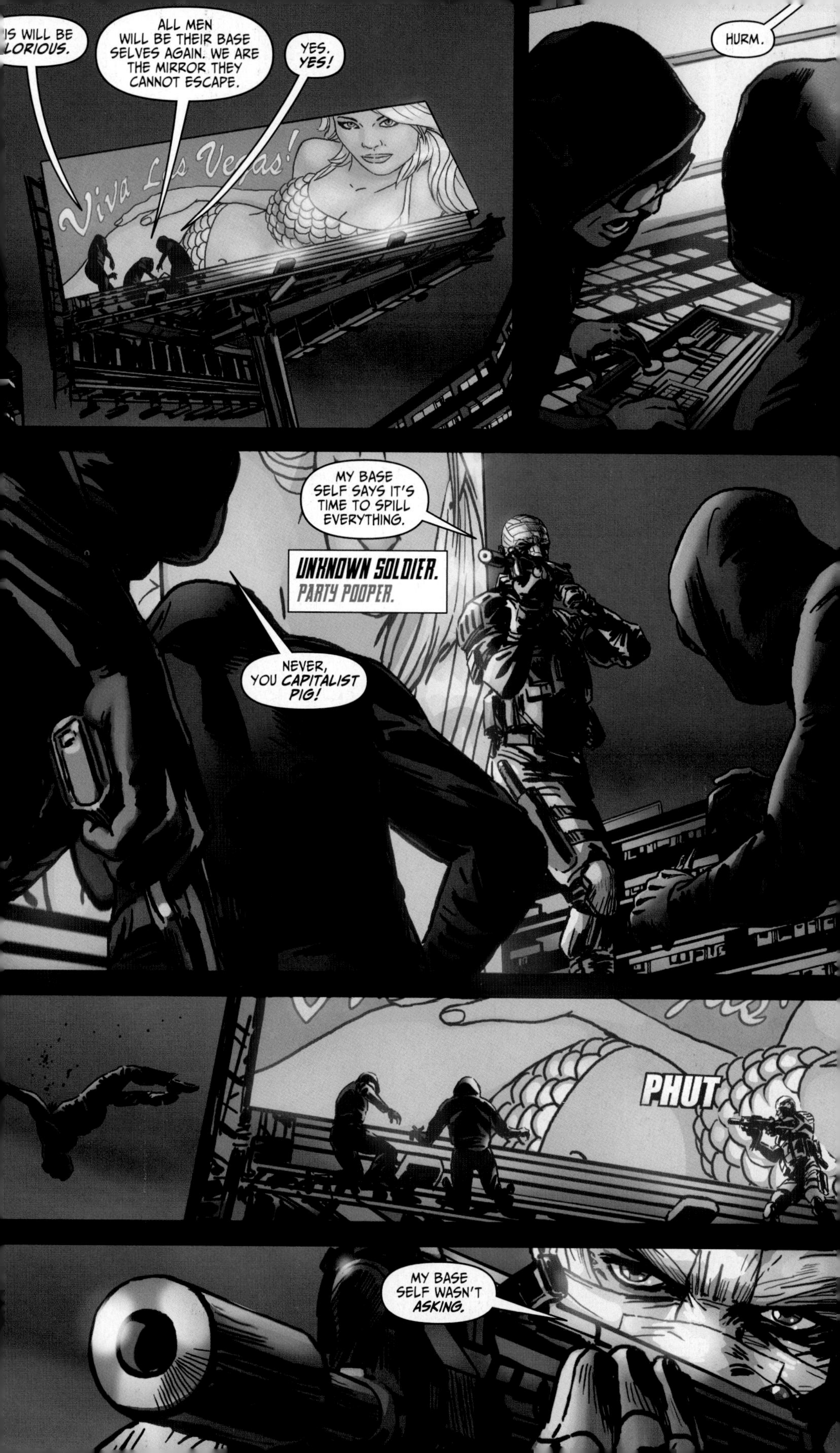

IS WILL BE
LORIOUS.
ALL MEN WILL BE THEIR BASE SELVES AGAIN. WE ARE THE MIRROR THEY CANNOT ESCAPE.
YES. YES!
Viva Las Vegas!
HURM.
MY BASE SELF SAYS IT'S TIME TO SPILL EVERYTHING.
UNKNOWN SOLDIER.
PARTY POOPER.
NEVER, YOU CAPITALIST PIG!
PHUT
MY BASE SELF WASN'T ASKING.

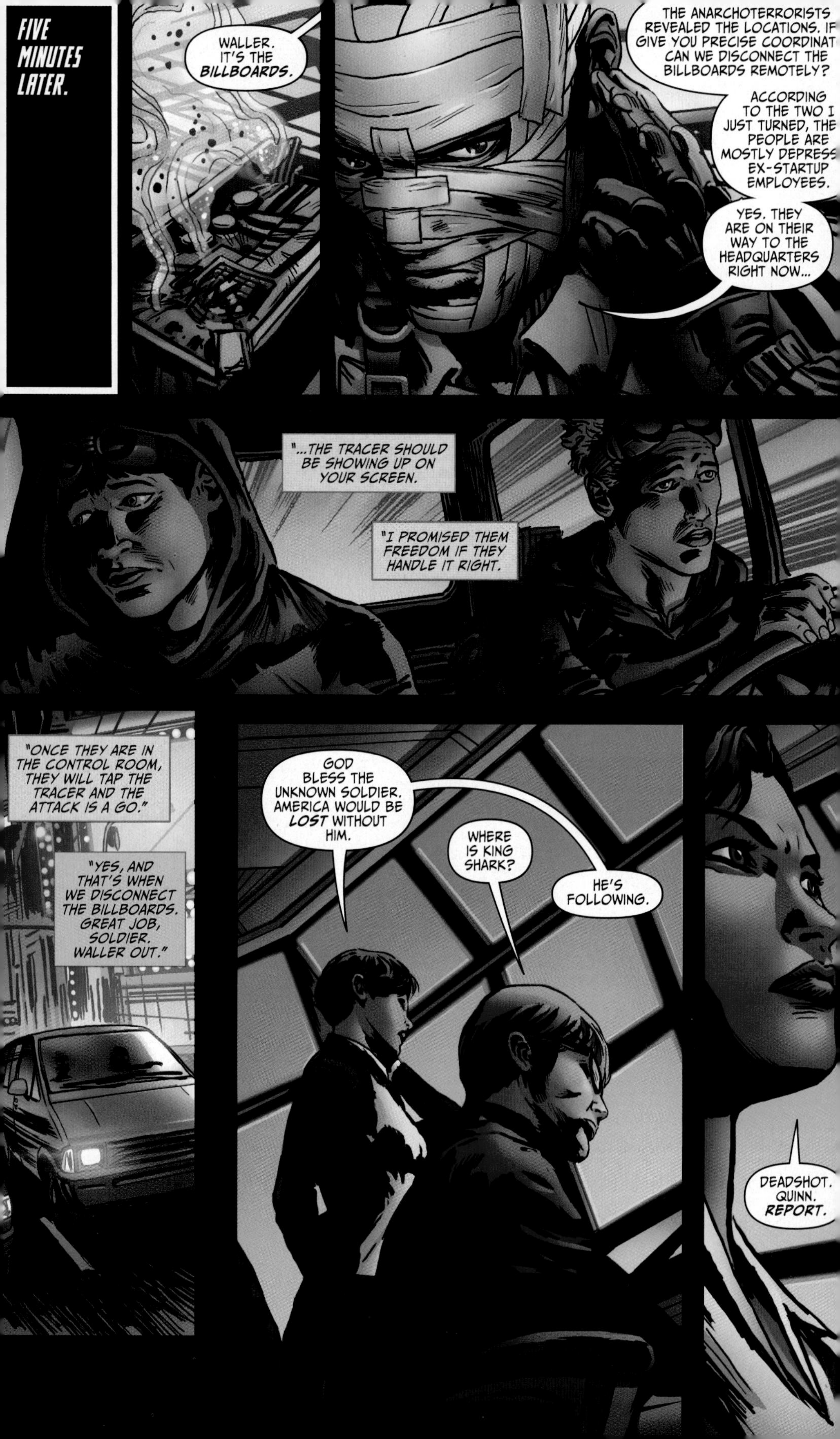
FIVE MINUTES LATER.
WALLER. IT'S THE *BILLBOARDS.*
THE ANARCHOTERRORISTS REVEALED THE LOCATIONS. IF GIVE YOU PRECISE COORDINAT CAN WE DISCONNECT THE BILLBOARDS REMOTELY?
ACCORDING TO THE TWO I JUST TURNED, THE PEOPLE ARE MOSTLY DEPRESS EX-STARTUP EMPLOYEES.
YES. THEY ARE ON THEIR WAY TO THE HEADQUARTERS RIGHT NOW...
"...THE TRACER SHOULD BE SHOWING UP ON YOUR SCREEN.
"I PROMISED THEM FREEDOM IF THEY HANDLE IT RIGHT.
"ONCE THEY ARE IN THE CONTROL ROOM, THEY WILL TAP THE TRACER AND THE ATTACK IS A GO."
"YES, AND THAT'S WHEN WE DISCONNECT THE BILLBOARDS. GREAT JOB, SOLDIER. WALLER OUT."
GOD BLESS THE UNKNOWN SOLDIER. AMERICA WOULD BE *LOST* WITHOUT HIM.
WHERE IS KING SHARK?
HE'S FOLLOWING.
DEADSHOT. QUINN. *REPORT.*

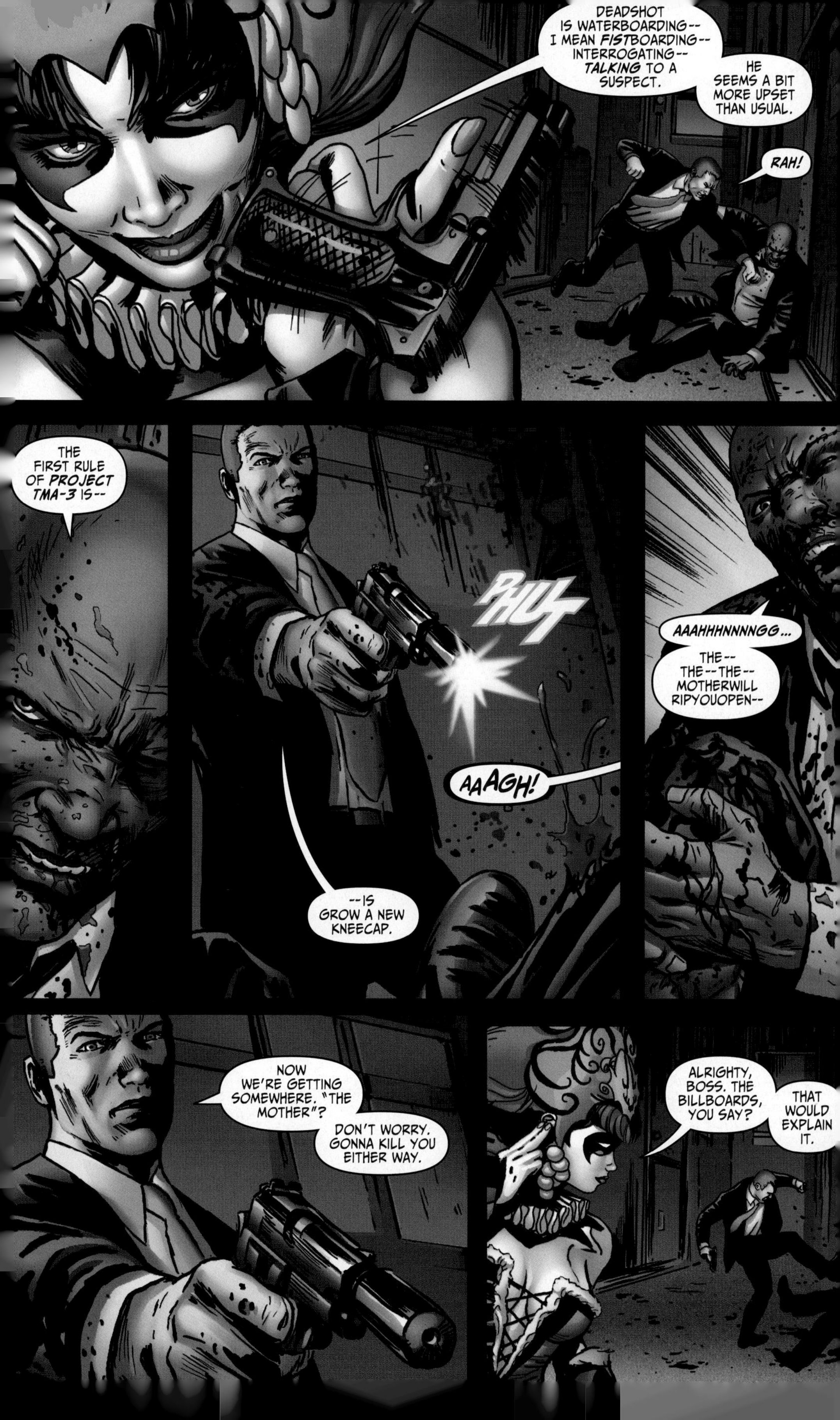
DEADSHOT IS WATERBOARDING-- I MEAN FISTBOARDING-- INTERROGATING-- TALKING TO A SUSPECT.
HE SEEMS A BIT MORE UPSET THAN USUAL.
RAH!
THE FIRST RULE OF PROJECT TMA-3 IS--
PHUT
--IS GROW A NEW KNEECAP.
AAAGH!
AAAHHHNNNGG...
THE-- THE--THE-- MOTHERWILL RIPYOUOPEN--
NOW WE'RE GETTING SOMEWHERE. "THE MOTHER"?
DON'T WORRY. GONNA KILL YOU EITHER WAY.
ALRIGHTY, BOSS. THE BILLBOARDS, YOU SAY?
THAT WOULD EXPLAIN IT.

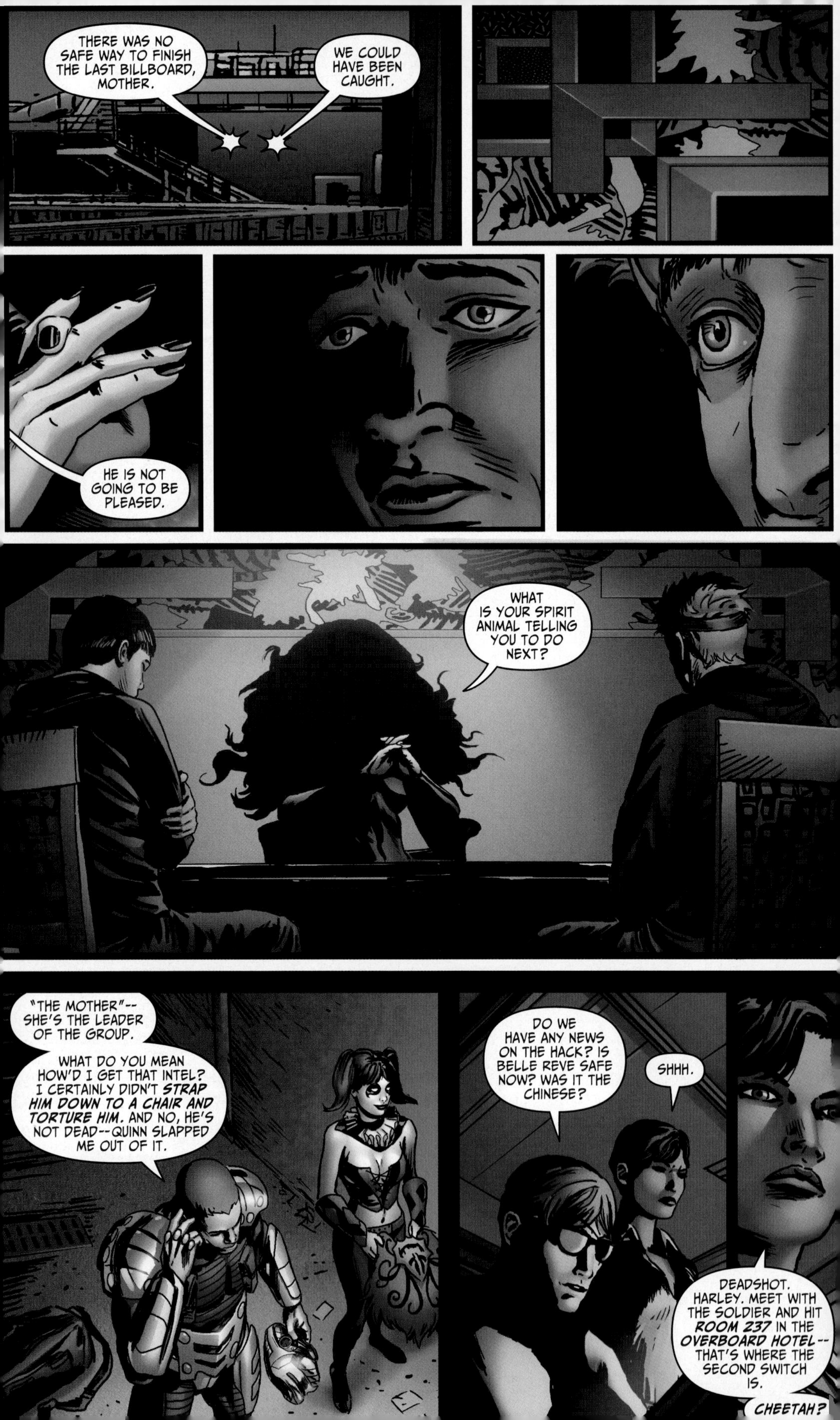
THERE WAS NO SAFE WAY TO FINISH THE LAST BILLBOARD, MOTHER.
WE COULD HAVE BEEN CAUGHT.
HE IS NOT GOING TO BE PLEASED.
WHAT IS YOUR SPIRIT ANIMAL TELLING YOU TO DO NEXT?
"THE MOTHER"-- SHE'S THE LEADER OF THE GROUP.
WHAT DO YOU MEAN HOW'D I GET THAT INTEL? I CERTAINLY DIDN'T STRAP HIM DOWN TO A CHAIR AND TORTURE HIM. AND NO, HE'S NOT DEAD--QUINN SLAPPED ME OUT OF IT.
DO WE HAVE ANY NEWS ON THE HACK? IS BELLE REVE SAFE NOW? WAS IT THE CHINESE?
SHHH.
DEADSHOT. HARLEY. MEET WITH THE SOLDIER AND HIT ROOM 237 IN THE OVERBOARD HOTEL-- THAT'S WHERE THE SECOND SWITCH IS.
CHEETAH?

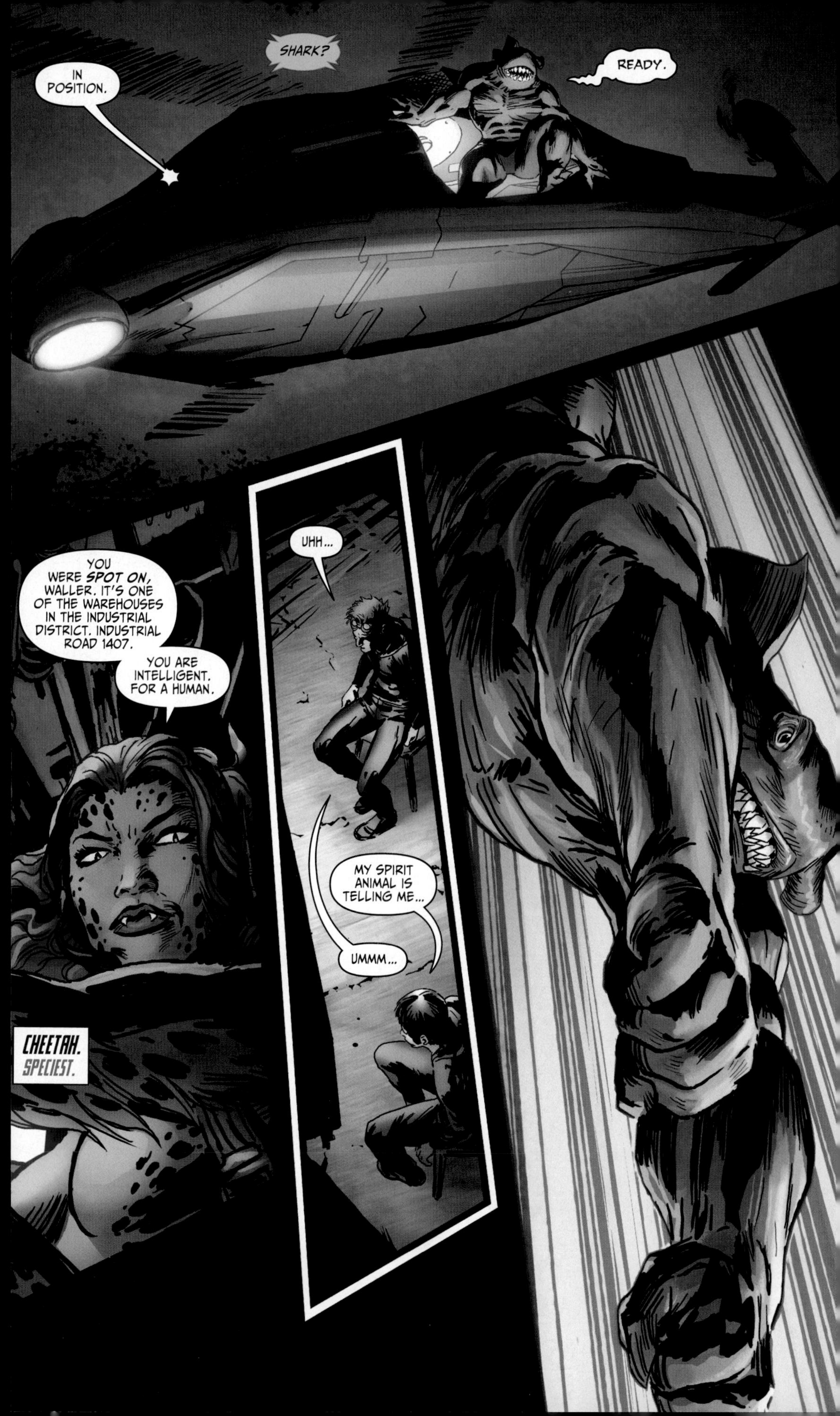

SHARK?
IN POSITION.
READY.
YOU WERE **SPOT ON**, WALLER. IT'S ONE OF THE WAREHOUSES IN THE INDUSTRIAL DISTRICT. INDUSTRIAL ROAD 1407.
YOU ARE INTELLIGENT. FOR A HUMAN.
CHEETAH. SPECIEST.
UHH...
MY SPIRIT ANIMAL IS TELLING ME...
UMMM...

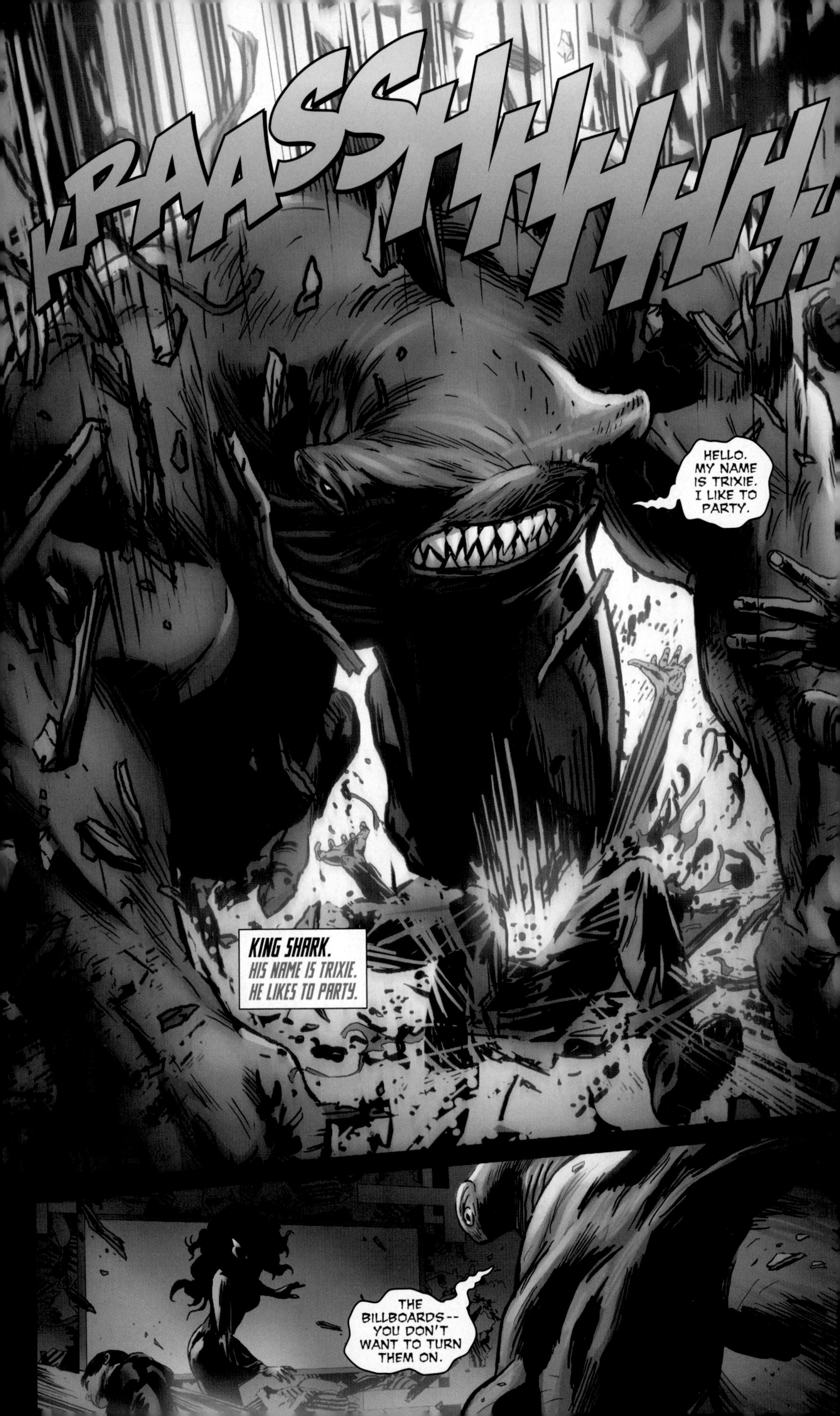
KRAASHHHHH
HELLO. MY NAME IS TRIXIE. I LIKE TO PARTY.
KING SHARK. HIS NAME IS TRIXIE. HE LIKES TO PARTY.
THE BILLBOARDS-- YOU DON'T WANT TO TURN THEM ON.

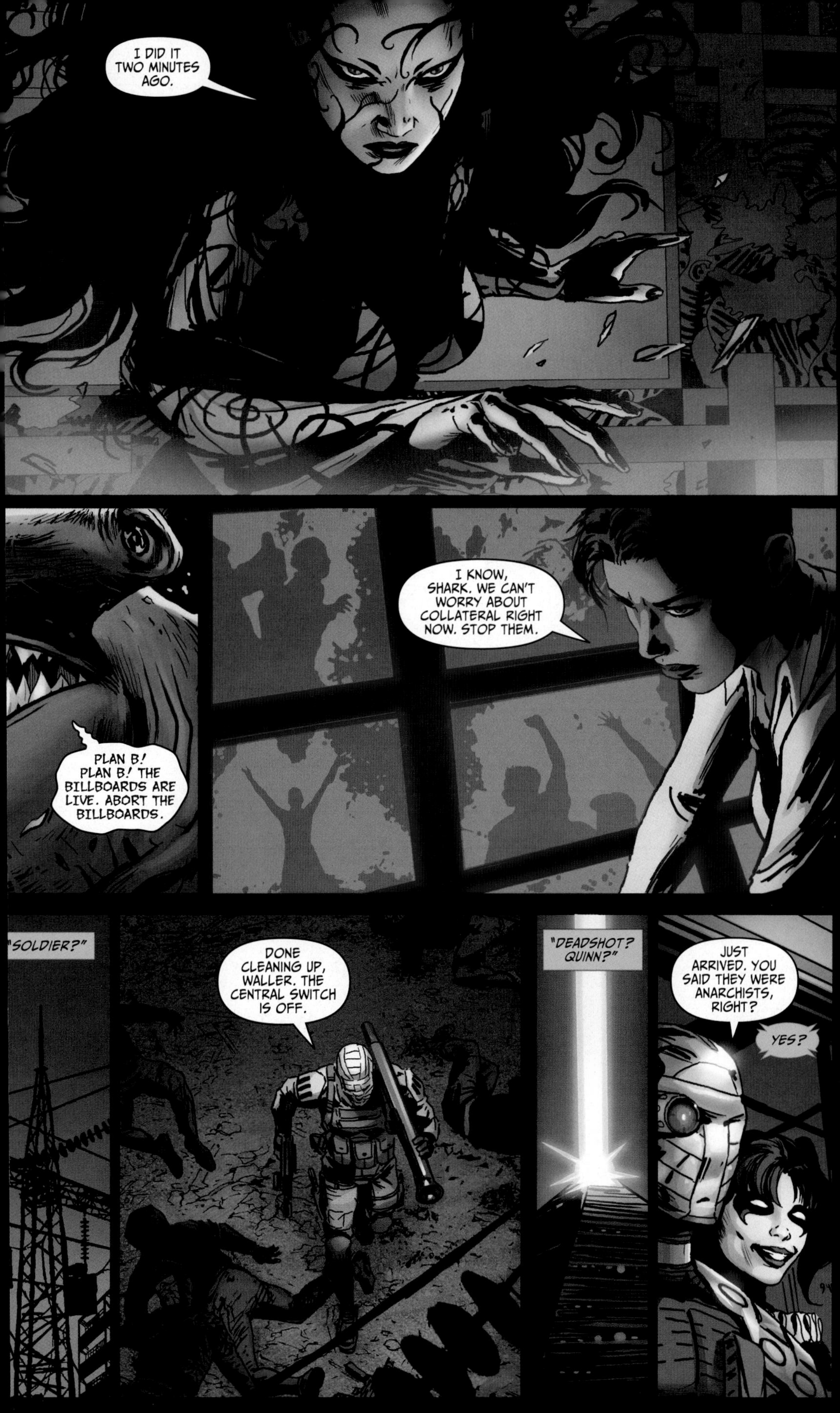

I DID IT TWO MINUTES AGO.
PLAN B! PLAN B! THE BILLBOARDS ARE LIVE. ABORT THE BILLBOARDS.
I KNOW, SHARK. WE CAN'T WORRY ABOUT COLLATERAL RIGHT NOW. STOP THEM.
"SOLDIER?"
DONE CLEANING UP, WALLER. THE CENTRAL SWITCH IS OFF.
"DEADSHOT? QUINN?"
JUST ARRIVED. YOU SAID THEY WERE ANARCHISTS, RIGHT?
YES?

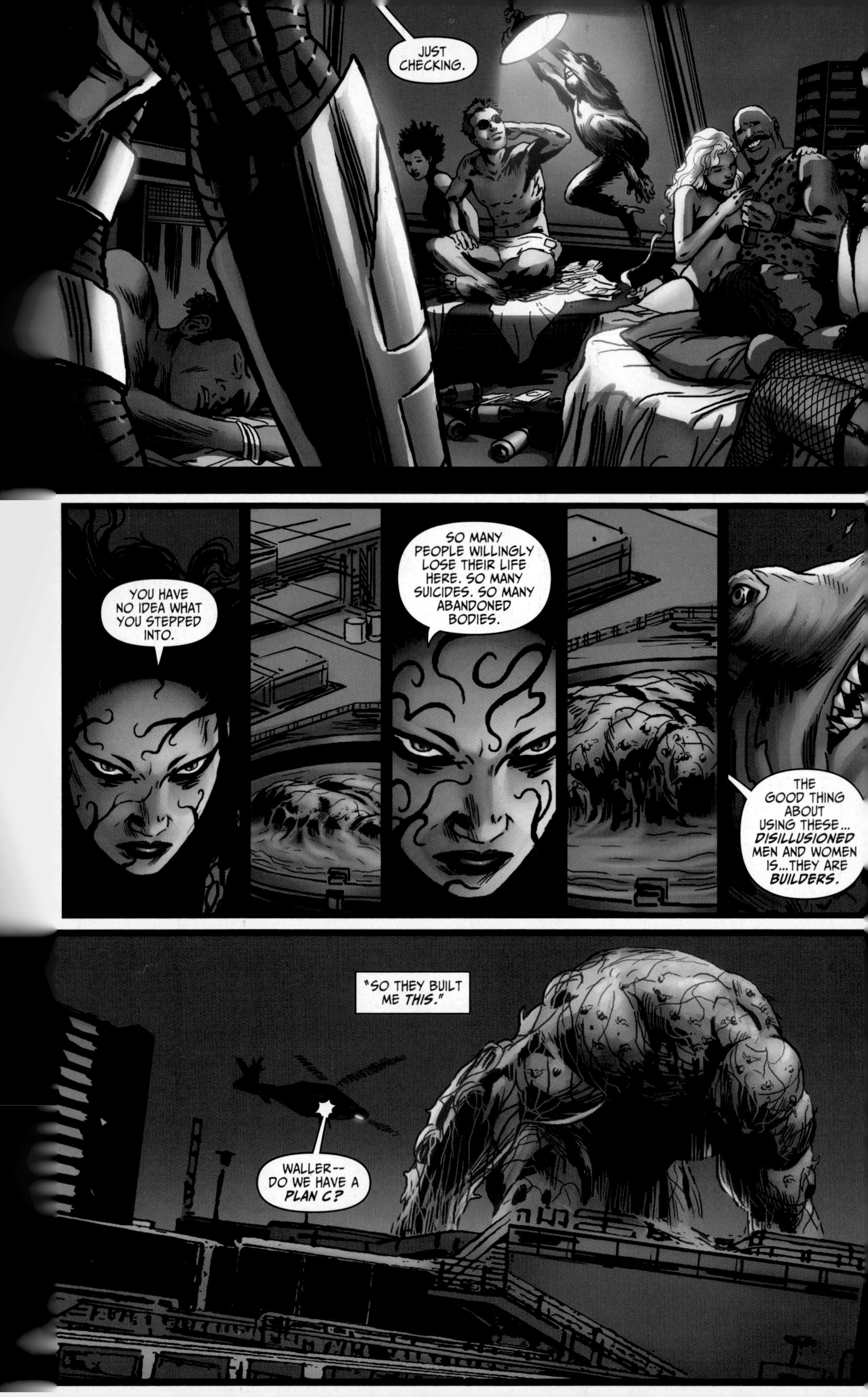
JUST CHECKING.
YOU HAVE NO IDEA WHAT YOU STEPPED INTO.
SO MANY PEOPLE WILLINGLY LOSE THEIR LIFE HERE. SO MANY SUICIDES. SO MANY ABANDONED BODIES.
THE GOOD THING ABOUT USING THESE... DISILLUSIONED MEN AND WOMEN IS...THEY ARE BUILDERS.
"SO THEY BUILT ME THIS."
WALLER-- DO WE HAVE A PLAN C?

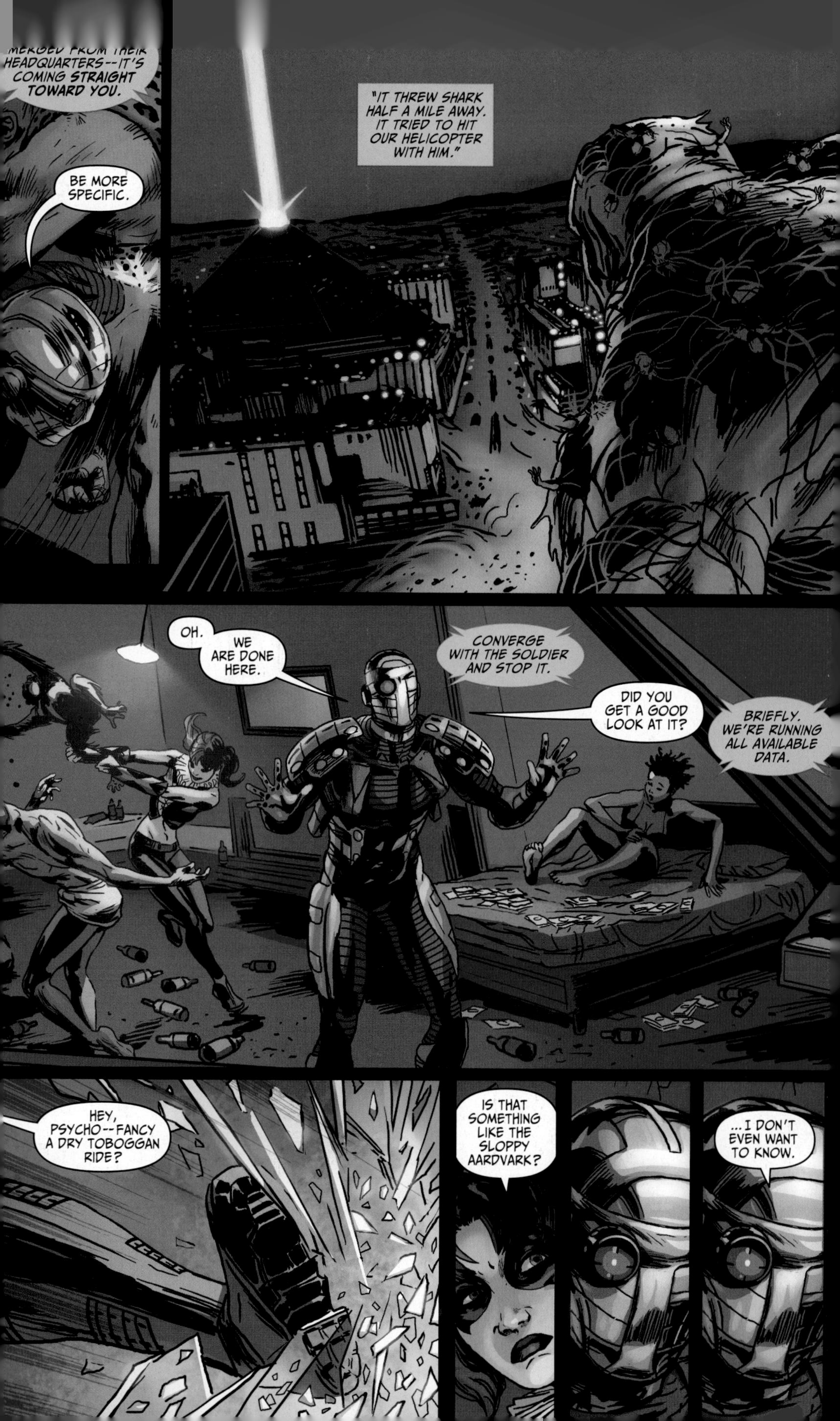

...MERGED FROM THEIR HEADQUARTERS--IT'S COMING STRAIGHT TOWARD YOU.
BE MORE SPECIFIC.
"IT THREW SHARK HALF A MILE AWAY. IT TRIED TO HIT OUR HELICOPTER WITH HIM."
OH.
WE ARE DONE HERE.
CONVERGE WITH THE SOLDIER AND STOP IT.
DID YOU GET A GOOD LOOK AT IT?
BRIEFLY. WE'RE RUNNING ALL AVAILABLE DATA.
HEY, PSYCHO--FANCY A DRY TOBOGGAN RIDE?
IS THAT SOMETHING LIKE THE SLOPPY AARDVARK?
...I DON'T EVEN WANT TO KNOW.

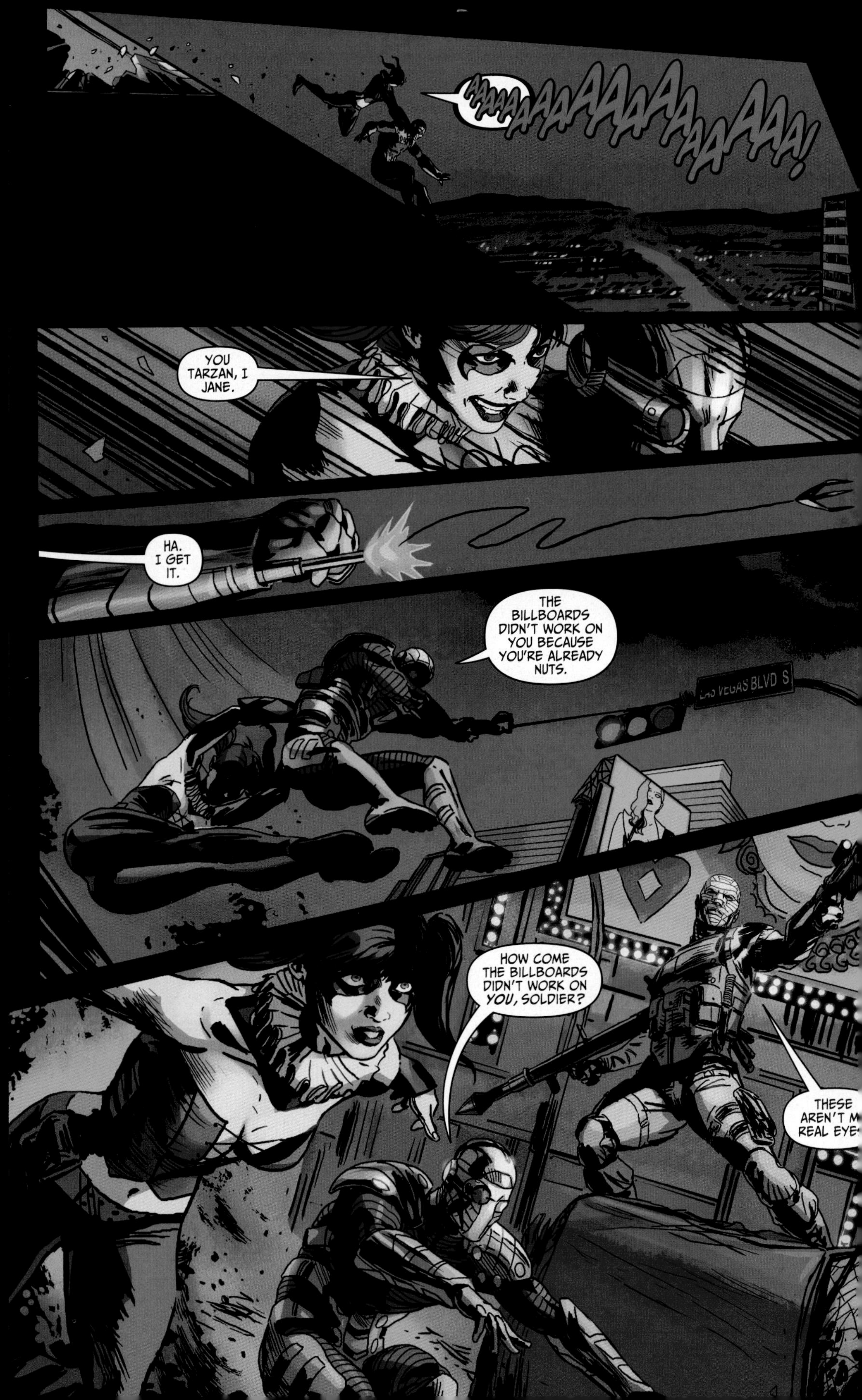
AAAAAAAAAAAAAAAAAAAAA!
YOU TARZAN, I JANE.
HA. I GET IT.
THE BILLBOARDS DIDN'T WORK ON YOU BECAUSE YOU'RE ALREADY NUTS.
LAS VEGAS BLVD S
HOW COME THE BILLBOARDS DIDN'T WORK ON *YOU*, SOLDIER?
THESE AREN'T M
REAL EYE

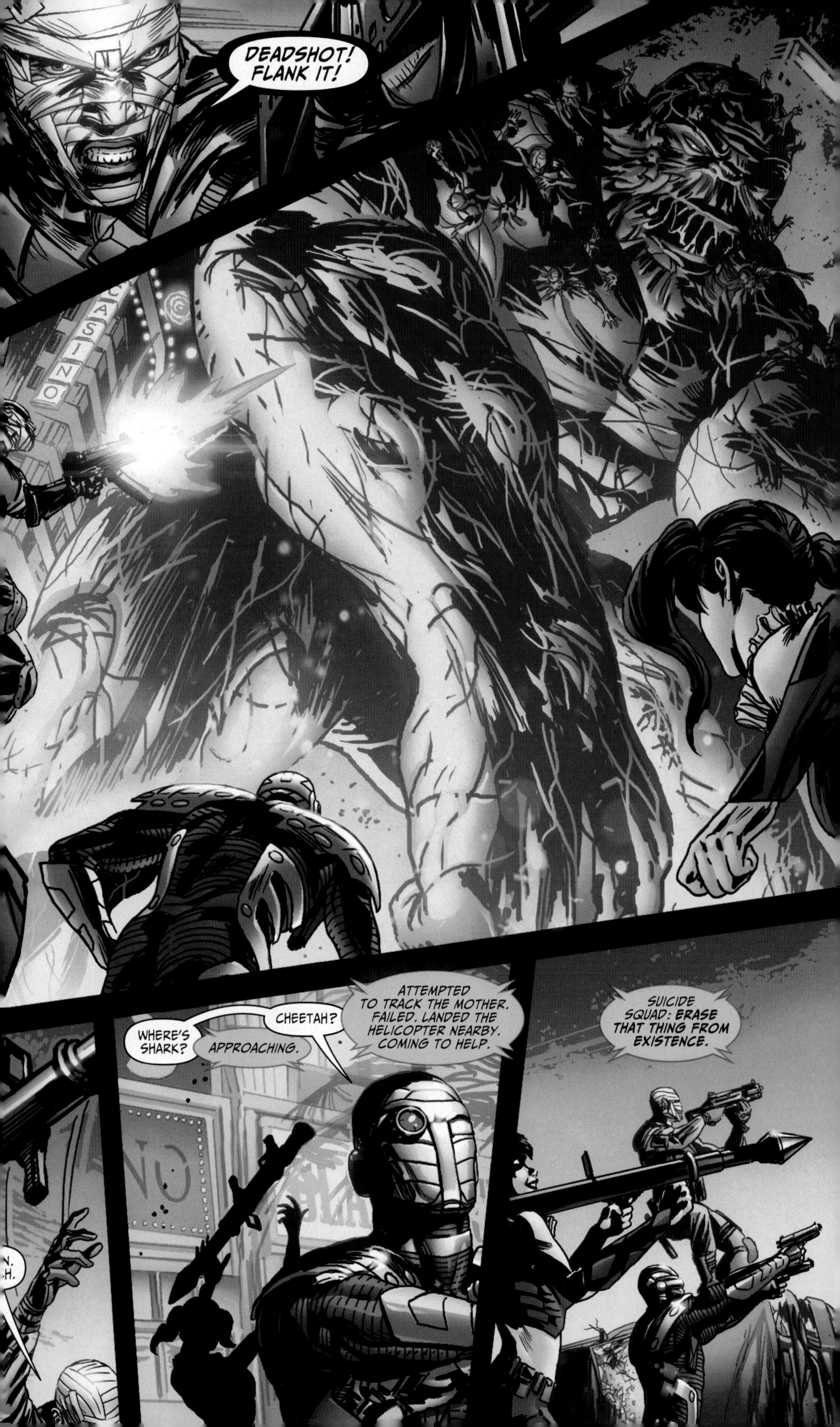
DEADSHOT! FLANK IT!
CASINO
WHERE'S SHARK?
CHEETAH?
APPROACHING.
ATTEMPTED TO TRACK THE MOTHER. FAILED. LANDED THE HELICOPTER NEARBY. COMING TO HELP.
SUICIDE SQUAD: ERASE THAT THING FROM EXISTENCE.

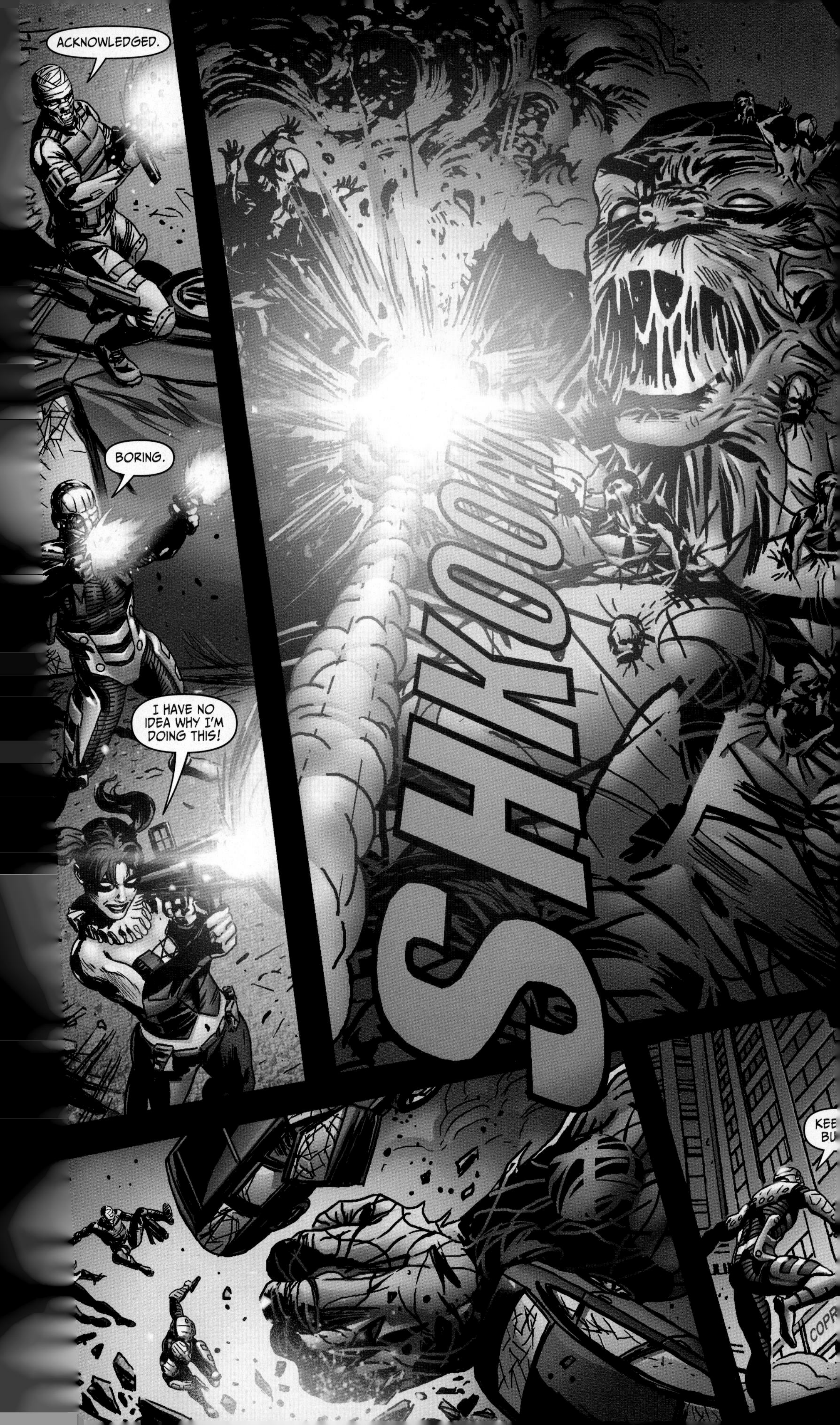
ACKNOWLEDGED.
BORING.
I HAVE NO IDEA WHY I'M DOING THIS!
SHKOOM

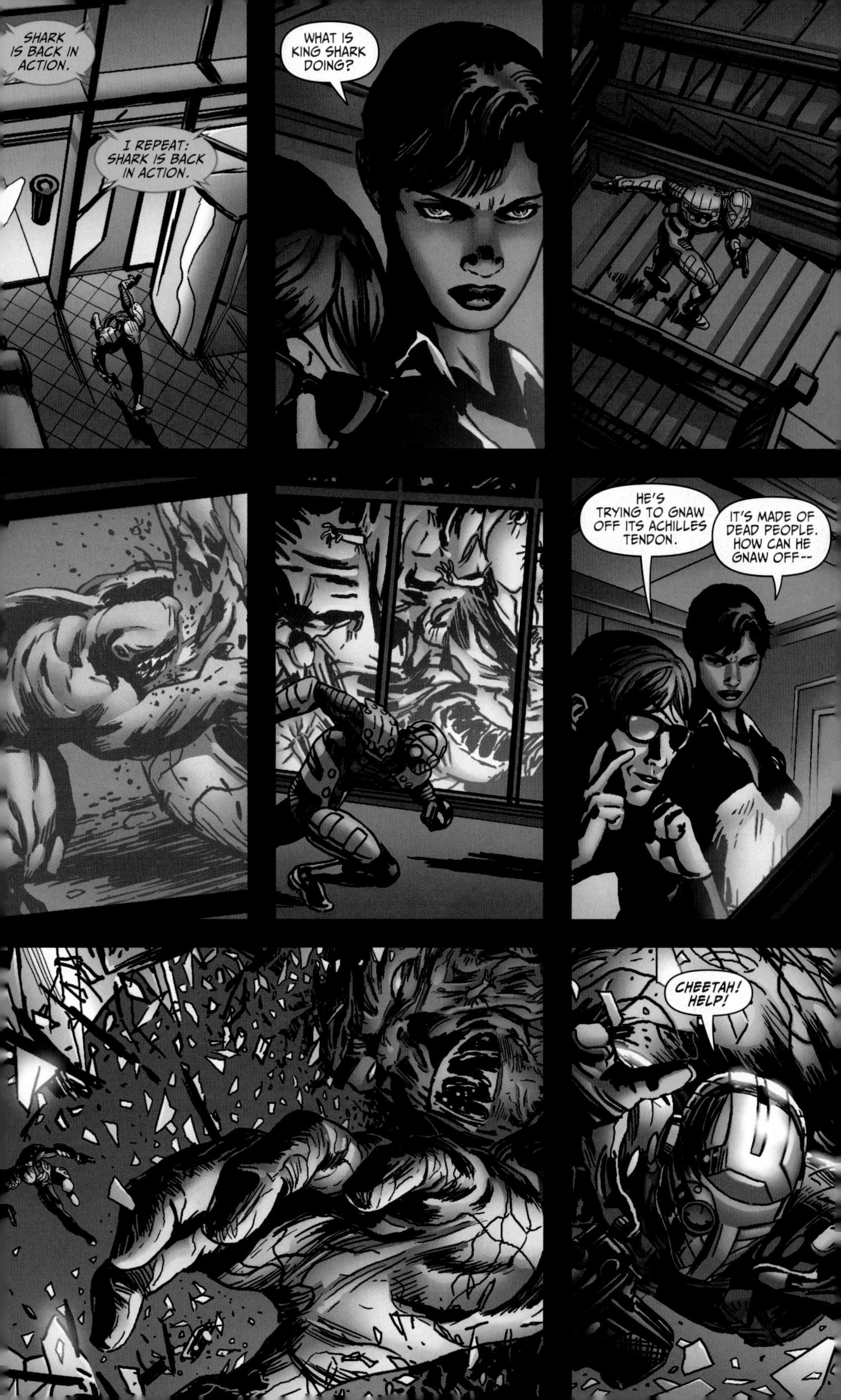
SHARK IS BACK IN ACTION.
I REPEAT: SHARK IS BACK IN ACTION.
WHAT IS KING SHARK DOING?
HE'S TRYING TO GNAW OFF ITS ACHILLES TENDON.
IT'S MADE OF DEAD PEOPLE. HOW CAN HE GNAW OFF--
CHEETAH! HELP!

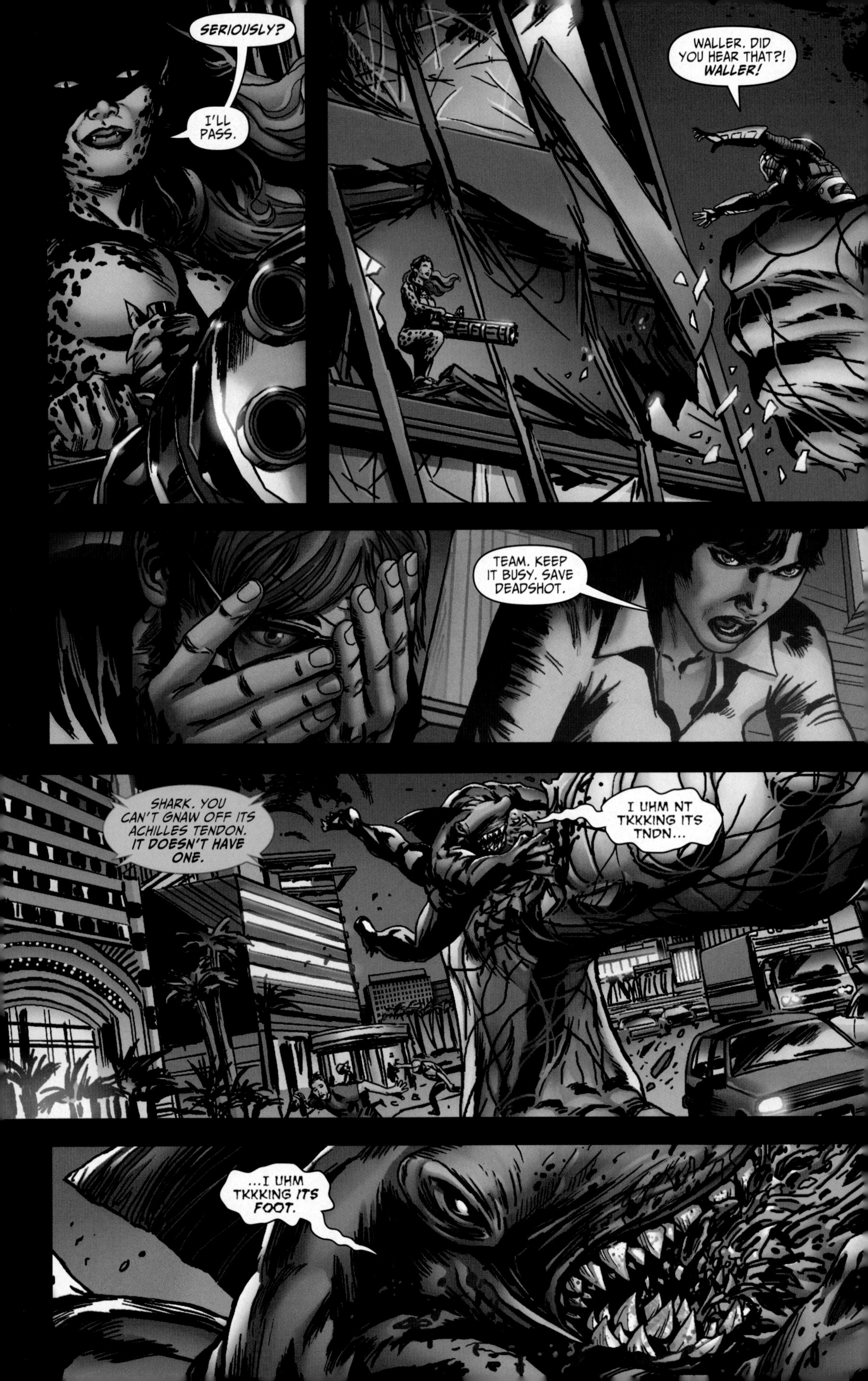
SERIOUSLY?
I'LL PASS.
WALLER. DID YOU HEAR THAT?! WALLER!
TEAM. KEEP IT BUSY. SAVE DEADSHOT.
SHARK. YOU CAN'T GNAW OFF ITS ACHILLES TENDON. IT DOESN'T HAVE ONE.
I UHM NT TKKKING ITS TNDN...
...I UHM TKKKING ITS FOOT.

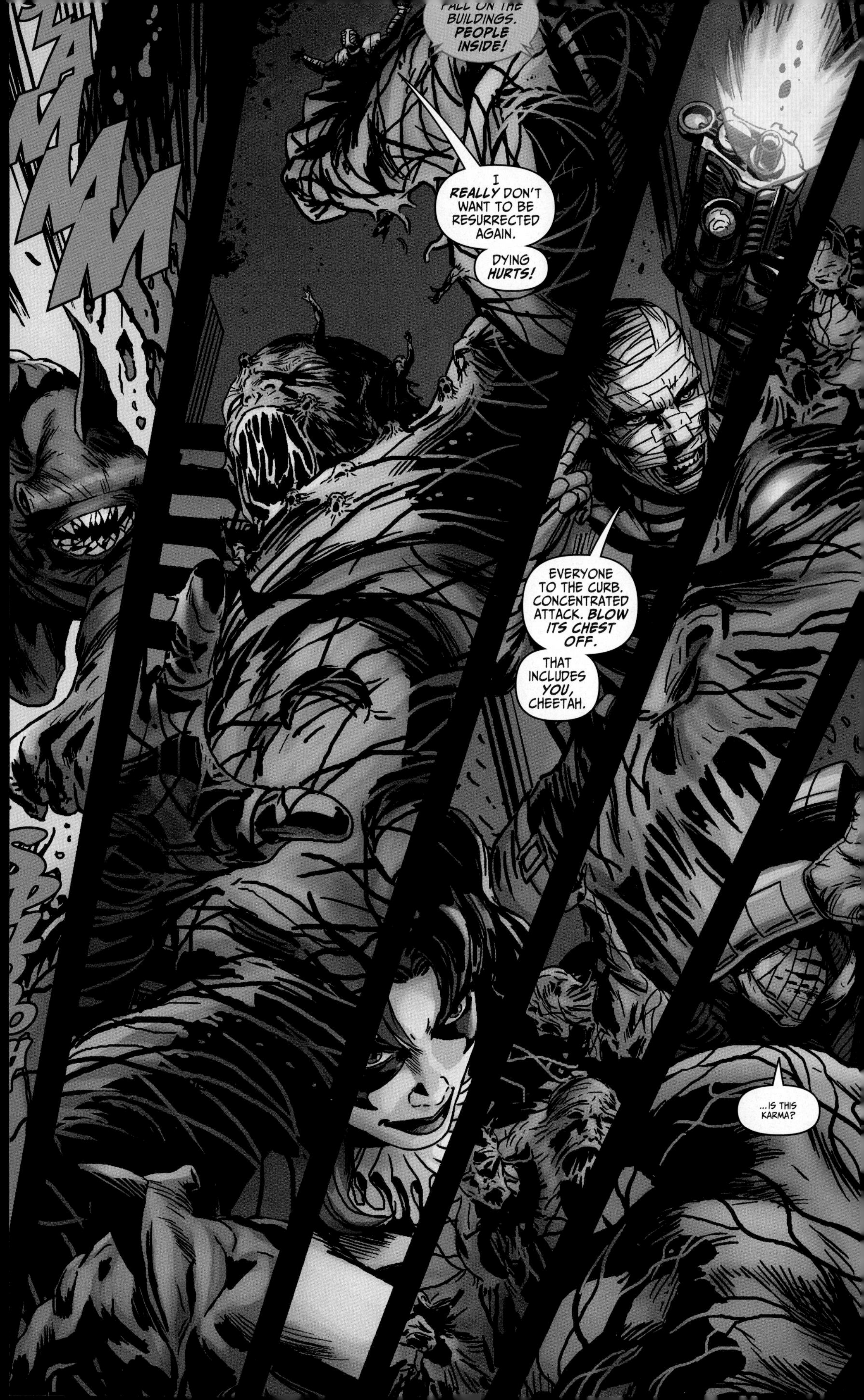
BUILDINGS. PEOPLE INSIDE!
I REALLY DON'T WANT TO BE RESURRECTED AGAIN.
DYING HURTS!
EVERYONE TO THE CURB. CONCENTRATED ATTACK. BLOW ITS CHEST OFF.
THAT INCLUDES YOU, CHEETAH.
...IS THIS KARMA?

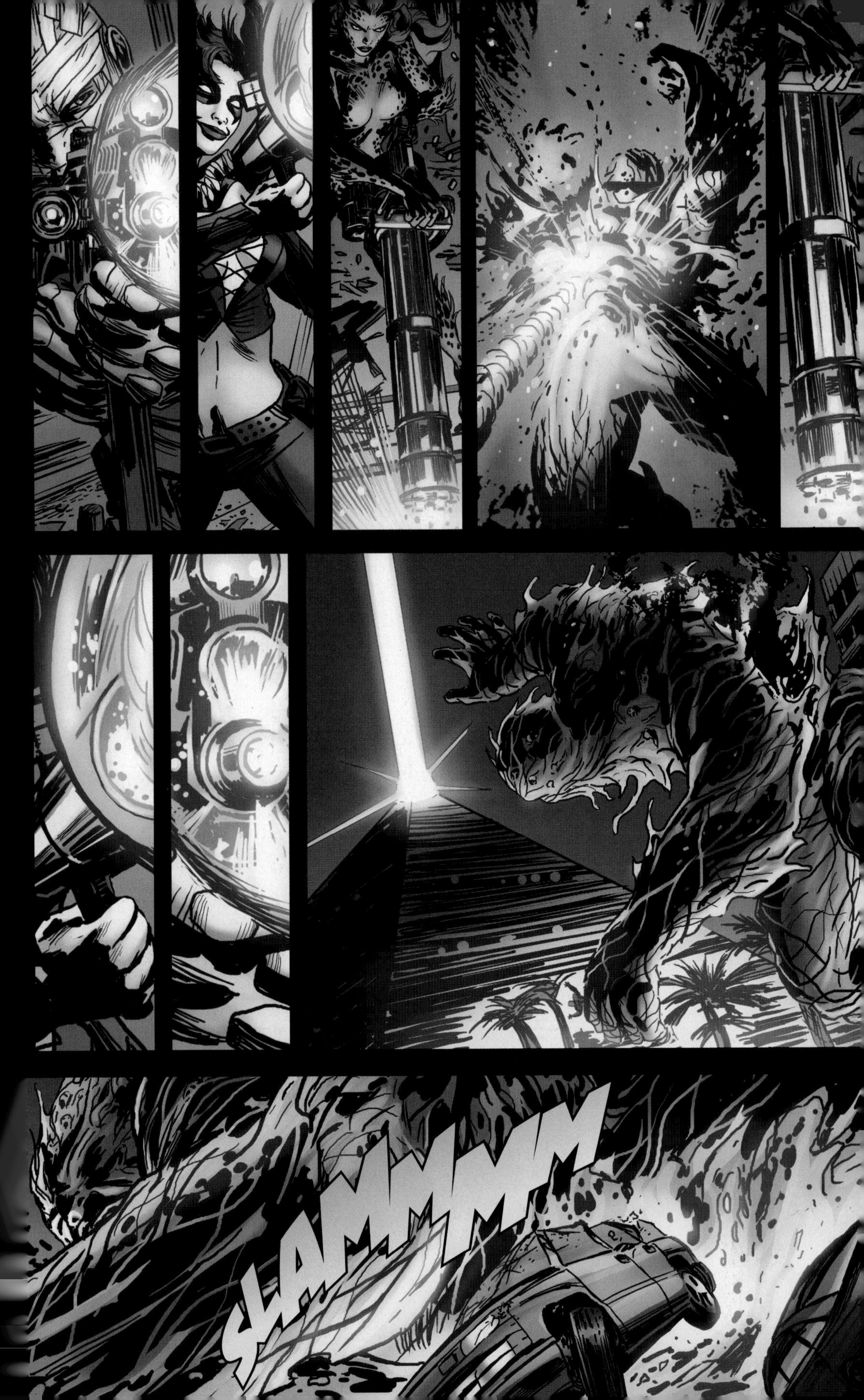
SLAMMMM

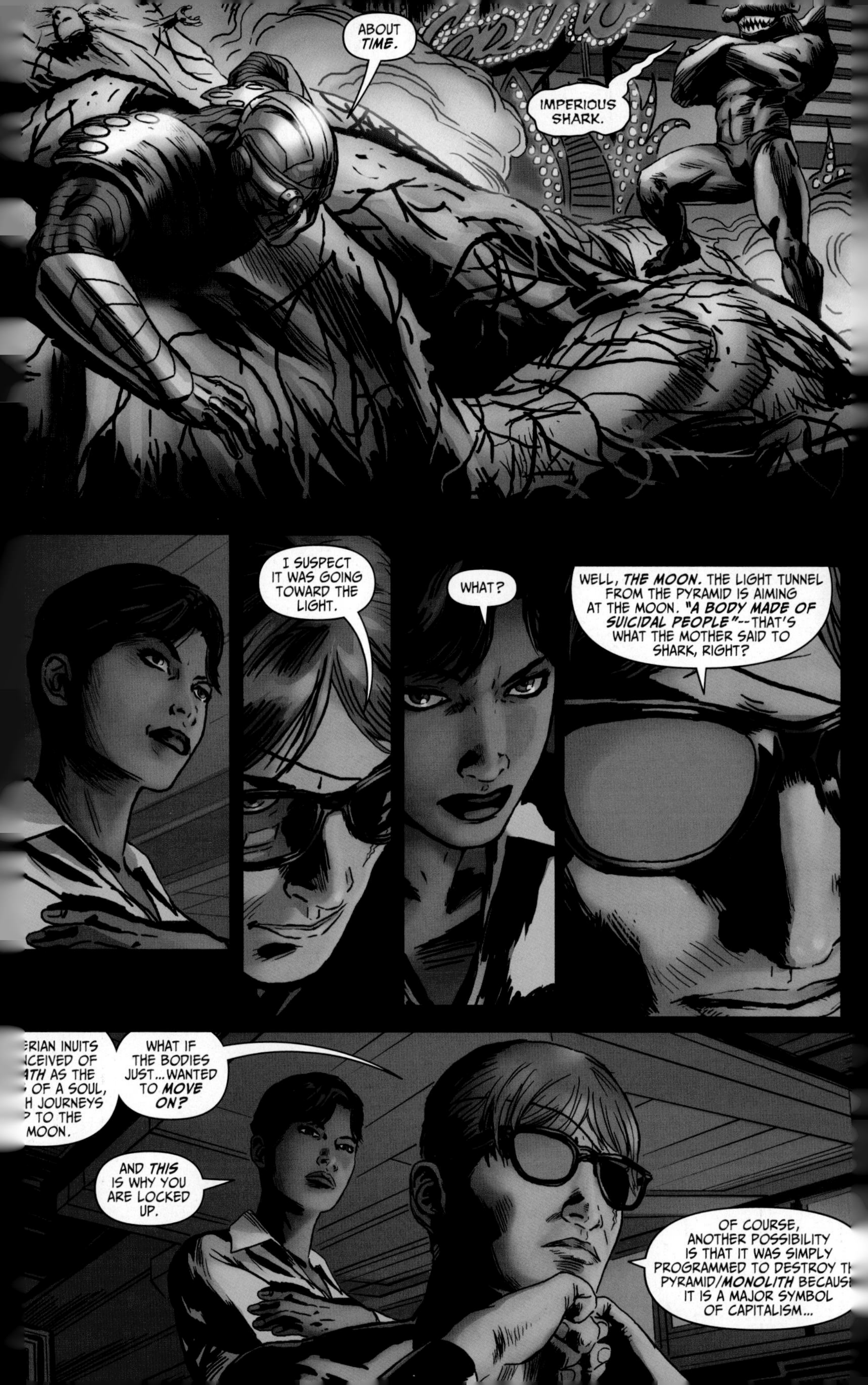
ABOUT *TIME.*
IMPERIOUS SHARK.
I SUSPECT IT WAS GOING TOWARD THE LIGHT.
WHAT?
WELL, *THE MOON.* THE LIGHT TUNNEL FROM THE PYRAMID IS AIMING AT THE MOON. *"A BODY MADE OF SUICIDAL PEOPLE"*--THAT'S WHAT THE MOTHER SAID TO SHARK, RIGHT?
ERIAN INUITS NCEIVED OF *ATH* AS THE OF A SOUL, H JOURNEYS P TO THE MOON.
WHAT IF THE BODIES JUST...WANTED TO *MOVE ON?*
AND *THIS* IS WHY YOU ARE LOCKED UP.
OF COURSE, ANOTHER POSSIBILITY IS THAT IT WAS SIMPLY PROGRAMMED TO DESTROY TH PYRAMID/*MONOLITH* BECAUS IT IS A MAJOR SYMBOL OF CAPITALISM...

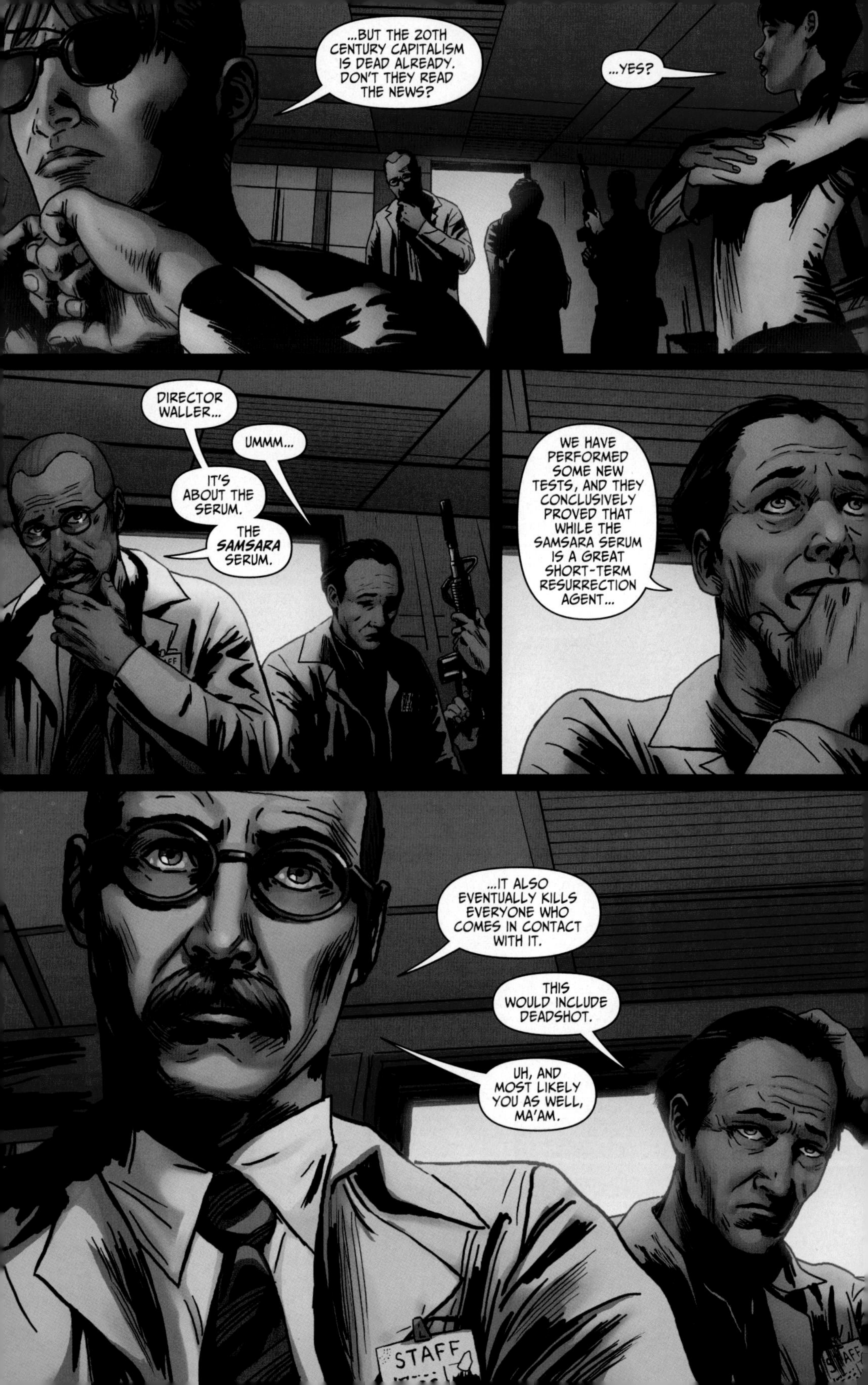
...BUT THE 20TH CENTURY CAPITALISM IS DEAD ALREADY. DON'T THEY READ THE NEWS?
...YES?
DIRECTOR WALLER...
UMMM...
IT'S ABOUT THE SERUM.
THE *SAMSARA* SERUM.
WE HAVE PERFORMED SOME NEW TESTS, AND THEY CONCLUSIVELY PROVED THAT WHILE THE SAMSARA SERUM IS A GREAT SHORT-TERM RESURRECTION AGENT...
...IT ALSO EVENTUALLY KILLS EVERYONE WHO COMES IN CONTACT WITH IT.
THIS WOULD INCLUDE DEADSHOT.
UH, AND MOST LIKELY YOU AS WELL, MA'AM.
STAFF

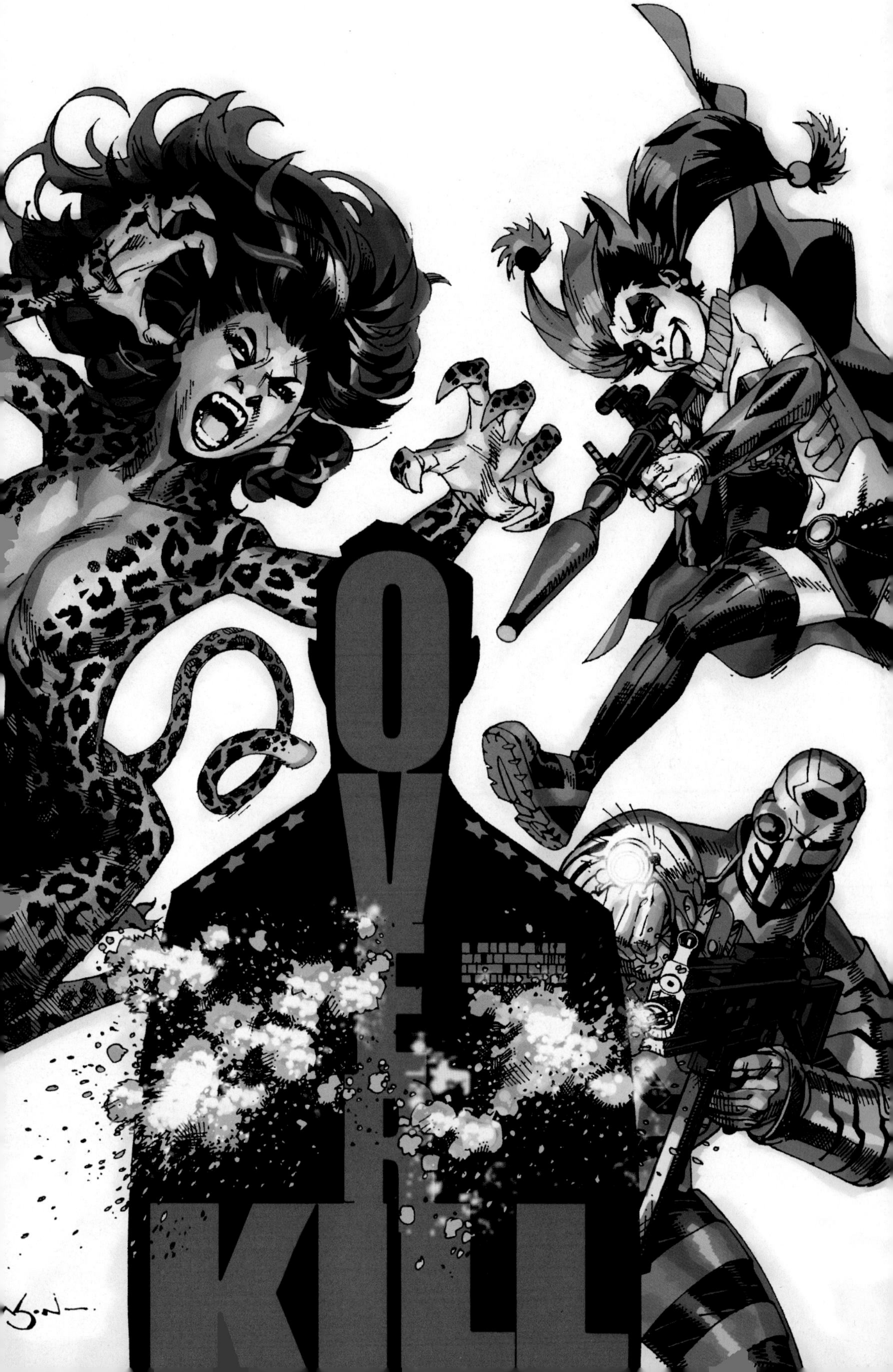
OVER
KILL

SLASH 'N' BURN

ALES KOT writer **RICK LEONARDI** penciller **ANDY OWENS, DEREK FRIDOLFS & MARC DEERING** inkers cover by **JASON PEARSON**

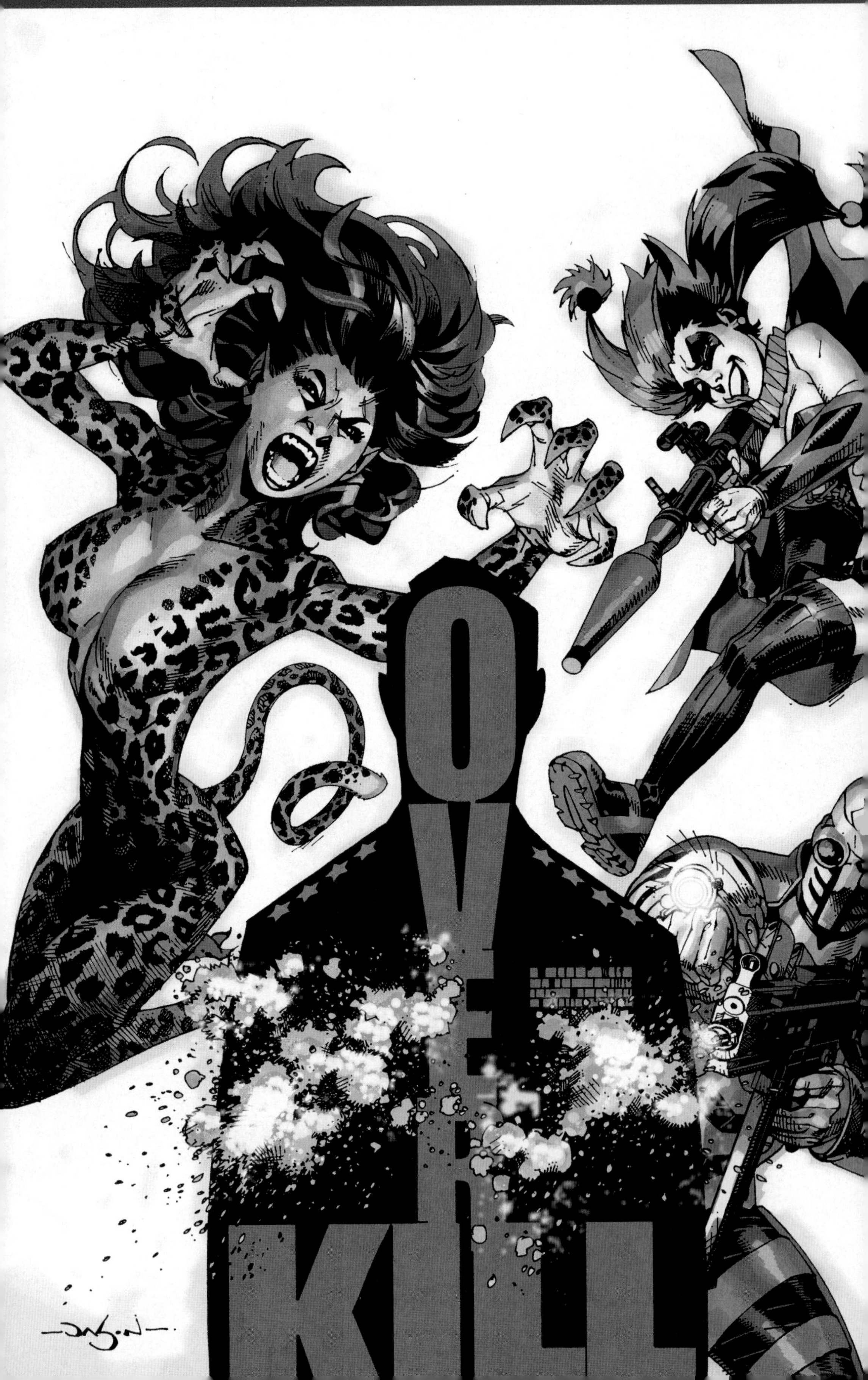
OVERKILL

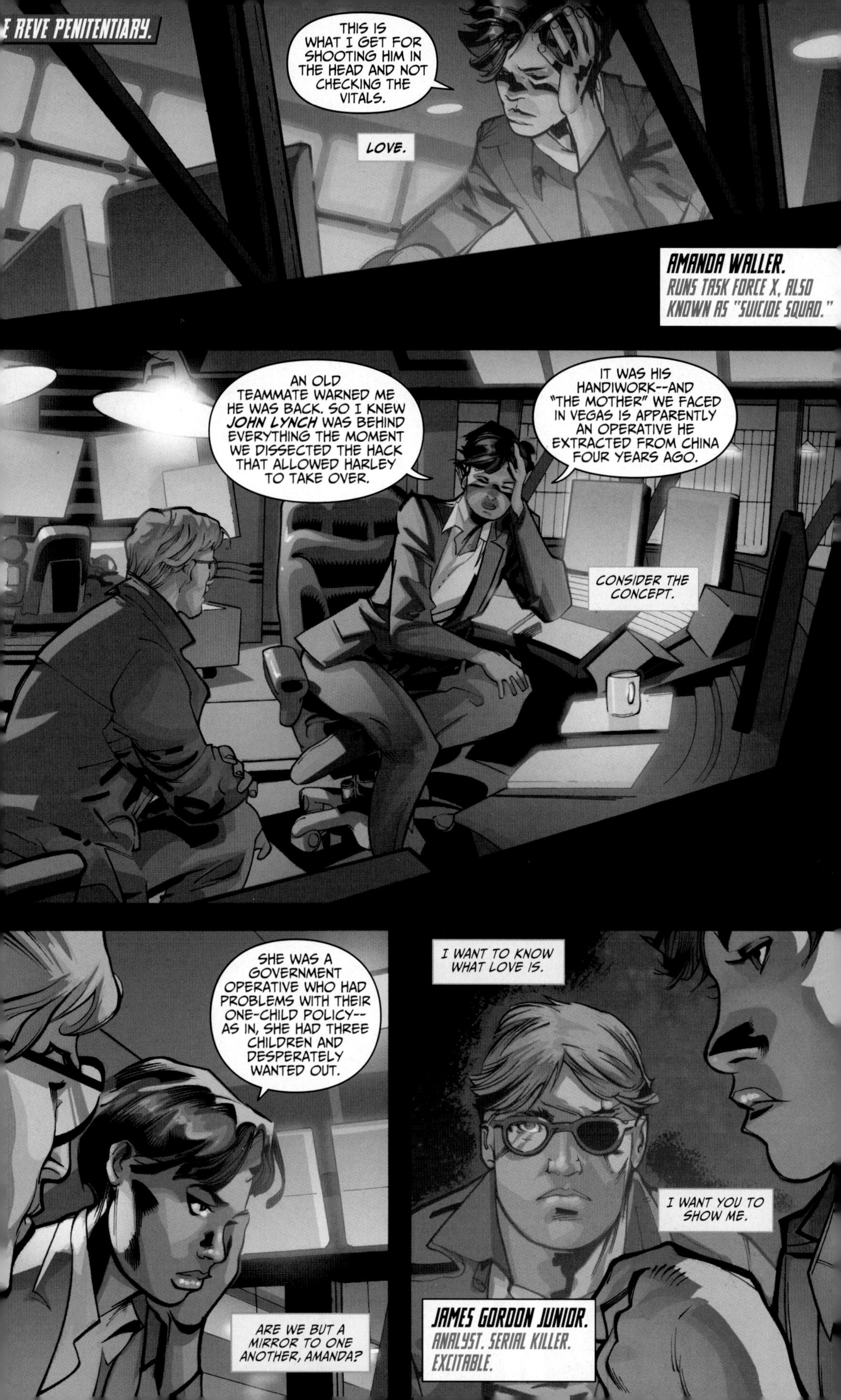
E REVE PENITENTIARY.
THIS IS WHAT I GET FOR SHOOTING HIM IN THE HEAD AND NOT CHECKING THE VITALS.
LOVE.
AMANDA WALLER.
RUNS TASK FORCE X, ALSO KNOWN AS "SUICIDE SQUAD."
AN OLD TEAMMATE WARNED ME HE WAS BACK. SO I KNEW JOHN LYNCH WAS BEHIND EVERYTHING THE MOMENT WE DISSECTED THE HACK THAT ALLOWED HARLEY TO TAKE OVER.
IT WAS HIS HANDIWORK--AND "THE MOTHER" WE FACED IN VEGAS IS APPARENTLY AN OPERATIVE HE EXTRACTED FROM CHINA FOUR YEARS AGO.
CONSIDER THE CONCEPT.
SHE WAS A GOVERNMENT OPERATIVE WHO HAD PROBLEMS WITH THEIR ONE-CHILD POLICY--AS IN, SHE HAD THREE CHILDREN AND DESPERATELY WANTED OUT.
ARE WE BUT A MIRROR TO ONE ANOTHER, AMANDA?
I WANT TO KNOW WHAT LOVE IS.
I WANT YOU TO SHOW ME.
JAMES GORDON JUNIOR.
ANALYST. SERIAL KILLER. EXCITABLE.

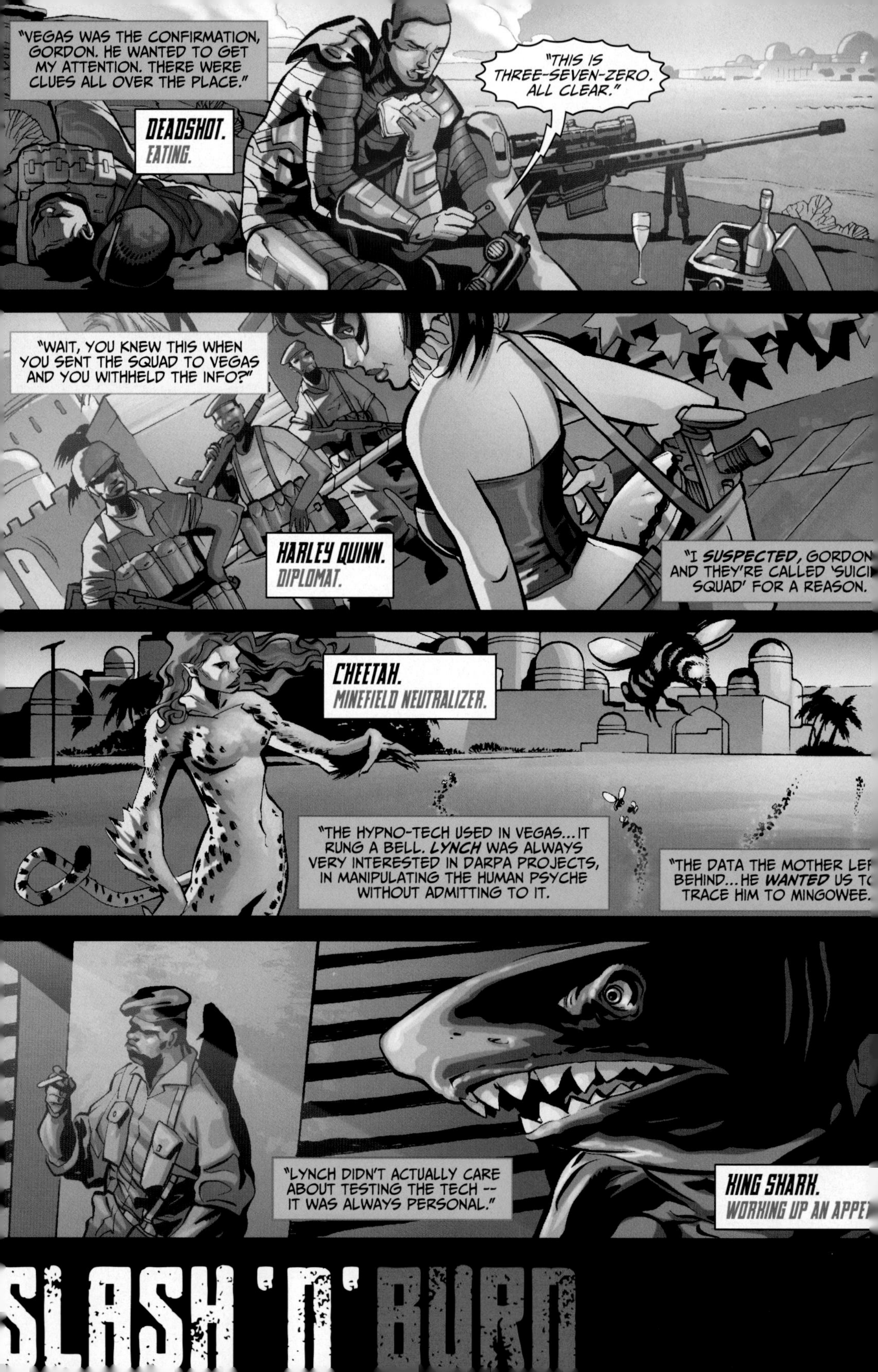
"VEGAS WAS THE CONFIRMATION, GORDON. HE WANTED TO GET MY ATTENTION. THERE WERE CLUES ALL OVER THE PLACE."
DEADSHOT. EATING.
"THIS IS THREE-SEVEN-ZERO. ALL CLEAR."
"WAIT, YOU KNEW THIS WHEN YOU SENT THE SQUAD TO VEGAS AND YOU WITHHELD THE INFO?"
HARLEY QUINN. DIPLOMAT.
"I SUSPECTED, GORDON AND THEY'RE CALLED 'SUICI SQUAD' FOR A REASON.
CHEETAH. MINEFIELD NEUTRALIZER.
"THE HYPNO-TECH USED IN VEGAS... IT RUNG A BELL. LYNCH WAS ALWAYS VERY INTERESTED IN DARPA PROJECTS, IN MANIPULATING THE HUMAN PSYCHE WITHOUT ADMITTING TO IT.
"THE DATA THE MOTHER LEF BEHIND... HE WANTED US T TRACE HIM TO MINGOWEE.
"LYNCH DIDN'T ACTUALLY CARE ABOUT TESTING THE TECH -- IT WAS ALWAYS PERSONAL."
KING SHARK. WORKING UP AN APPE
SLASH 'N' BURN

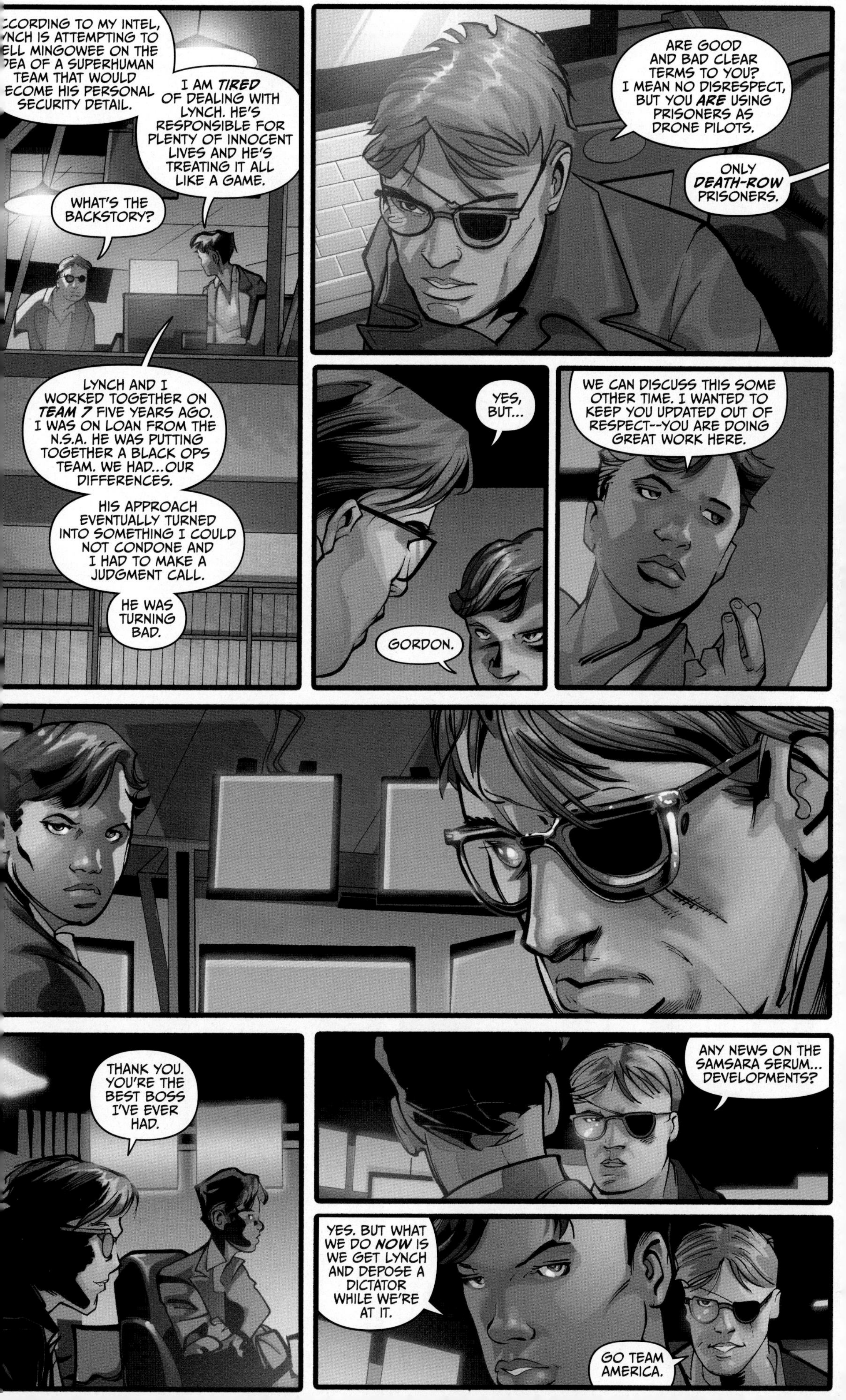
CCORDING TO MY INTEL, YNCH IS ATTEMPTING TO ELL MINGOWEE ON THE DEA OF A SUPERHUMAN TEAM THAT WOULD ECOME HIS PERSONAL SECURITY DETAIL.
I AM TIRED OF DEALING WITH LYNCH. HE'S RESPONSIBLE FOR PLENTY OF INNOCENT LIVES AND HE'S TREATING IT ALL LIKE A GAME.
WHAT'S THE BACKSTORY?
LYNCH AND I WORKED TOGETHER ON TEAM 7 FIVE YEARS AGO. I WAS ON LOAN FROM THE N.S.A. HE WAS PUTTING TOGETHER A BLACK OPS TEAM. WE HAD...OUR DIFFERENCES.
HIS APPROACH EVENTUALLY TURNED INTO SOMETHING I COULD NOT CONDONE AND I HAD TO MAKE A JUDGMENT CALL.
HE WAS TURNING BAD.
ARE GOOD AND BAD CLEAR TERMS TO YOU? I MEAN NO DISRESPECT, BUT YOU ARE USING PRISONERS AS DRONE PILOTS.
ONLY DEATH-ROW PRISONERS.
YES, BUT...
GORDON.
WE CAN DISCUSS THIS SOME OTHER TIME. I WANTED TO KEEP YOU UPDATED OUT OF RESPECT--YOU ARE DOING GREAT WORK HERE.
THANK YOU. YOU'RE THE BEST BOSS I'VE EVER HAD.
ANY NEWS ON THE SAMSARA SERUM... DEVELOPMENTS?
YES. BUT WHAT WE DO NOW IS WE GET LYNCH AND DEPOSE A DICTATOR WHILE WE'RE AT IT.
GO TEAM AMERICA.

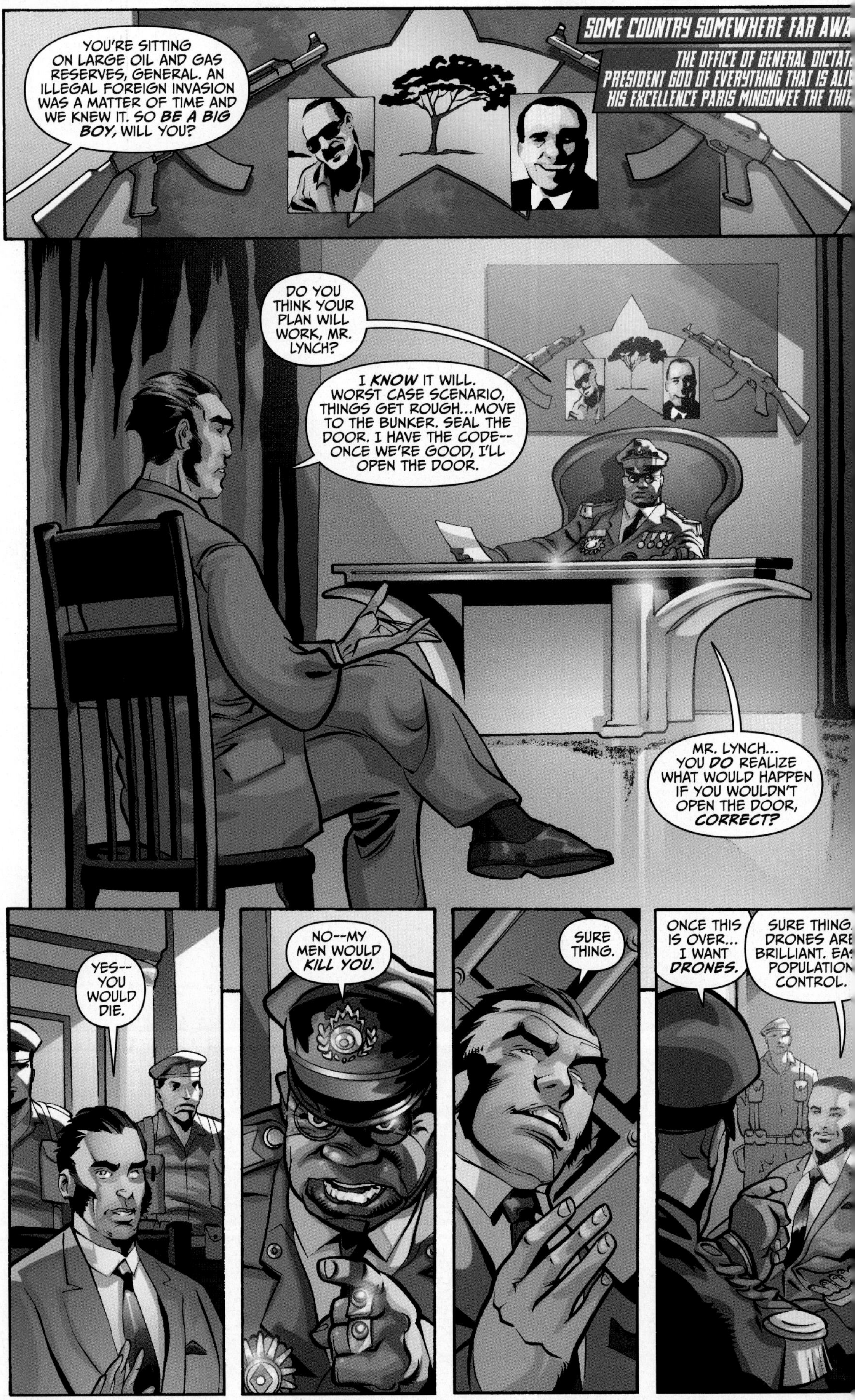
SOME COUNTRY SOMEWHERE FAR AWA
THE OFFICE OF GENERAL DICTAT PRESIDENT GOD OF EVERYTHING THAT IS ALI HIS EXCELLENCE PARIS MINGOWEE THE THI
YOU'RE SITTING ON LARGE OIL AND GAS RESERVES, GENERAL. AN ILLEGAL FOREIGN INVASION WAS A MATTER OF TIME AND WE KNEW IT. SO BE A BIG BOY, WILL YOU?
DO YOU THINK YOUR PLAN WILL WORK, MR. LYNCH?
I KNOW IT WILL. WORST CASE SCENARIO, THINGS GET ROUGH...MOVE TO THE BUNKER. SEAL THE DOOR. I HAVE THE CODE--ONCE WE'RE GOOD, I'LL OPEN THE DOOR.
MR. LYNCH... YOU DO REALIZE WHAT WOULD HAPPEN IF YOU WOULDN'T OPEN THE DOOR, CORRECT?
YES--YOU WOULD DIE.
NO--MY MEN WOULD KILL YOU.
SURE THING.
ONCE THIS IS OVER... I WANT DRONES.
SURE THING DRONES ARE BRILLIANT. EA POPULATION CONTROL.

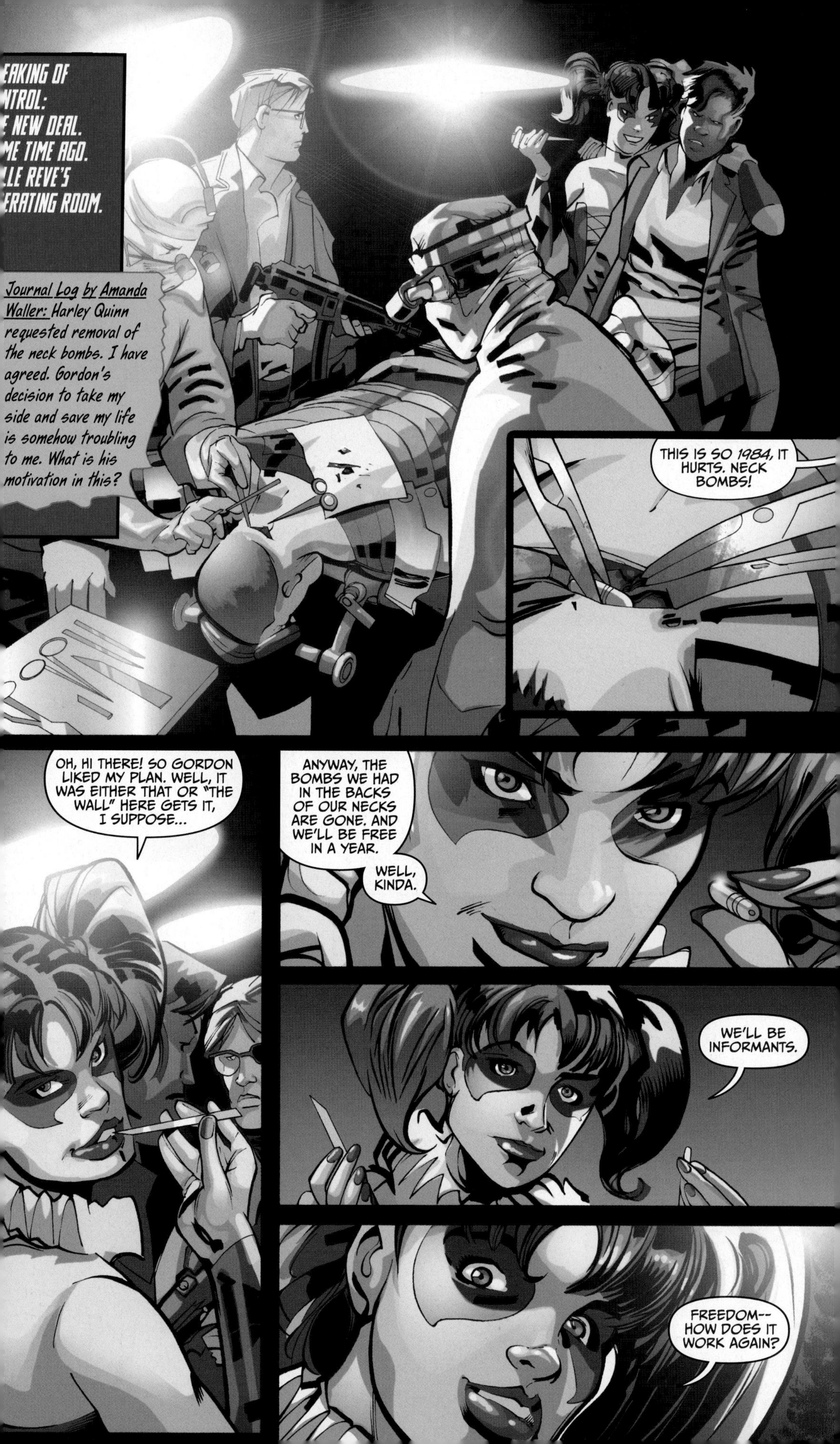
EAKING OF
NTROL:
E NEW DEAL.
ME TIME AGO.
LLE REVE'S
ERATING ROOM.
Journal Log by Amanda Waller: Harley Quinn requested removal of the neck bombs. I have agreed. Gordon's decision to take my side and save my life is somehow troubling to me. What is his motivation in this?
THIS IS SO 1984, IT HURTS. NECK BOMBS!
OH, HI THERE! SO GORDON LIKED MY PLAN. WELL, IT WAS EITHER THAT OR "THE WALL" HERE GETS IT, I SUPPOSE...
ANYWAY, THE BOMBS WE HAD IN THE BACKS OF OUR NECKS ARE GONE. AND WE'LL BE FREE IN A YEAR.
WELL, KINDA.
WE'LL BE INFORMANTS.
FREEDOM-- HOW DOES IT WORK AGAIN?

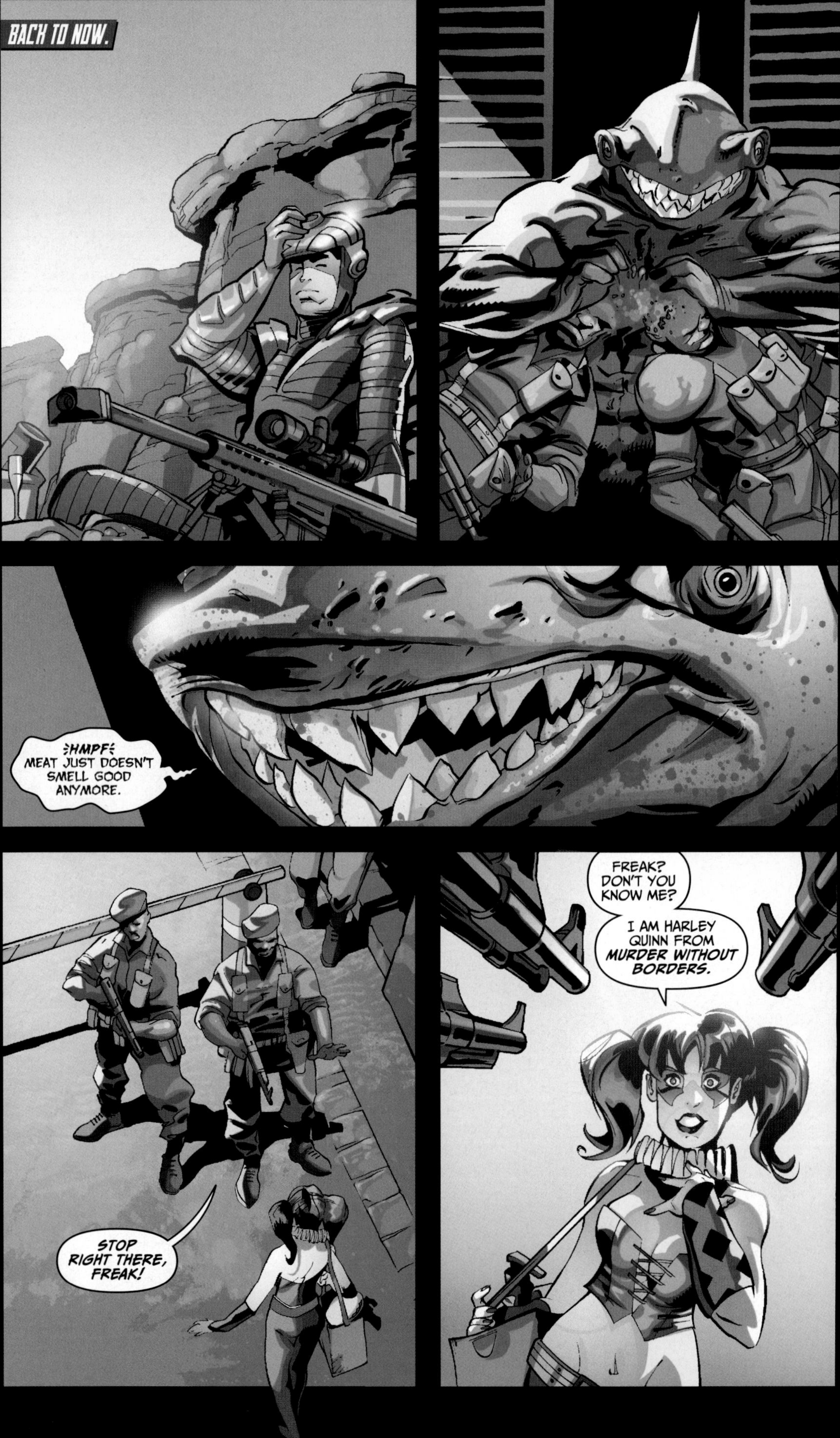
BACK TO NOW.
HMPF
MEAT JUST DOESN'T SMELL GOOD ANYMORE.
STOP RIGHT THERE, FREAK!
FREAK? DON'T YOU KNOW ME?
I AM HARLEY QUINN FROM MURDER WITHOUT BORDERS.

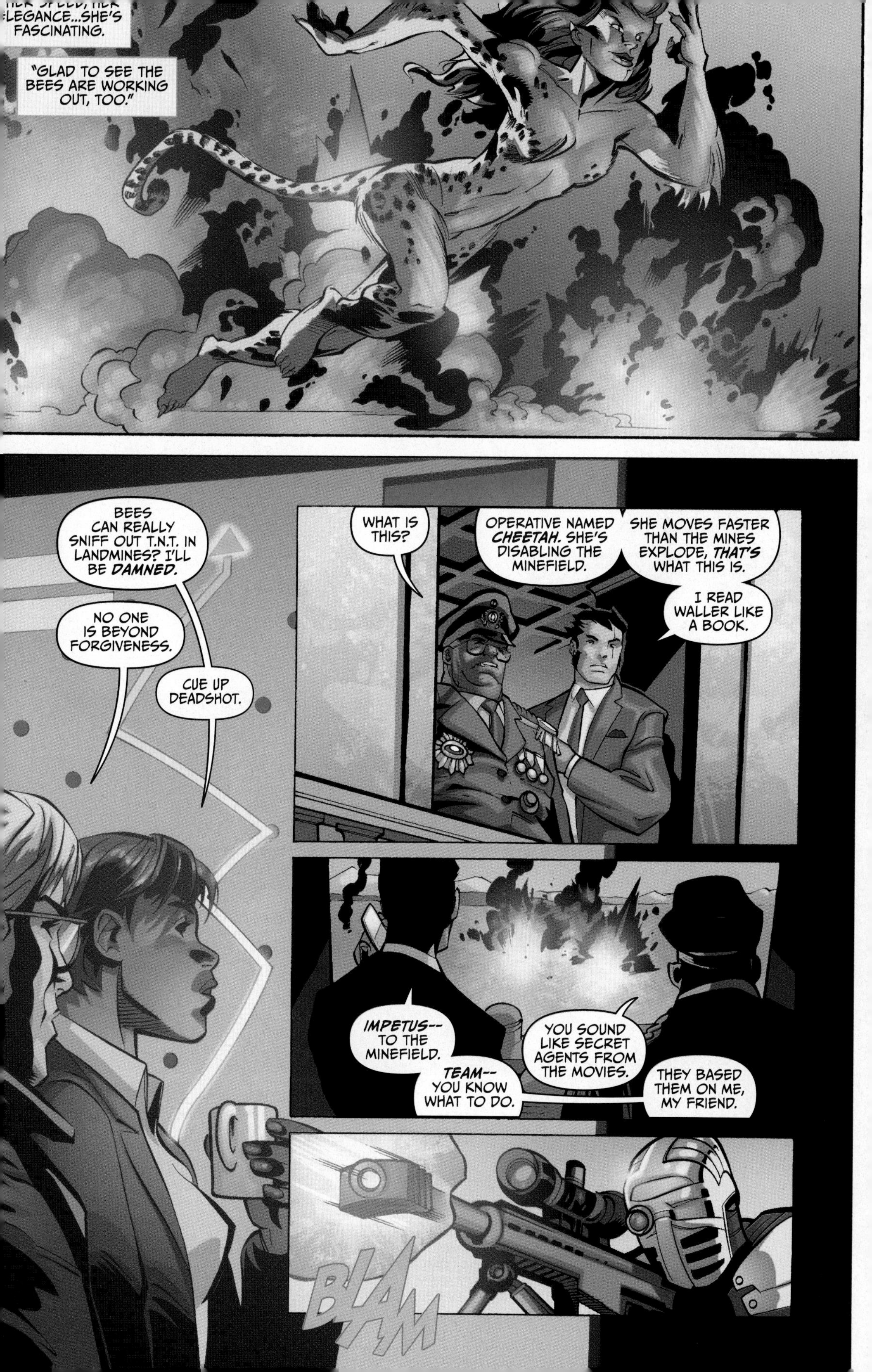

HER SPEED, HER ELEGANCE...SHE'S FASCINATING.
"GLAD TO SEE THE BEES ARE WORKING OUT, TOO."
BEES CAN REALLY SNIFF OUT T.N.T. IN LANDMINES? I'LL BE DAMNED.
NO ONE IS BEYOND FORGIVENESS.
CUE UP DEADSHOT.
WHAT IS THIS?
OPERATIVE NAMED CHEETAH. SHE'S DISABLING THE MINEFIELD.
SHE MOVES FASTER THAN THE MINES EXPLODE, THAT'S WHAT THIS IS.
I READ WALLER LIKE A BOOK.
IMPETUS-- TO THE MINEFIELD.
TEAM-- YOU KNOW WHAT TO DO.
YOU SOUND LIKE SECRET AGENTS FROM THE MOVIES.
THEY BASED THEM ON ME, MY FRIEND.
BLAM

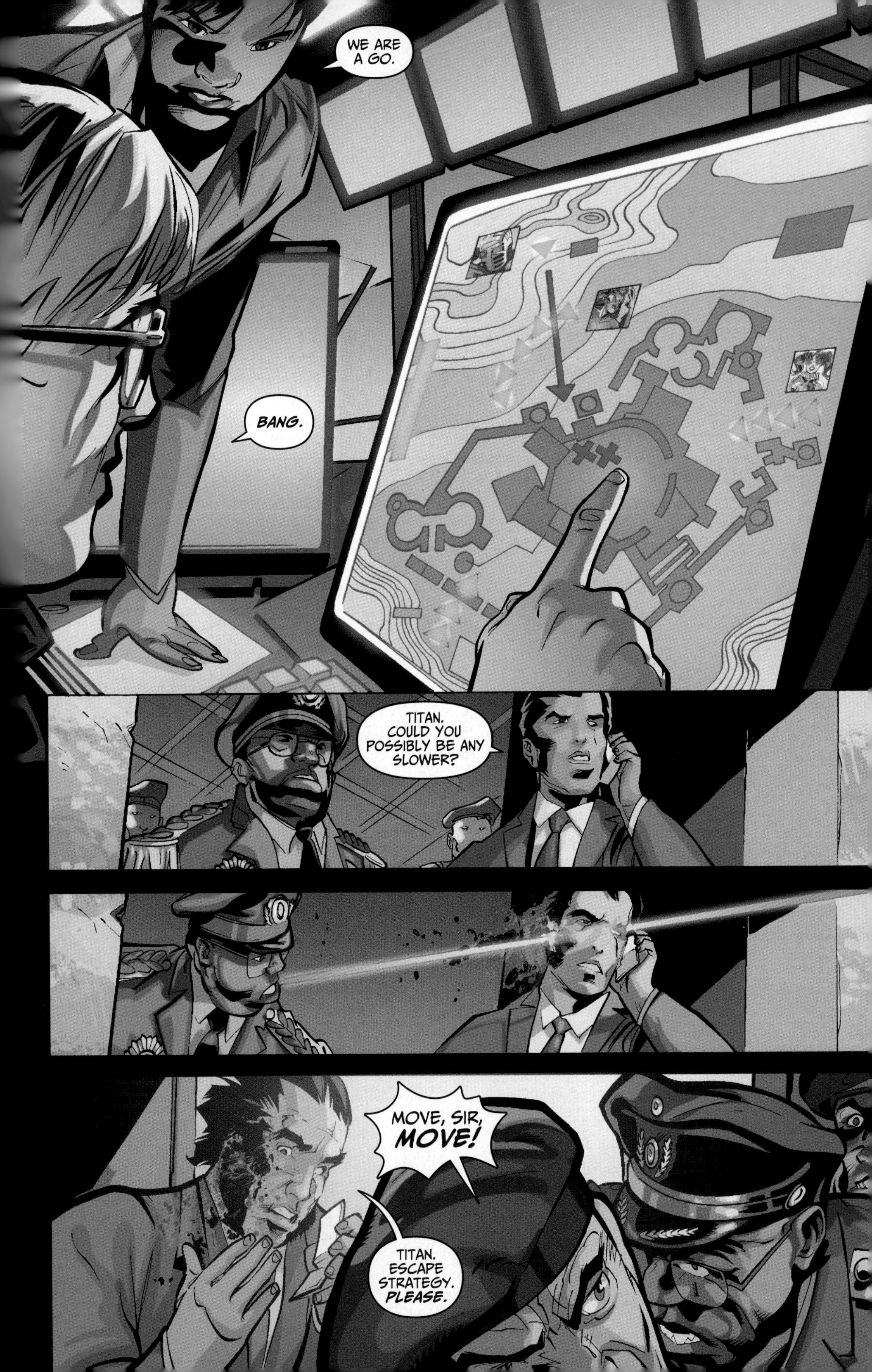
WE ARE A GO.
BANG.
TITAN. COULD YOU POSSIBLY BE ANY SLOWER?
MOVE, SIR, MOVE!
TITAN. ESCAPE STRATEGY. PLEASE.

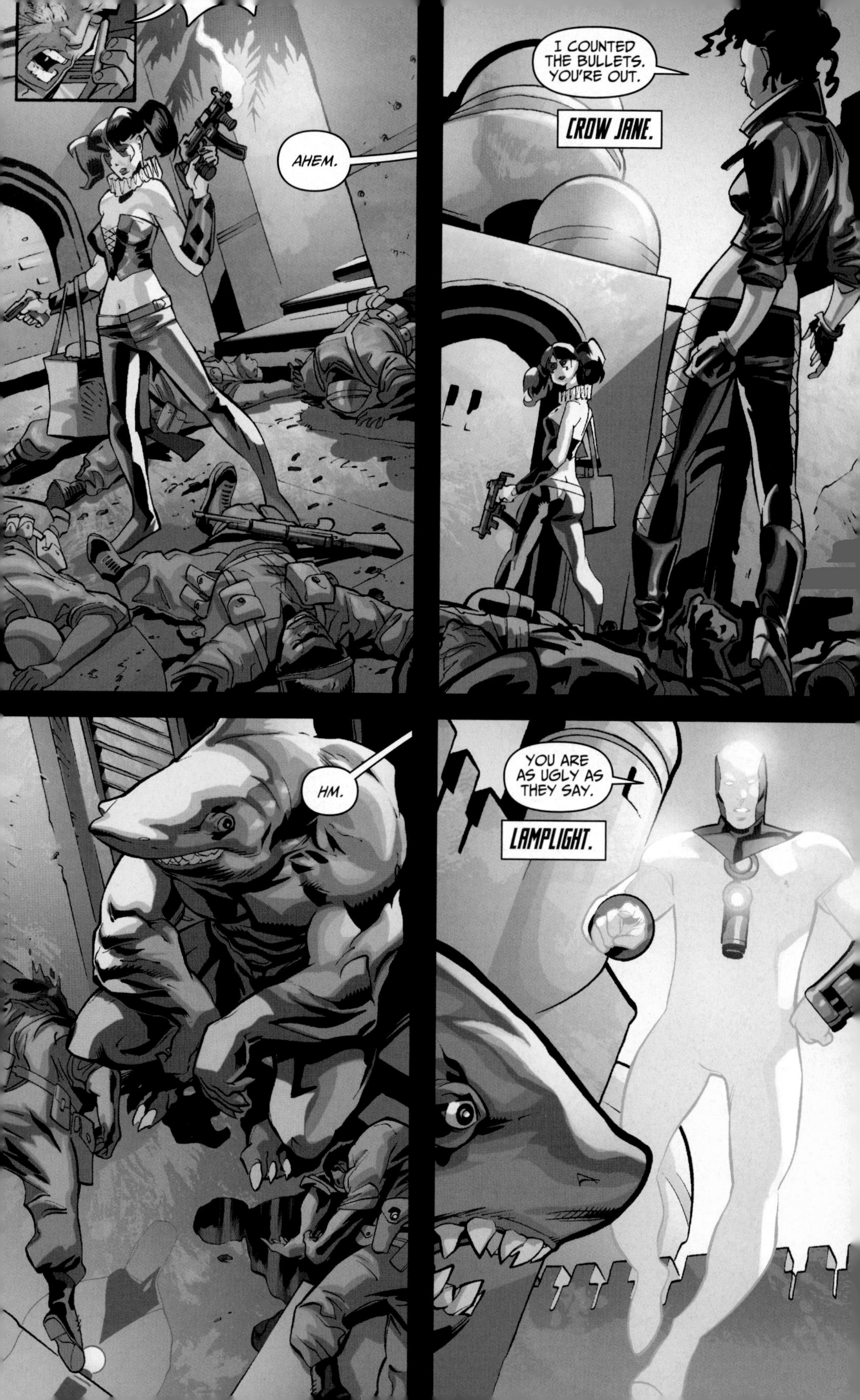
AHEM.
I COUNTED THE BULLETS. YOU'RE OUT.
CROW JANE.
HM.
YOU ARE AS UGLY AS THEY SAY.
LAMPLIGHT.

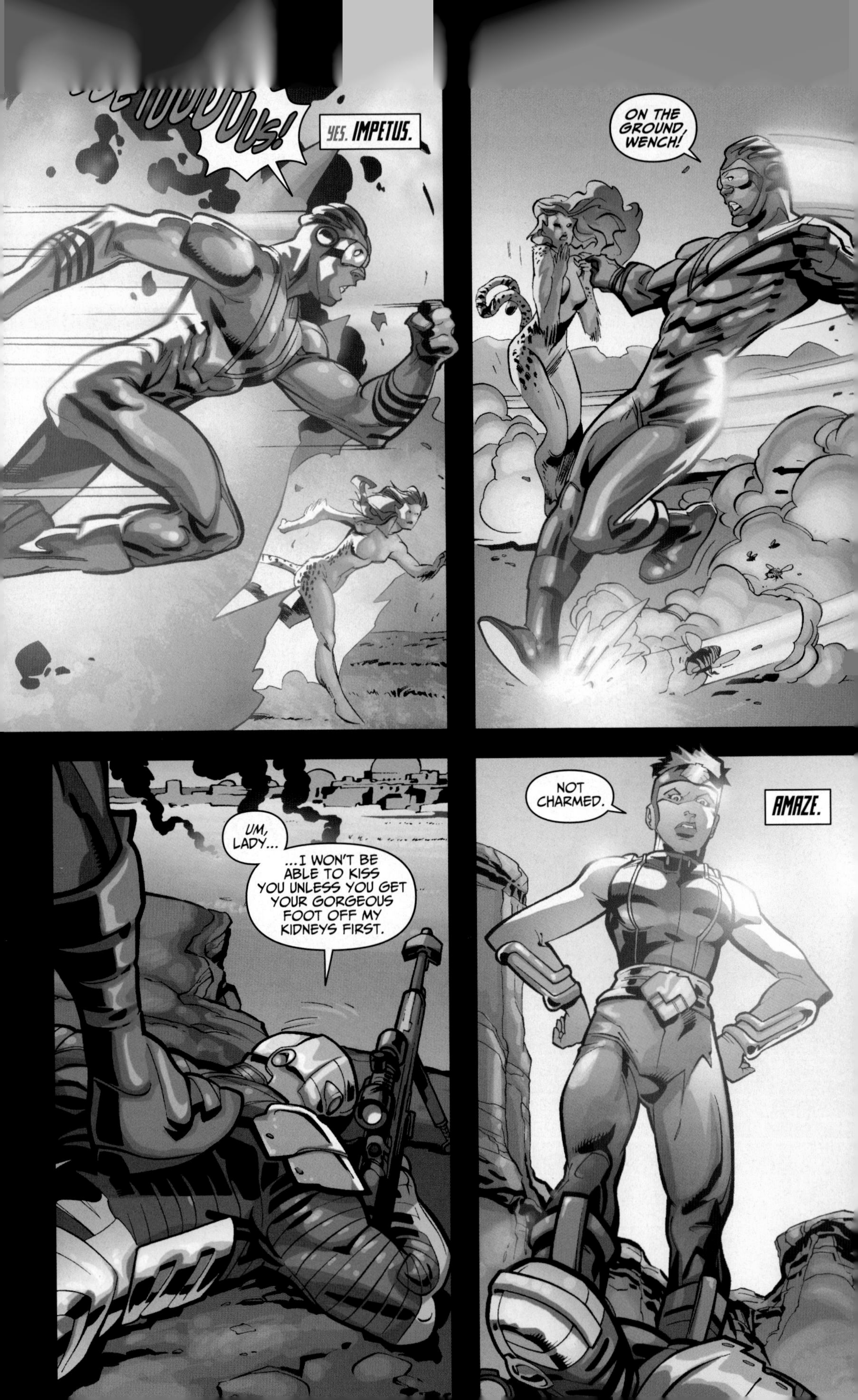
...US!
YES. IMPETUS.
ON THE GROUND, WENCH!
UM, LADY...
...I WON'T BE ABLE TO KISS YOU UNLESS YOU GET YOUR GORGEOUS FOOT OFF MY KIDNEYS FIRST.
NOT CHARMED.
AMAZE.

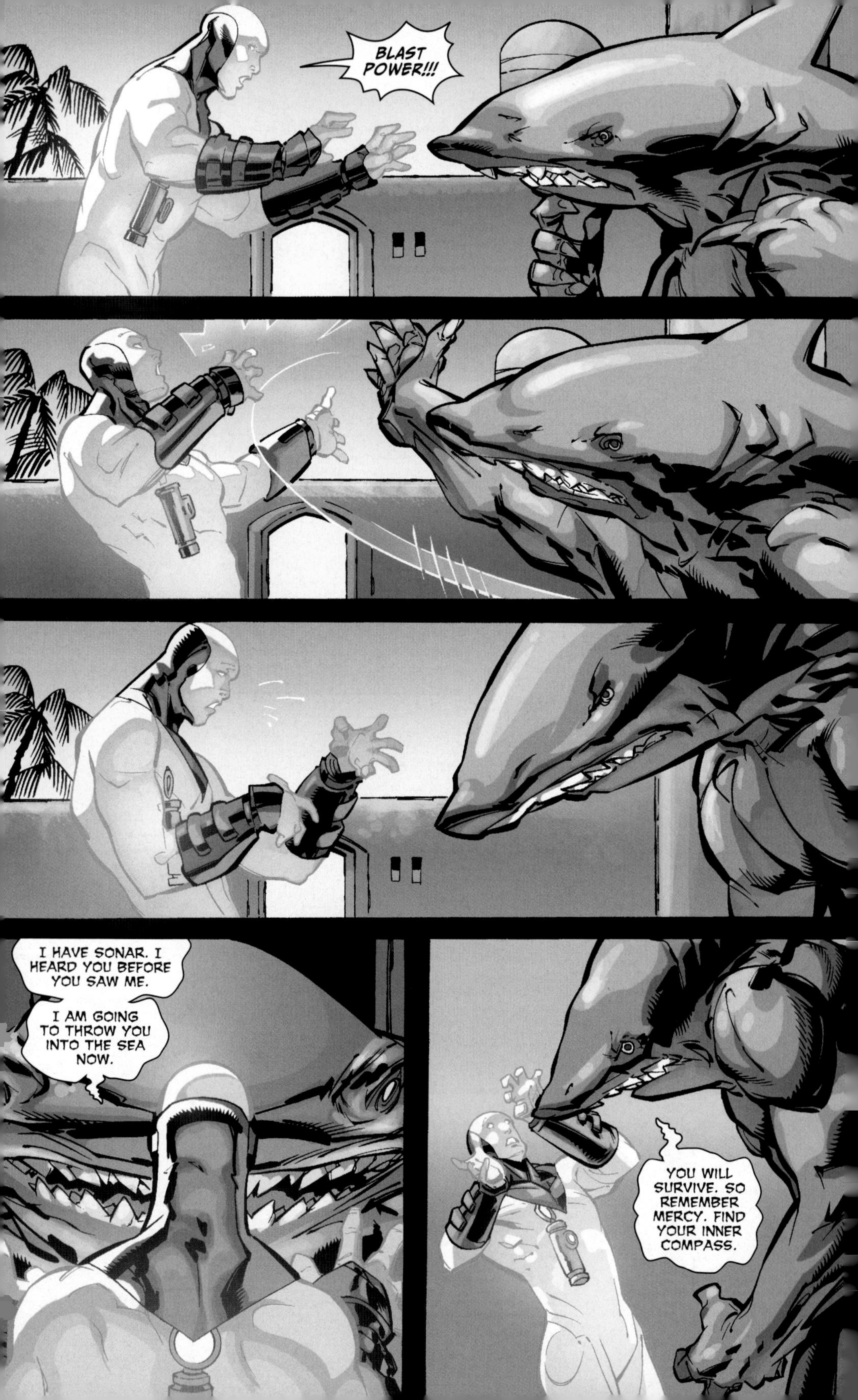
BLAST POWER!!!
I HAVE SONAR. I HEARD YOU BEFORE YOU SAW ME.
I AM GOING TO THROW YOU INTO THE SEA NOW.
YOU WILL SURVIVE. SO REMEMBER MERCY. FIND YOUR INNER COMPASS.

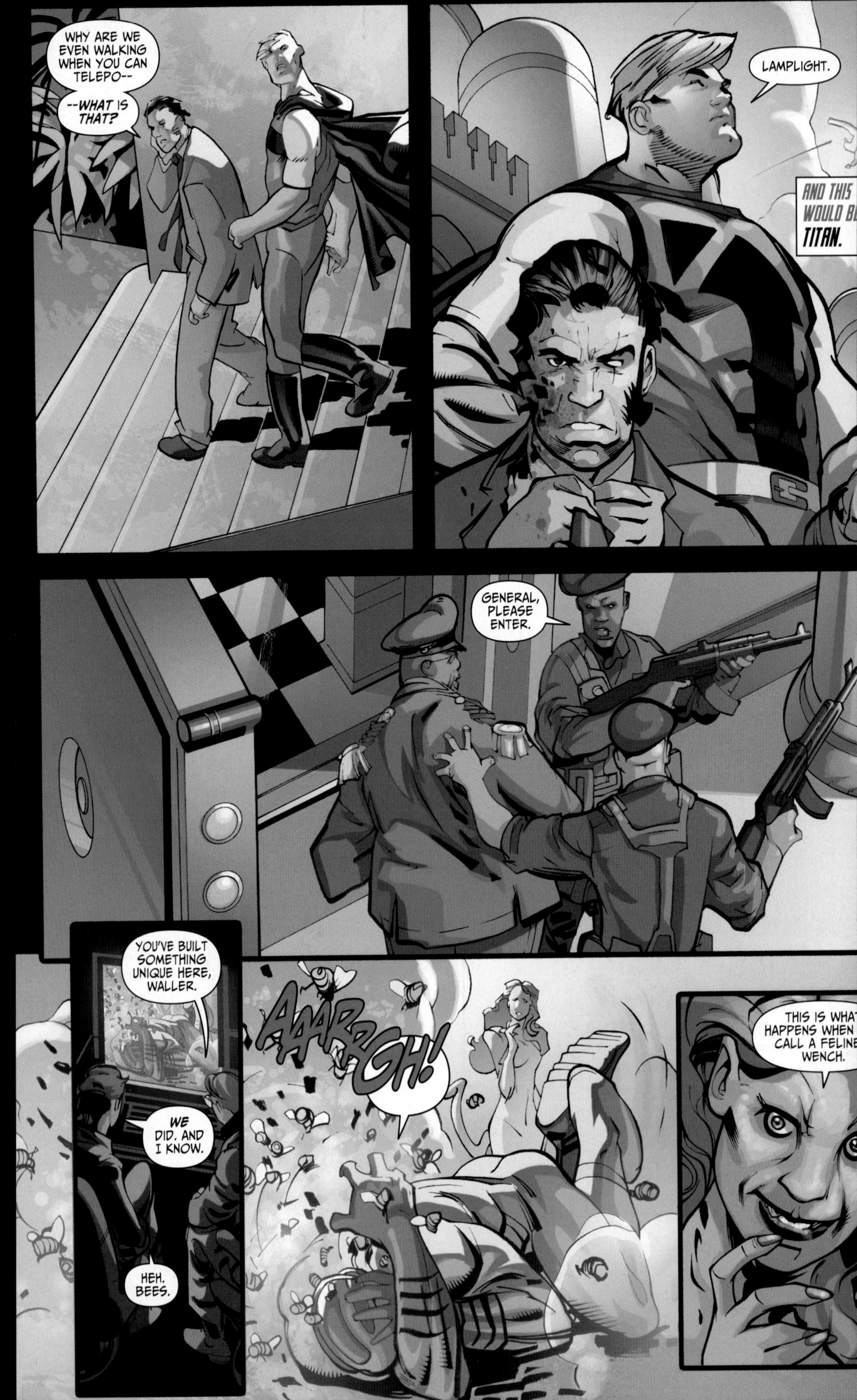
WHY ARE WE EVEN WALKING WHEN YOU CAN TELEPO--
--WHAT IS THAT?
LAMPLIGHT.
AND THIS WOULD B
TITAN.
GENERAL, PLEASE ENTER.
YOU'VE BUILT SOMETHING UNIQUE HERE, WALLER.
WE DID. AND I KNOW.
HEH. BEES.
AAARRGH!
THIS IS WHAT HAPPENS WHEN CALL A FELINE WENCH.

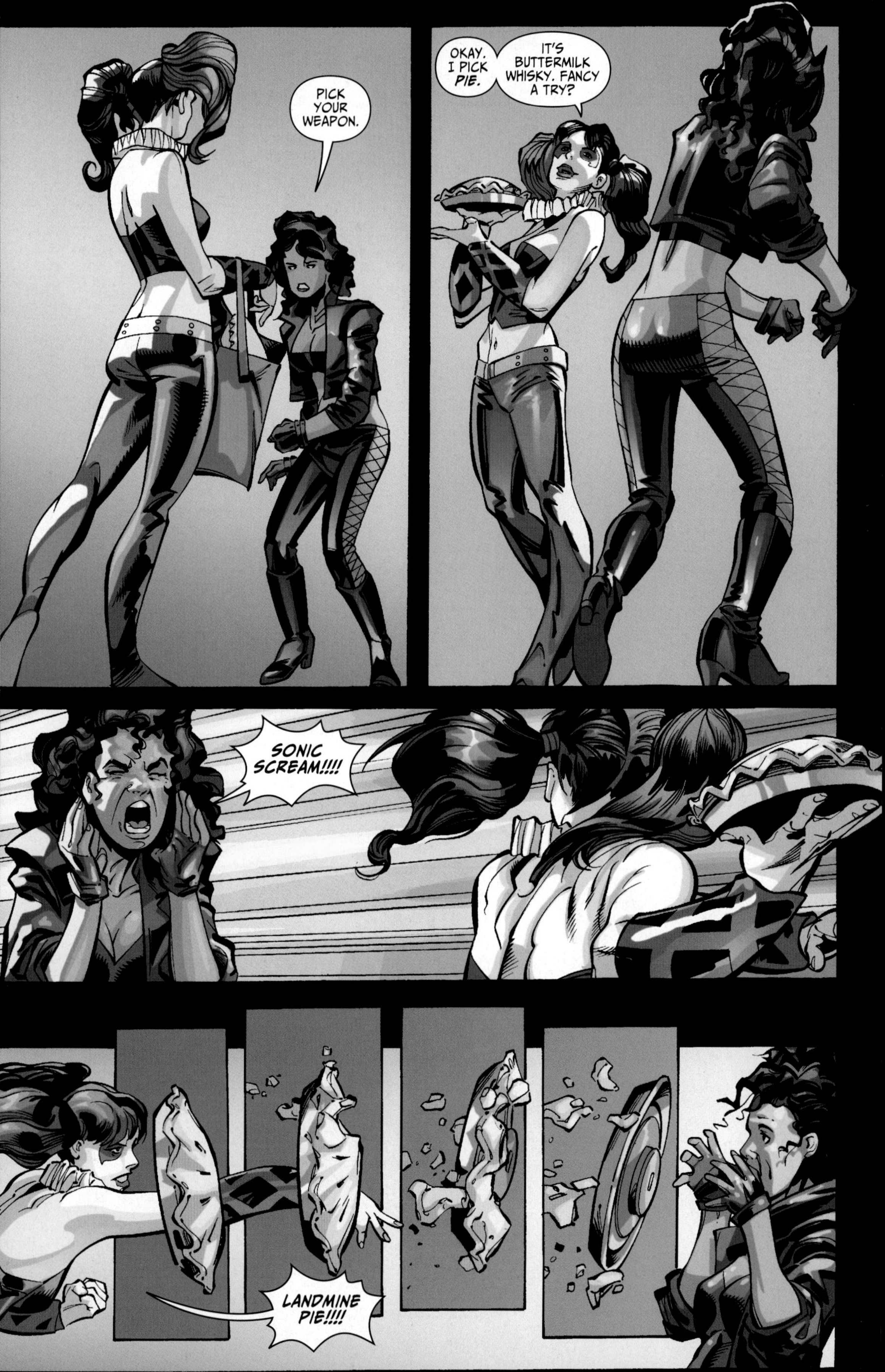
PICK YOUR WEAPON.
OKAY. I PICK PIE.
IT'S BUTTERMILK WHISKY. FANCY A TRY?
SONIC SCREAM!!!!
LANDMINE PIE!!!!

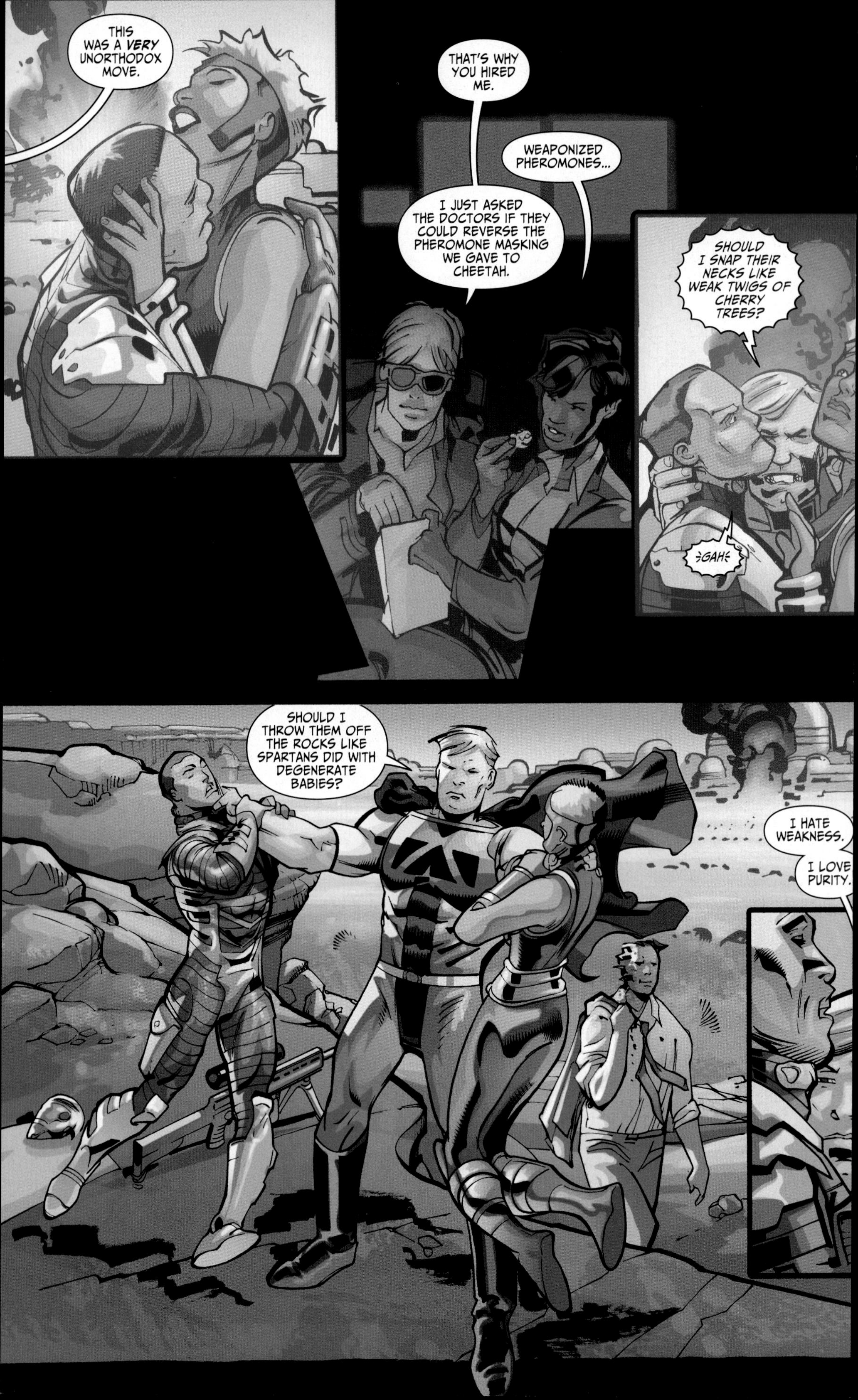
THIS WAS A VERY UNORTHODOX MOVE.
THAT'S WHY YOU HIRED ME.
WEAPONIZED PHEROMONES...
I JUST ASKED THE DOCTORS IF THEY COULD REVERSE THE PHEROMONE MASKING WE GAVE TO CHEETAH.
SHOULD I SNAP THEIR NECKS LIKE WEAK TWIGS OF CHERRY TREES?
GAH
SHOULD I THROW THEM OFF THE ROCKS LIKE SPARTANS DID WITH DEGENERATE BABIES?
I HATE WEAKNESS.
I LOVE PURITY.

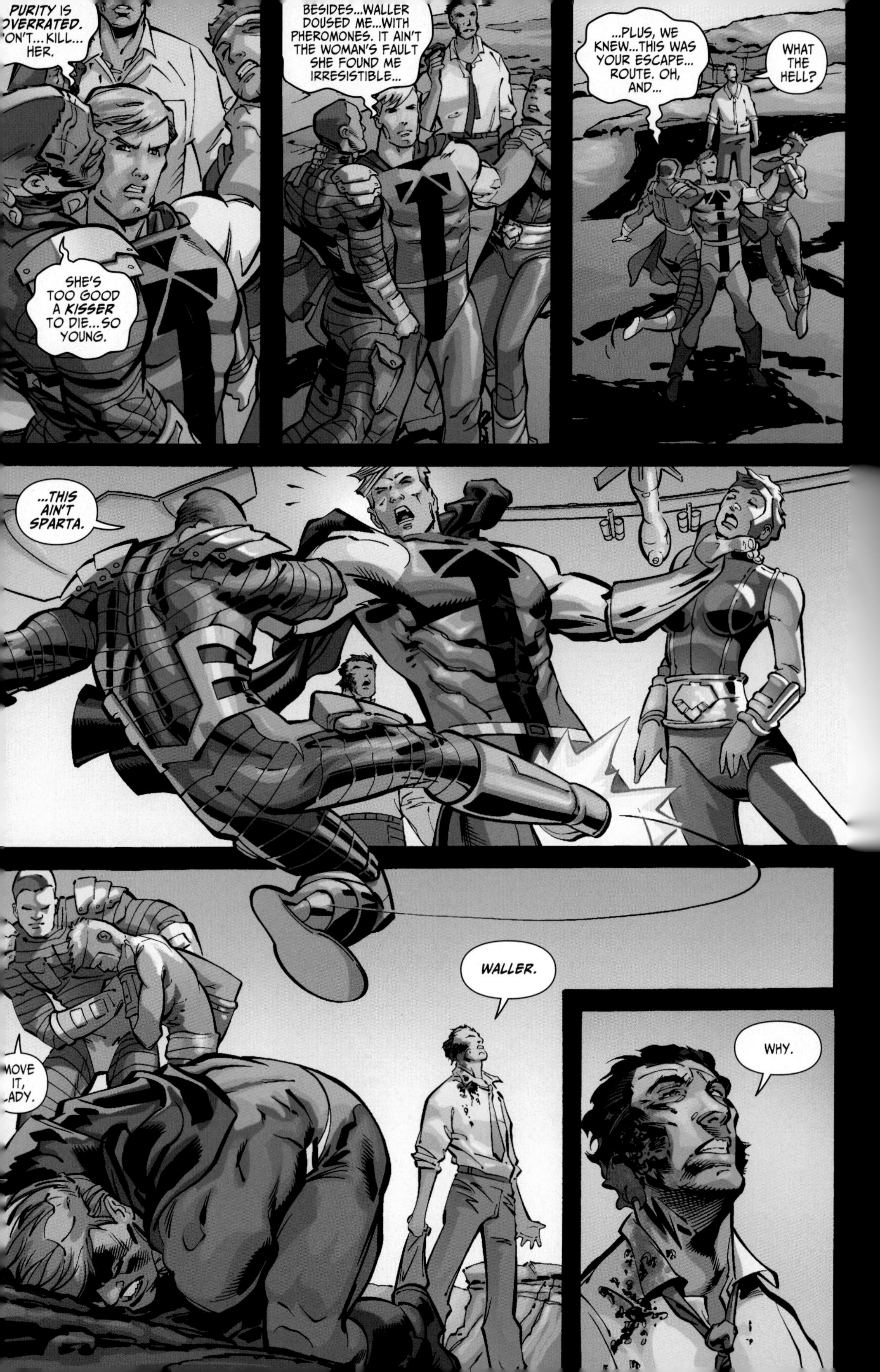
PURITY IS OVERRATED. DON'T...KILL... HER.
SHE'S TOO GOOD A KISSER TO DIE...SO YOUNG.
BESIDES...WALLER DOUSED ME...WITH PHEROMONES. IT AIN'T THE WOMAN'S FAULT SHE FOUND ME IRRESISTIBLE...
...PLUS, WE KNEW...THIS WAS YOUR ESCAPE... ROUTE. OH, AND...
WHAT THE HELL?
...THIS AIN'T SPARTA.
MOVE IT, LADY.
WALLER.
WHY.

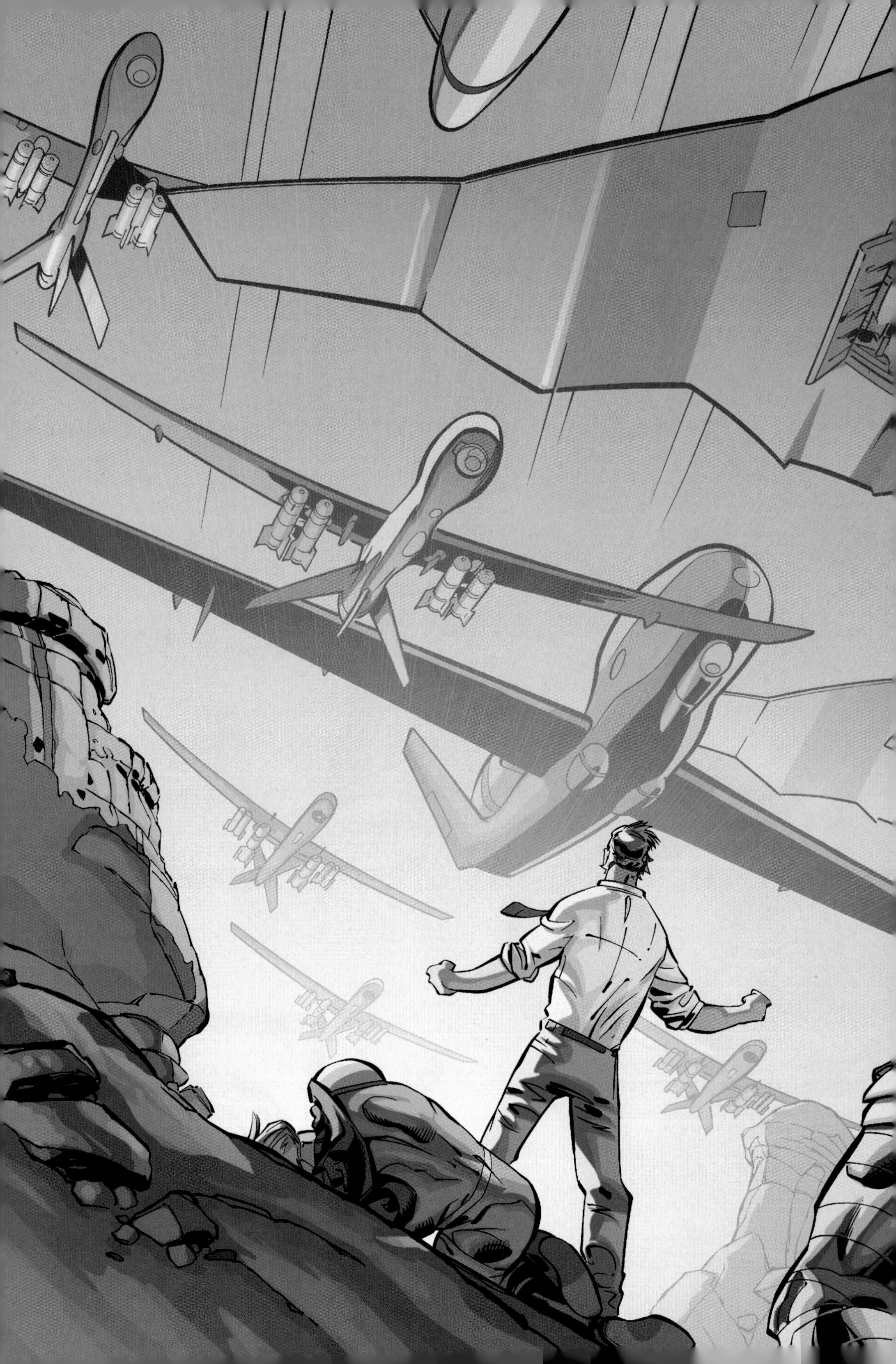

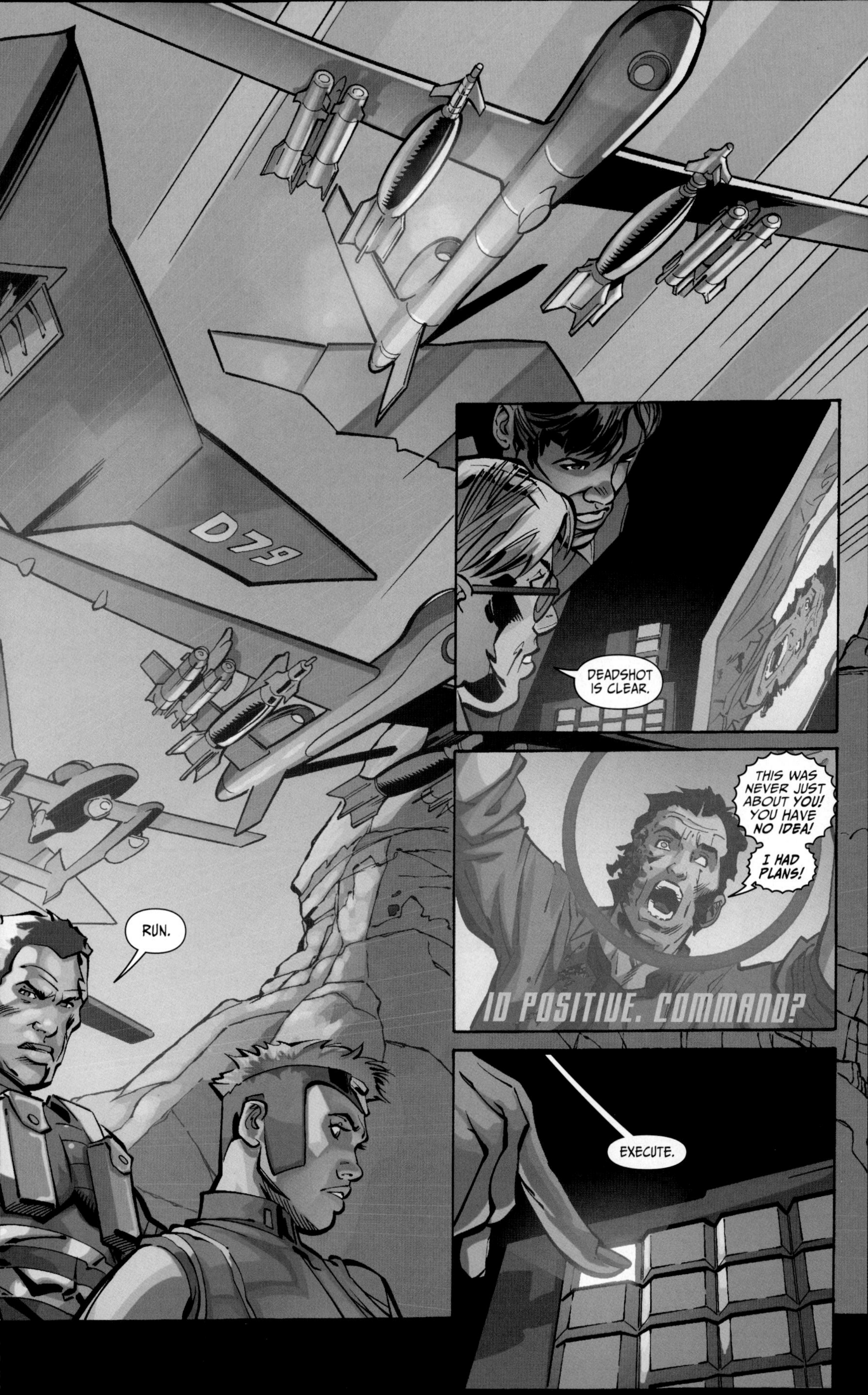
RUN.
DEADSHOT IS CLEAR.
THIS WAS NEVER JUST ABOUT YOU! YOU HAVE NO IDEA!
I HAD PLANS!
ID POSITIVE. COMMAND?
EXECUTE.

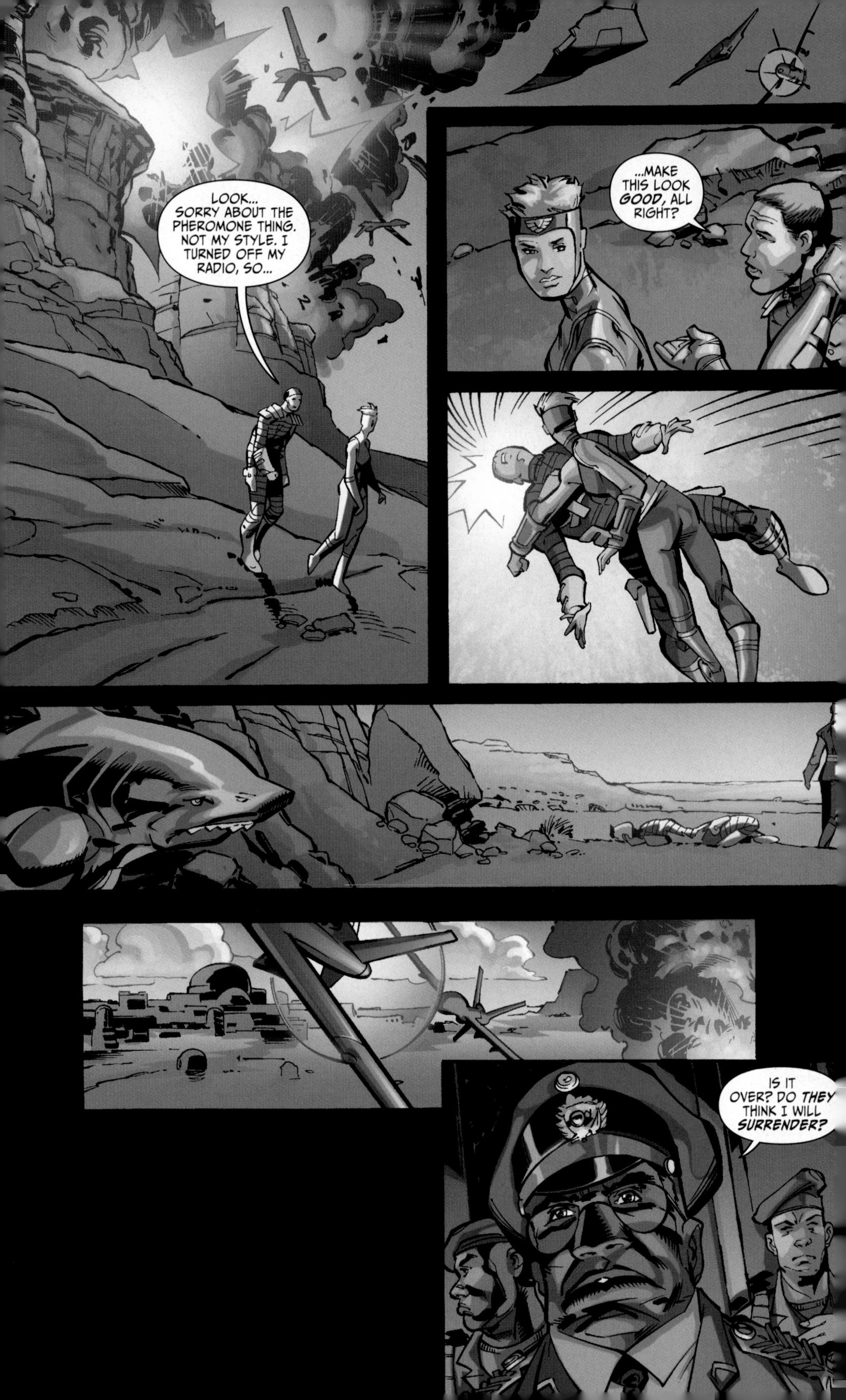
LOOK... SORRY ABOUT THE PHEROMONE THING. NOT MY STYLE. I TURNED OFF MY RADIO, SO...
...MAKE THIS LOOK GOOD, ALL RIGHT?
IS IT OVER? DO THEY THINK I WILL SURRENDER?

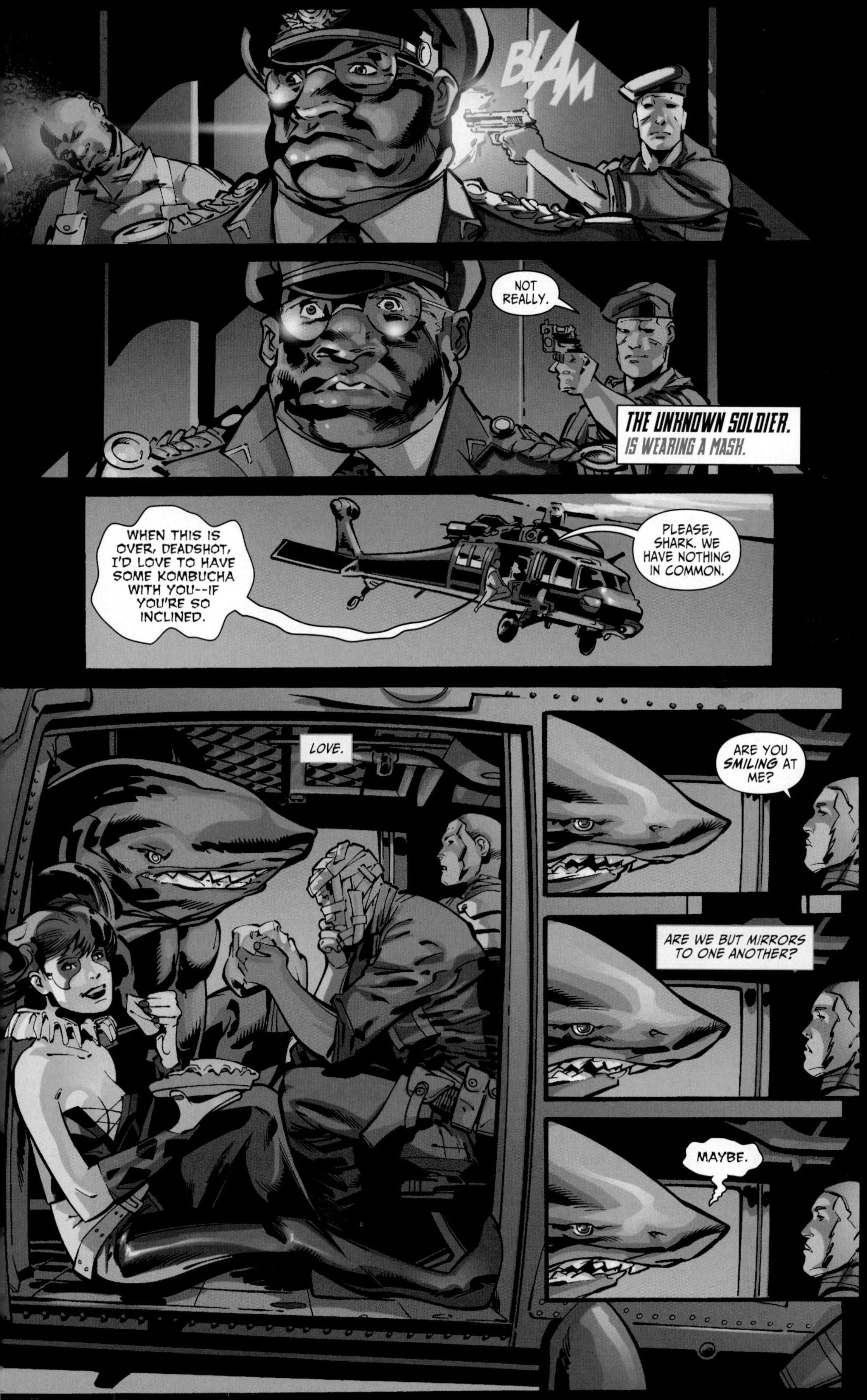
BLAM
NOT REALLY.
THE UNKNOWN SOLDIER.
IS WEARING A MASK.
WHEN THIS IS OVER, DEADSHOT, I'D LOVE TO HAVE SOME KOMBUCHA WITH YOU--IF YOU'RE SO INCLINED.
PLEASE, SHARK. WE HAVE NOTHING IN COMMON.
LOVE.
ARE YOU SMILING AT ME?
ARE WE BUT MIRRORS TO ONE ANOTHER?
MAYBE.

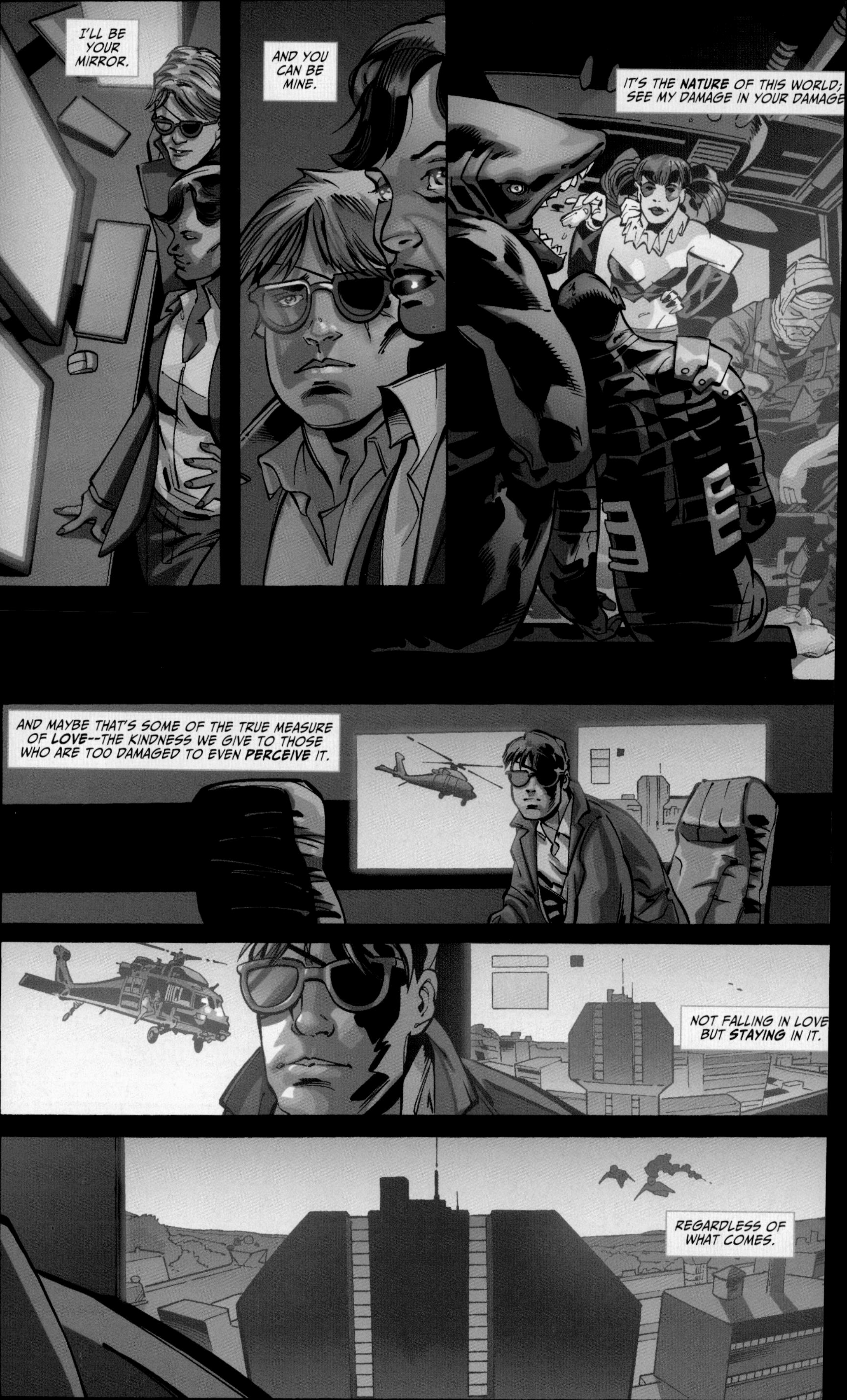
I'LL BE YOUR MIRROR.
AND YOU CAN BE MINE.
IT'S THE NATURE OF THIS WORLD; SEE MY DAMAGE IN YOUR DAMAGE
AND MAYBE THAT'S SOME OF THE TRUE MEASURE OF LOVE--THE KINDNESS WE GIVE TO THOSE WHO ARE TOO DAMAGED TO EVEN PERCEIVE IT.
NOT FALLING IN LOVE BUT STAYING IN IT.
REGARDLESS OF WHAT COMES.

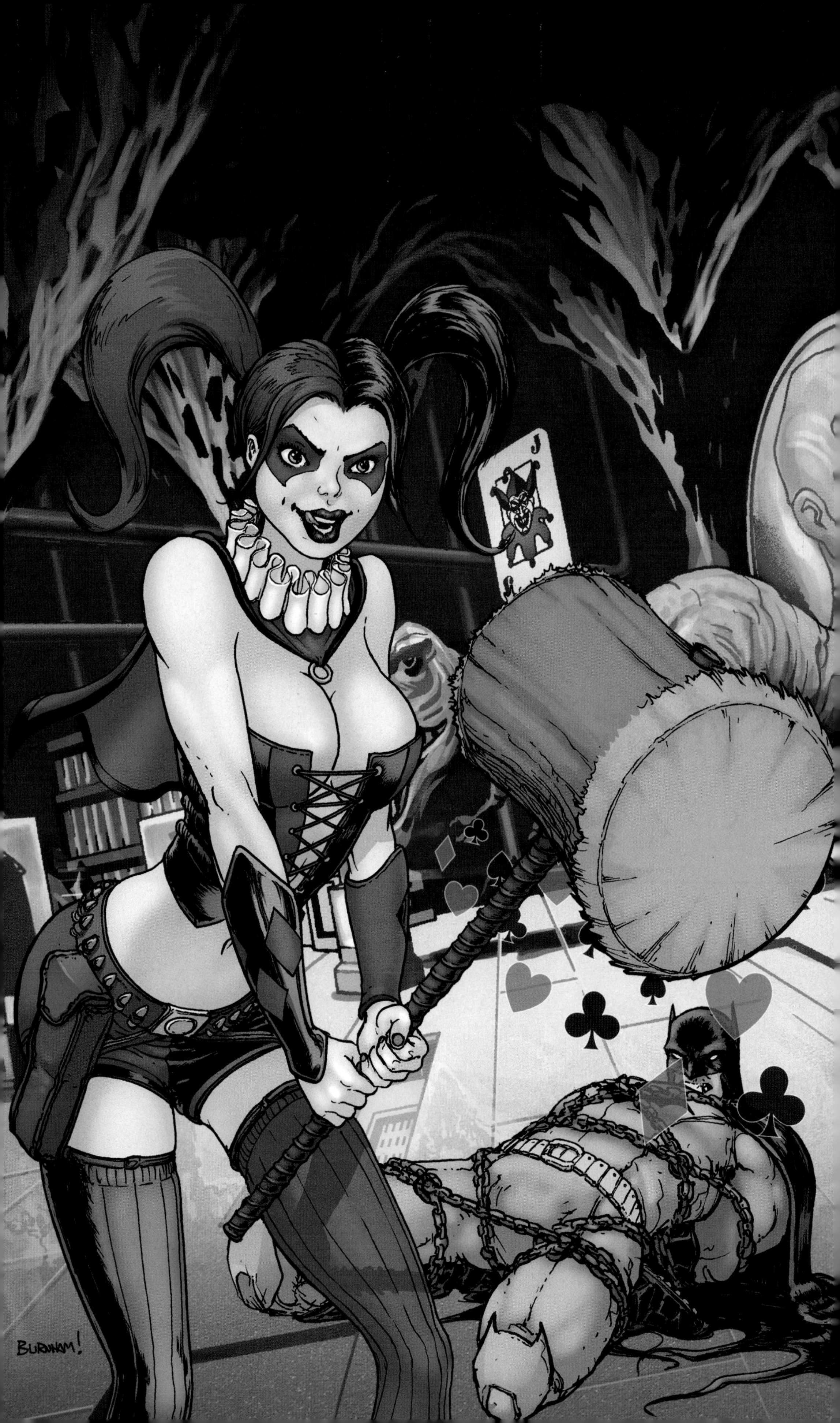
BURNHAM!

HARLEY LIVES

MATT KINDT writer **NEIL GOOGE** artist cover by **CHRIS BURNHAM & NATHAN FAIRBAIRN**

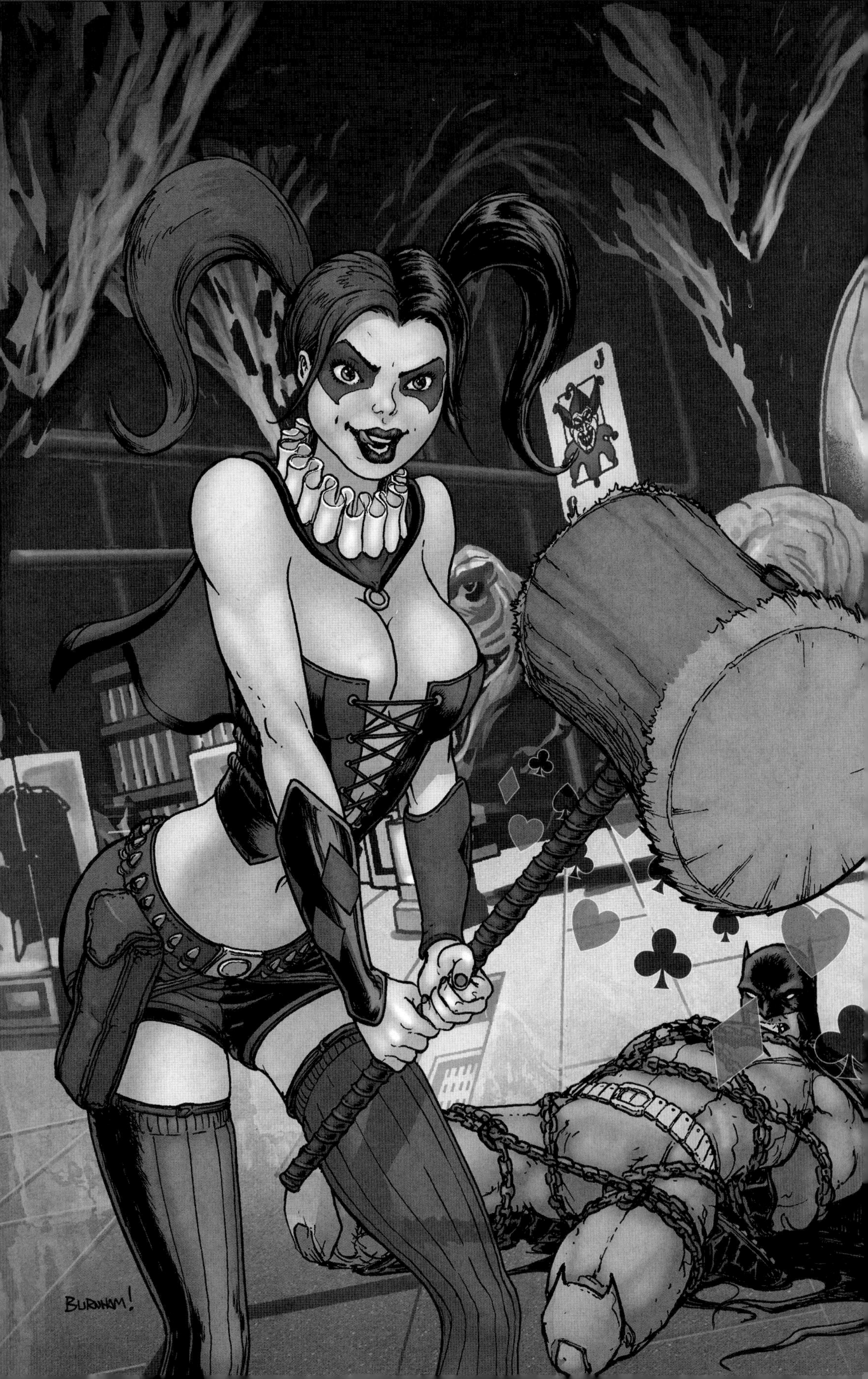

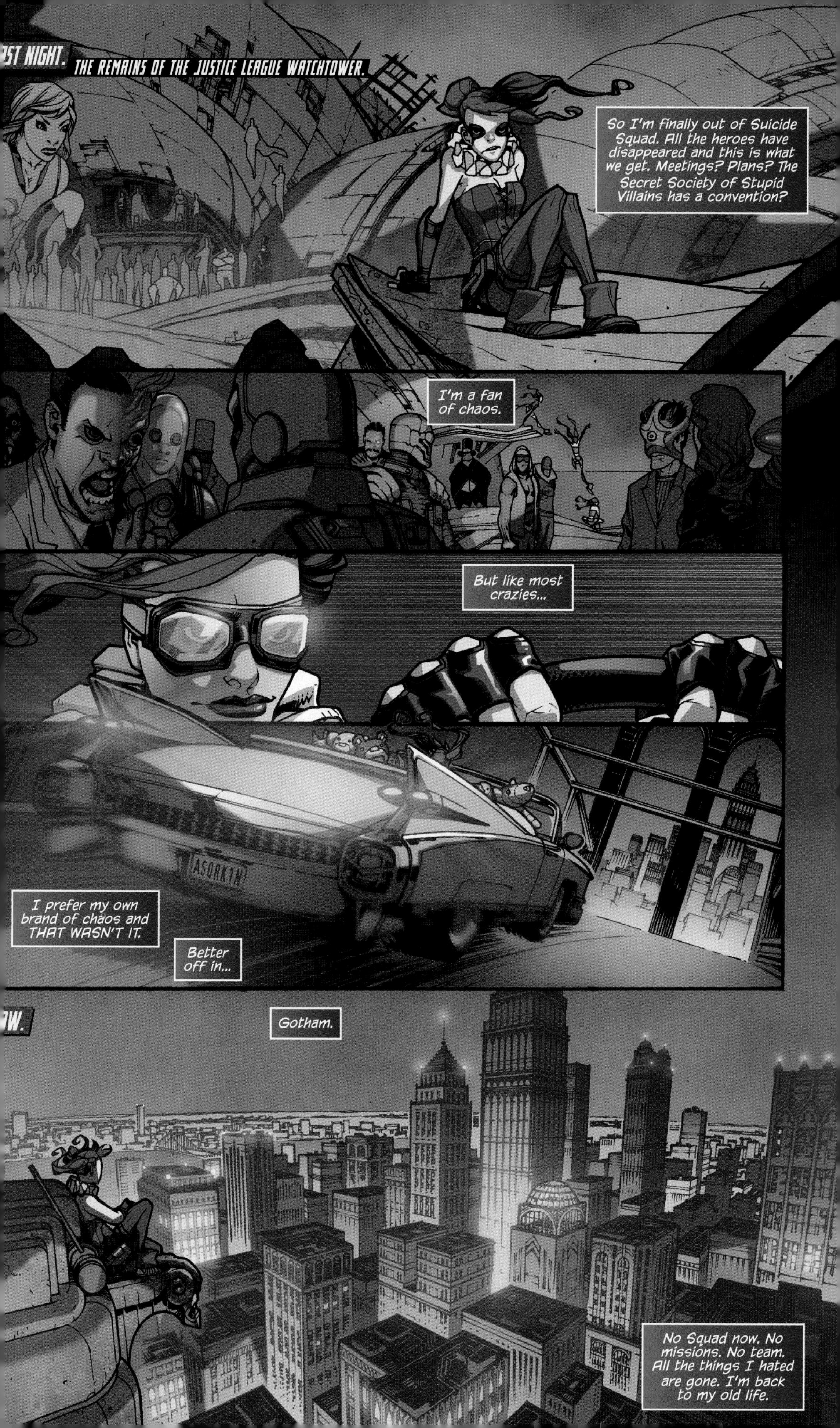

ST NIGHT.
THE REMAINS OF THE JUSTICE LEAGUE WATCHTOWER.
So I'm finally out of Suicide Squad. All the heroes have disappeared and this is what we get. Meetings? Plans? The Secret Society of Stupid Villains has a convention?
I'm a fan of chaos.
But like most crazies...
ASORK1N
I prefer my own brand of chaos and THAT WASN'T IT.
Better off in...
W.
Gotham.
No Squad now. No missions. No team. All the things I hated are gone. I'm back to my old life.

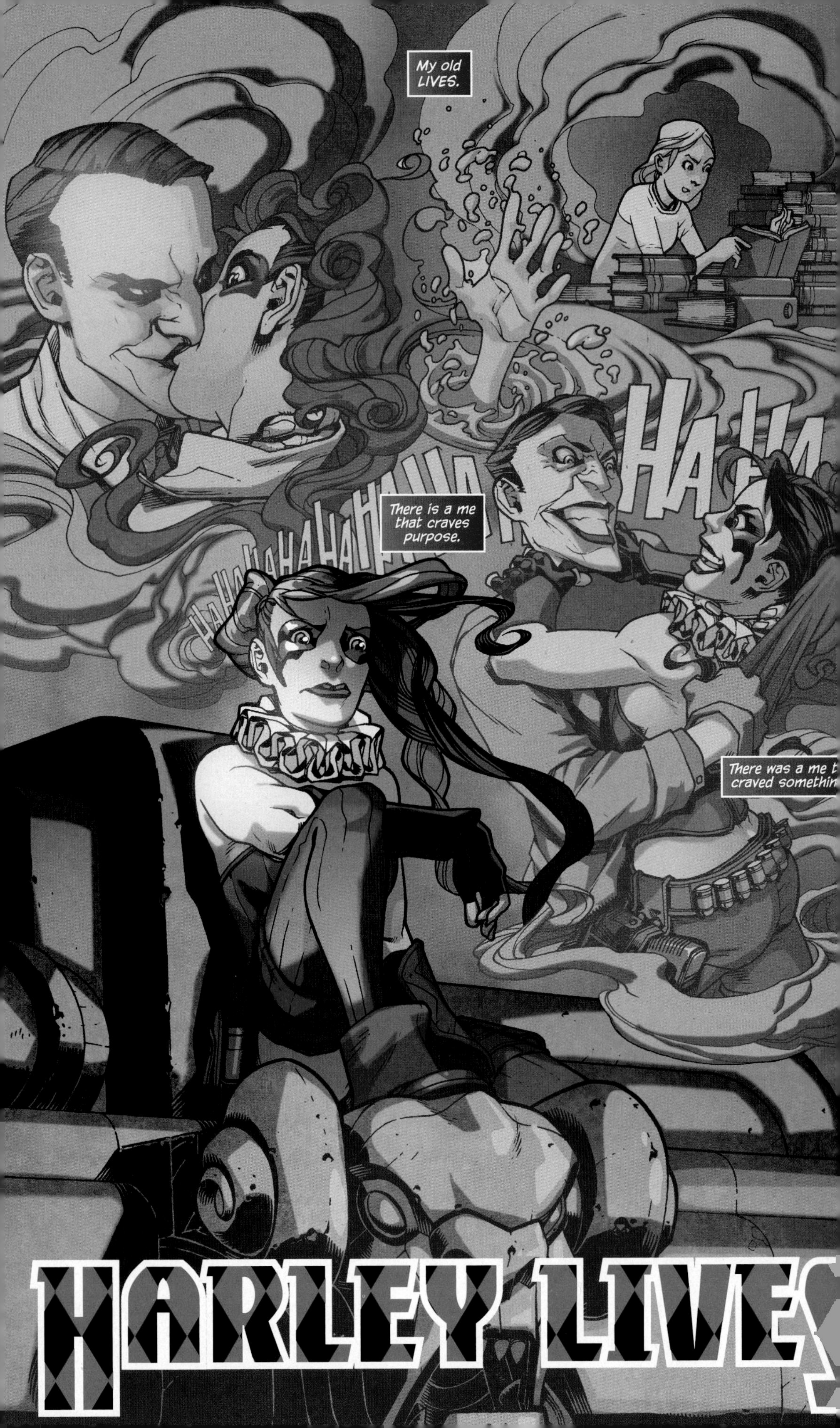
My old LIVES.
HAHAHAHAHAHA
There is a me that craves purpose.
HAHA
There was a me t
craved somethin
HARLEY LIVES

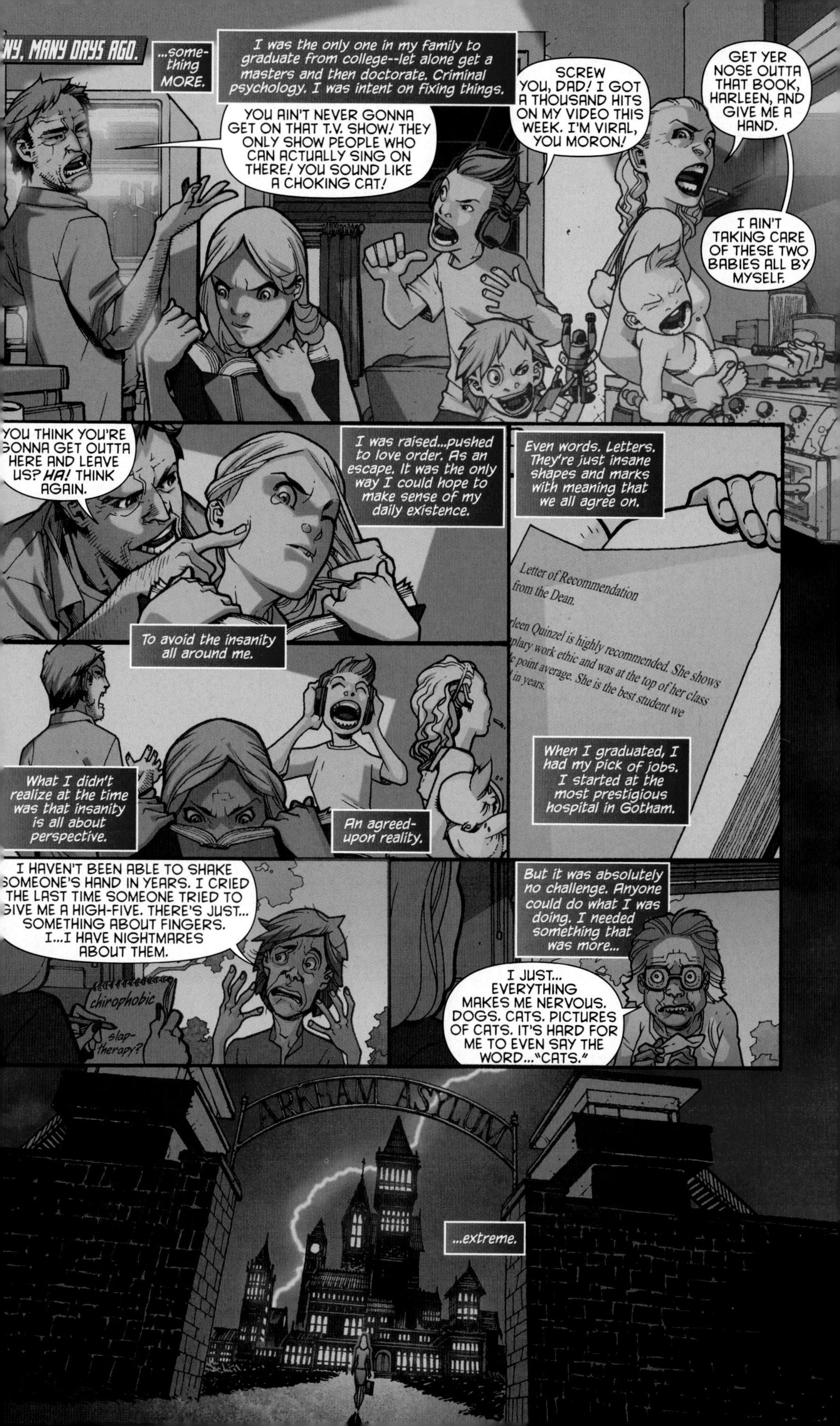
NY, MANY DAYS AGO.
...some-thing MORE.
I was the only one in my family to graduate from college--let alone get a masters and then doctorate. Criminal psychology. I was intent on fixing things.
YOU AIN'T NEVER GONNA GET ON THAT T.V. SHOW! THEY ONLY SHOW PEOPLE WHO CAN ACTUALLY SING ON THERE! YOU SOUND LIKE A CHOKING CAT!
SCREW YOU, DAD! I GOT A THOUSAND HITS ON MY VIDEO THIS WEEK. I'M VIRAL, YOU MORON!
GET YER NOSE OUTTA THAT BOOK, HARLEEN, AND GIVE ME A HAND.
I AIN'T TAKING CARE OF THESE TWO BABIES ALL BY MYSELF.
YOU THINK YOU'RE GONNA GET OUTTA HERE AND LEAVE US? HA! THINK AGAIN.
I was raised...pushed to love order. As an escape. It was the only way I could hope to make sense of my daily existence.
To avoid the insanity all around me.
What I didn't realize at the time was that insanity is all about perspective.
An agreed-upon reality.
Even words. Letters. They're just insane shapes and marks with meaning that we all agree on.
Letter of Recommendation
from the Dean.
rleen Quinzel is highly recommended. She shows
plary work ethic and was at the top of her class
e point average. She is the best student we
in years.
When I graduated, I had my pick of jobs. I started at the most prestigious hospital in Gotham.
I HAVEN'T BEEN ABLE TO SHAKE SOMEONE'S HAND IN YEARS. I CRIED THE LAST TIME SOMEONE TRIED TO GIVE ME A HIGH-FIVE. THERE'S JUST... SOMETHING ABOUT FINGERS. I...I HAVE NIGHTMARES ABOUT THEM.
chirophobic
slap-therapy?
But it was absolutely no challenge. Anyone could do what I was doing. I needed something that was more...
I JUST... EVERYTHING MAKES ME NERVOUS. DOGS. CATS. PICTURES OF CATS. IT'S HARD FOR ME TO EVEN SAY THE WORD..."CATS."
ARKHAM ASYLUM
...extreme.

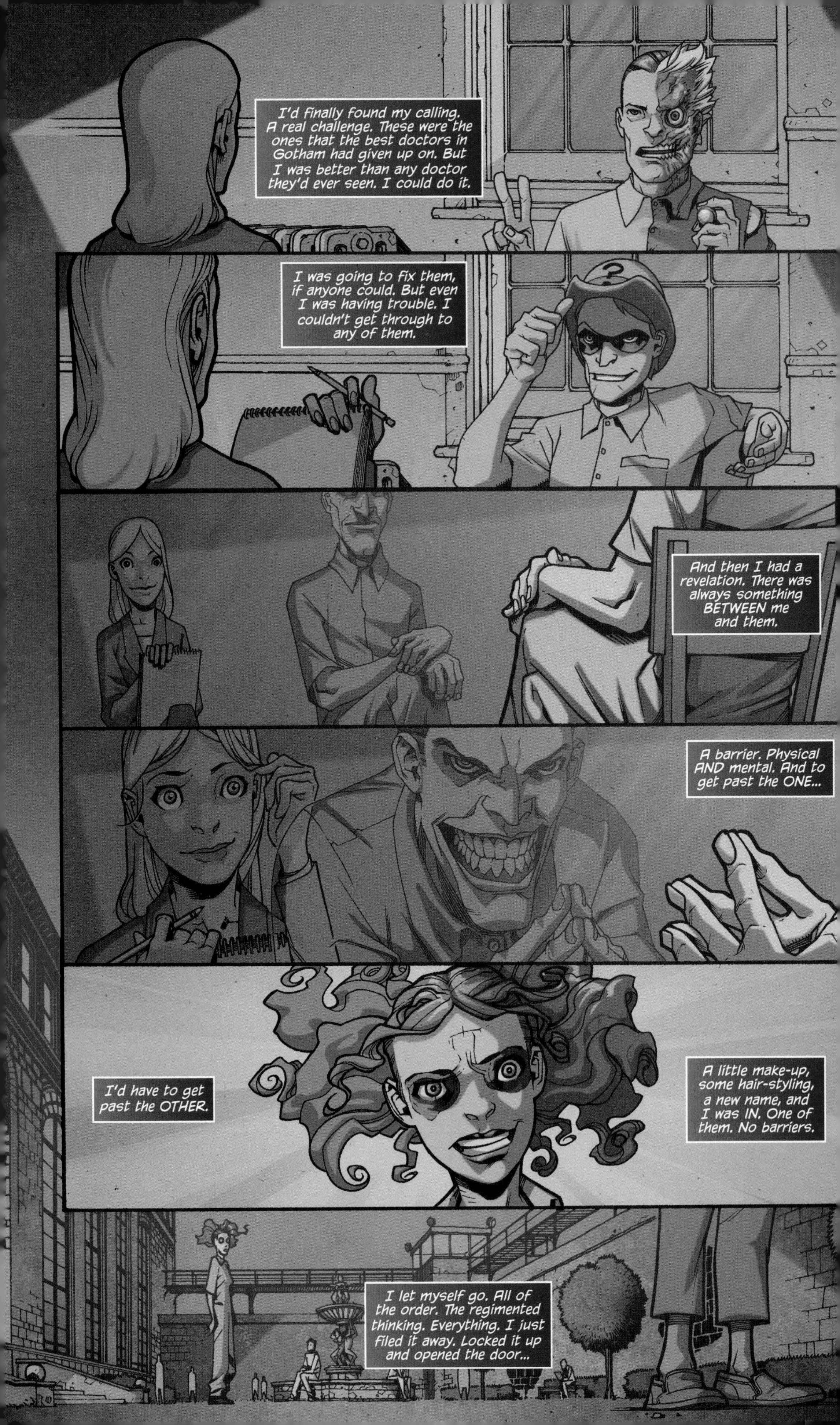
I'd finally found my calling. A real challenge. These were the ones that the best doctors in Gotham had given up on. But I was better than any doctor they'd ever seen. I could do it.
I was going to fix them, if anyone could. But even I was having trouble. I couldn't get through to any of them.
And then I had a revelation. There was always something BETWEEN me and them.
A barrier. Physical AND mental. And to get past the ONE...
I'd have to get past the OTHER.
A little make-up, some hair-styling, a new name, and I was IN. One of them. No barriers.
I let myself go. All of the order. The regimented thinking. Everything. I just filed it away. Locked it up and opened the door...

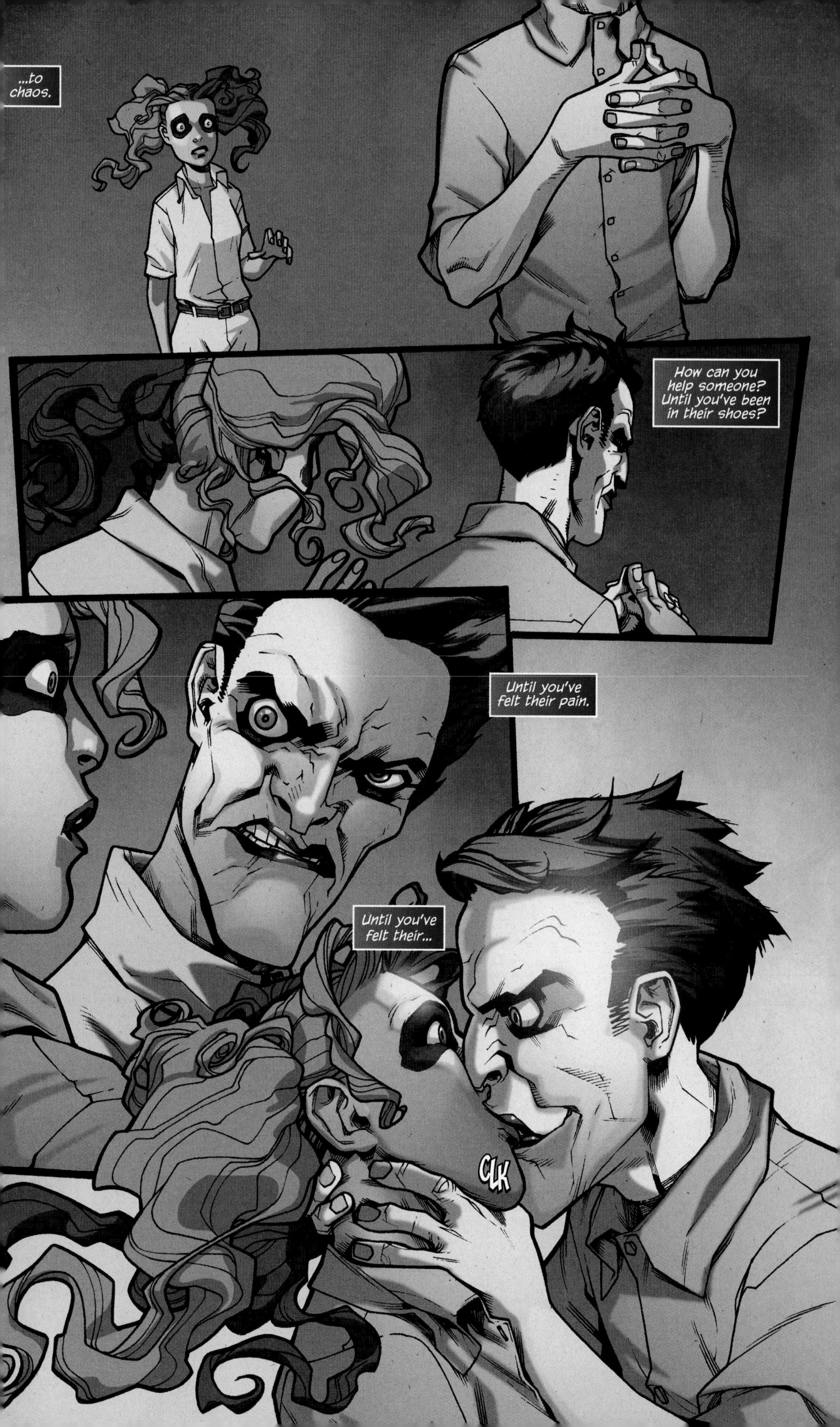
...to chaos.
How can you help someone? Until you've been in their shoes?
Until you've felt their pain.
Until you've felt their...
CLK

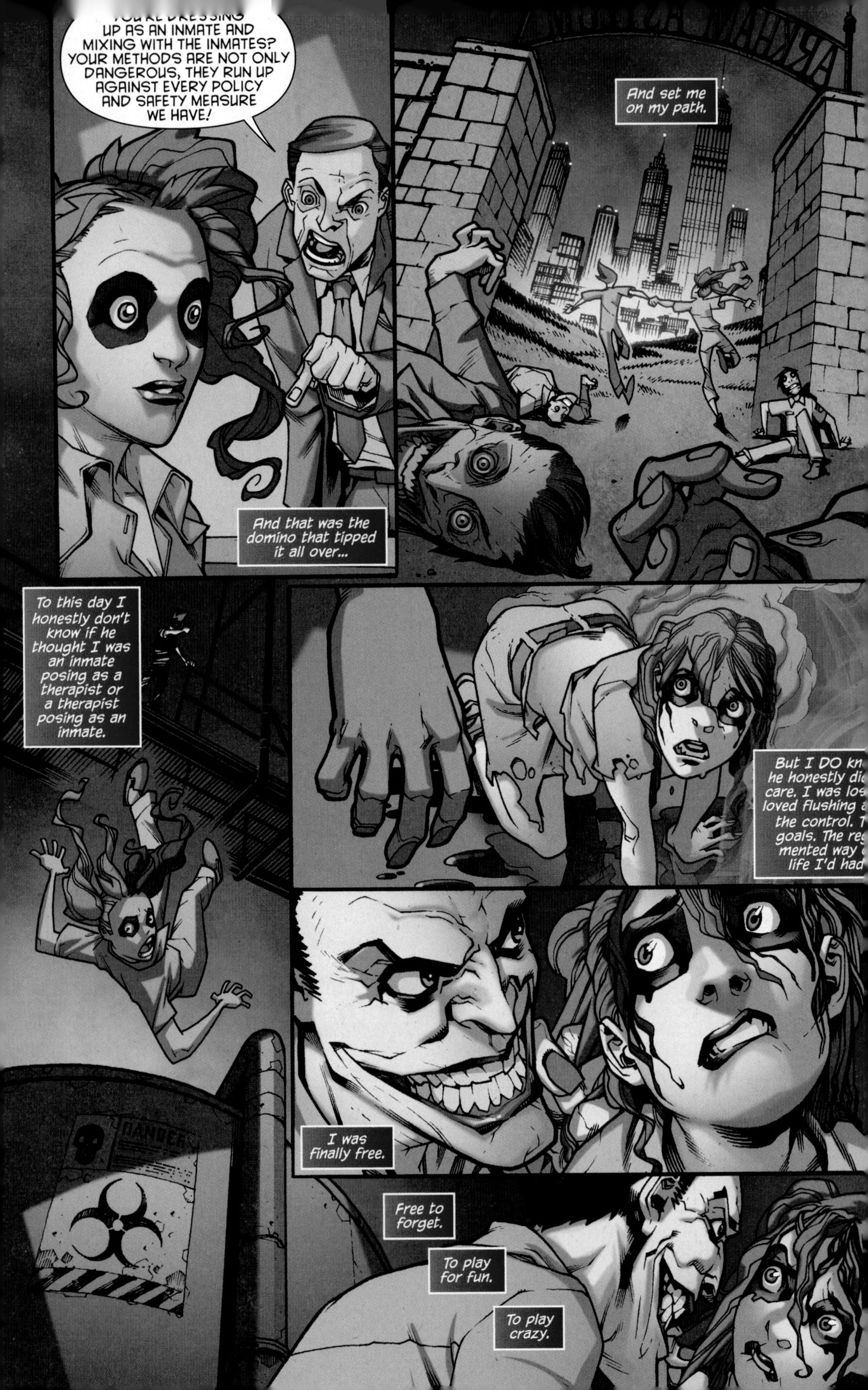
UP AS AN INMATE AND MIXING WITH THE INMATES? YOUR METHODS ARE NOT ONLY DANGEROUS, THEY RUN UP AGAINST EVERY POLICY AND SAFETY MEASURE WE HAVE!
And that was the domino that tipped it all over...
And set me on my path.
To this day I honestly don't know if he thought I was an inmate posing as a therapist or a therapist posing as an inmate.
But I DO kn he honestly di care. I was los loved flushing the control. goals. The re mented way life I'd had
I was finally free.
Free to forget.
To play for fun.
To play crazy.

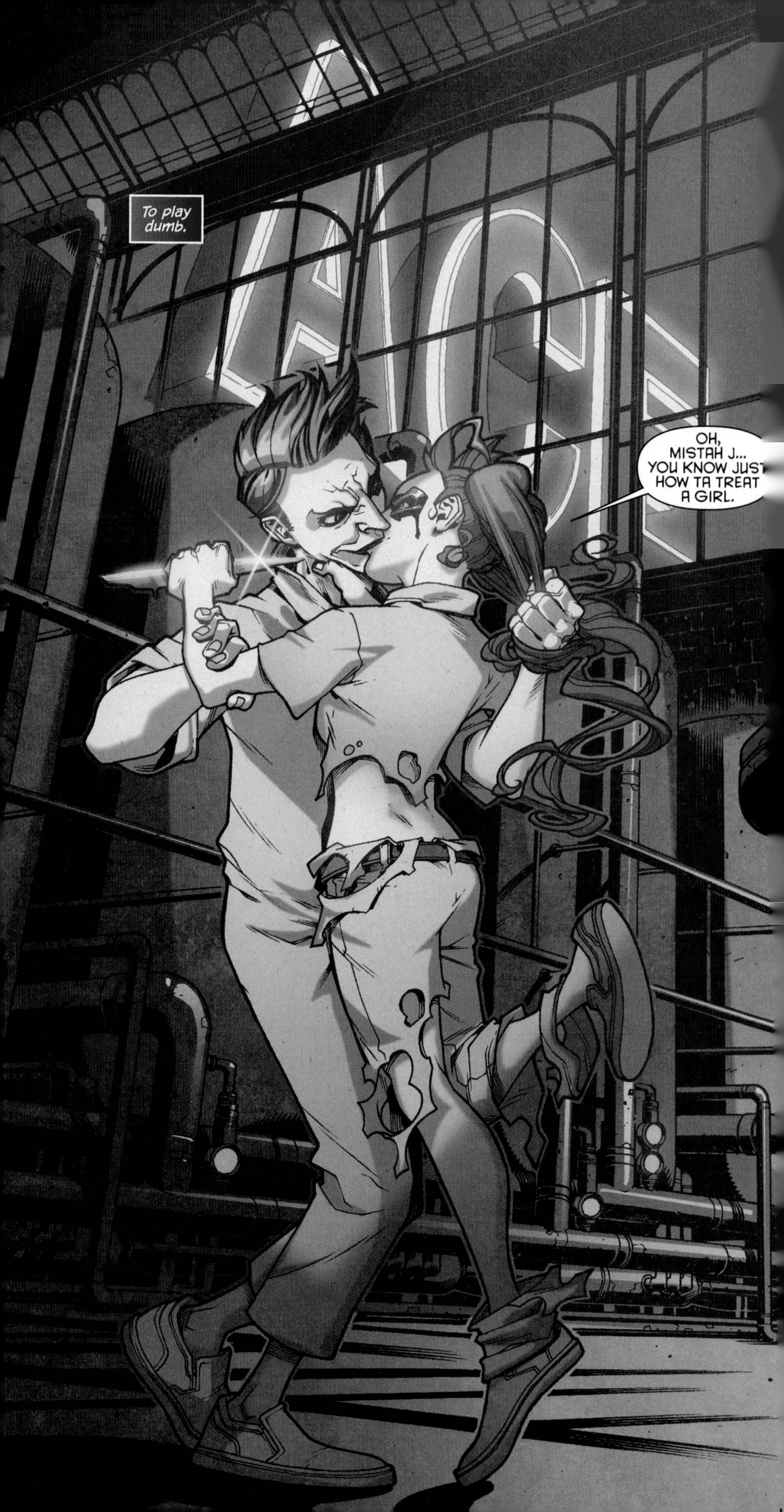
To play dumb.
OH, MISTAH J... YOU KNOW JUST HOW TA TREAT A GIRL.

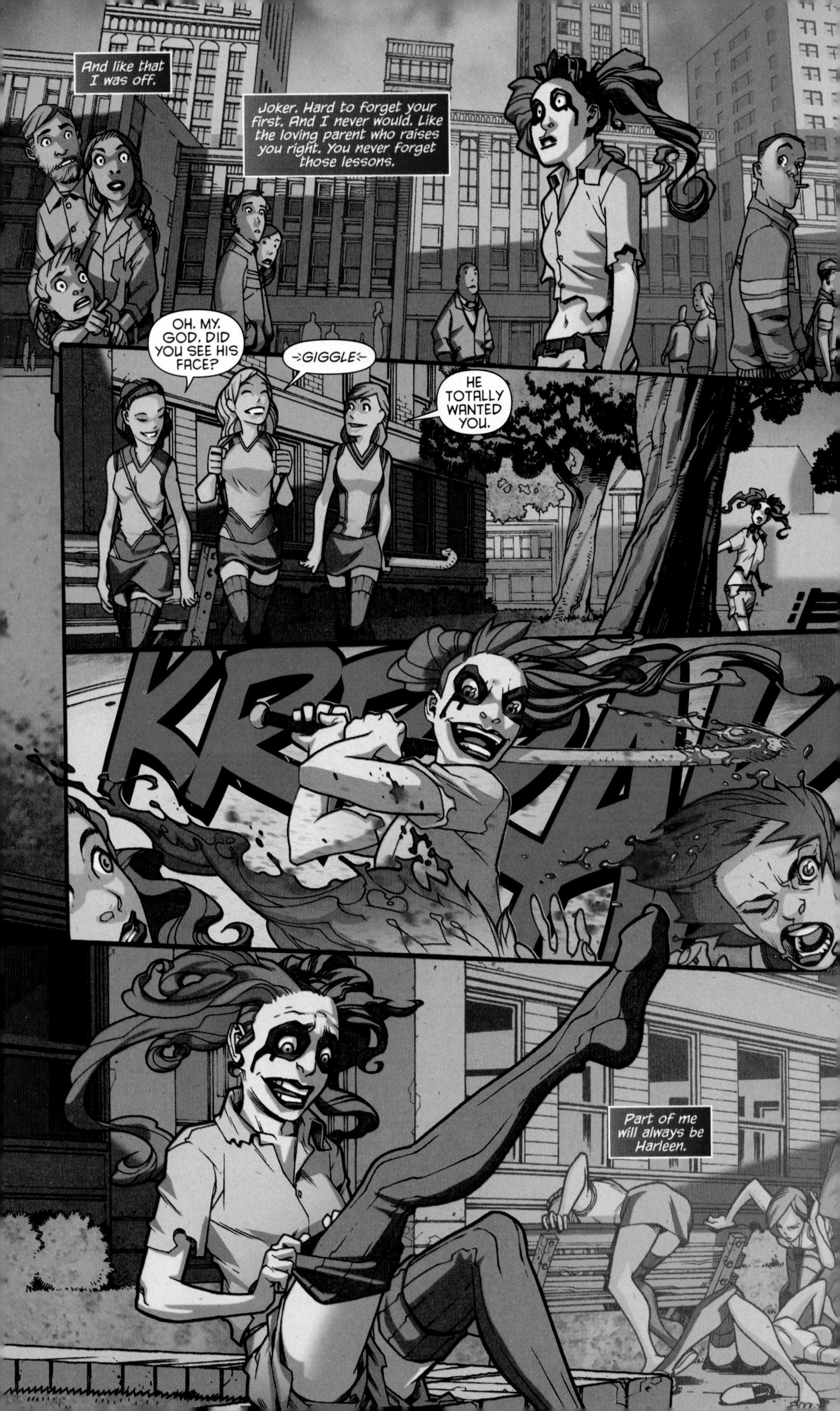
And like that I was off.
Joker. Hard to forget your first. And I never would. Like the loving parent who raises you right. You never forget those lessons.
OH. MY. GOD. DID YOU SEE HIS FACE?
~GIGGLE~
HE TOTALLY WANTED YOU.
Part of me will always be Harleen.

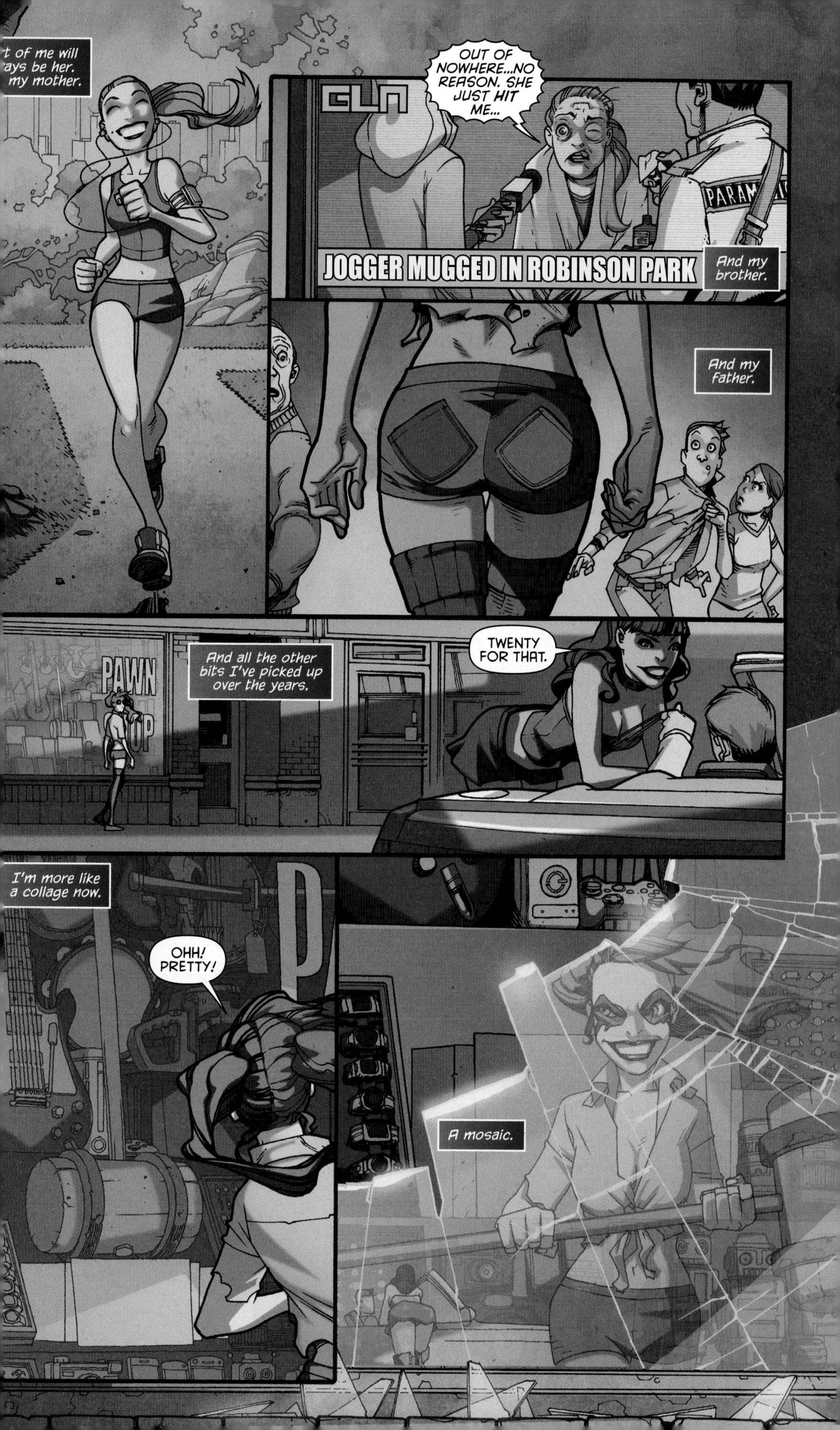

t of me will
ays be her.
my mother.
OUT OF NOWHERE...NO REASON. SHE JUST HIT ME...
GLN
JOGGER MUGGED IN ROBINSON PARK
And my brother.
And my father.
And all the other bits I've picked up over the years.
PAWN
TWENTY FOR THAT.
I'm more like a collage now.
OHH! PRETTY!
A mosaic.

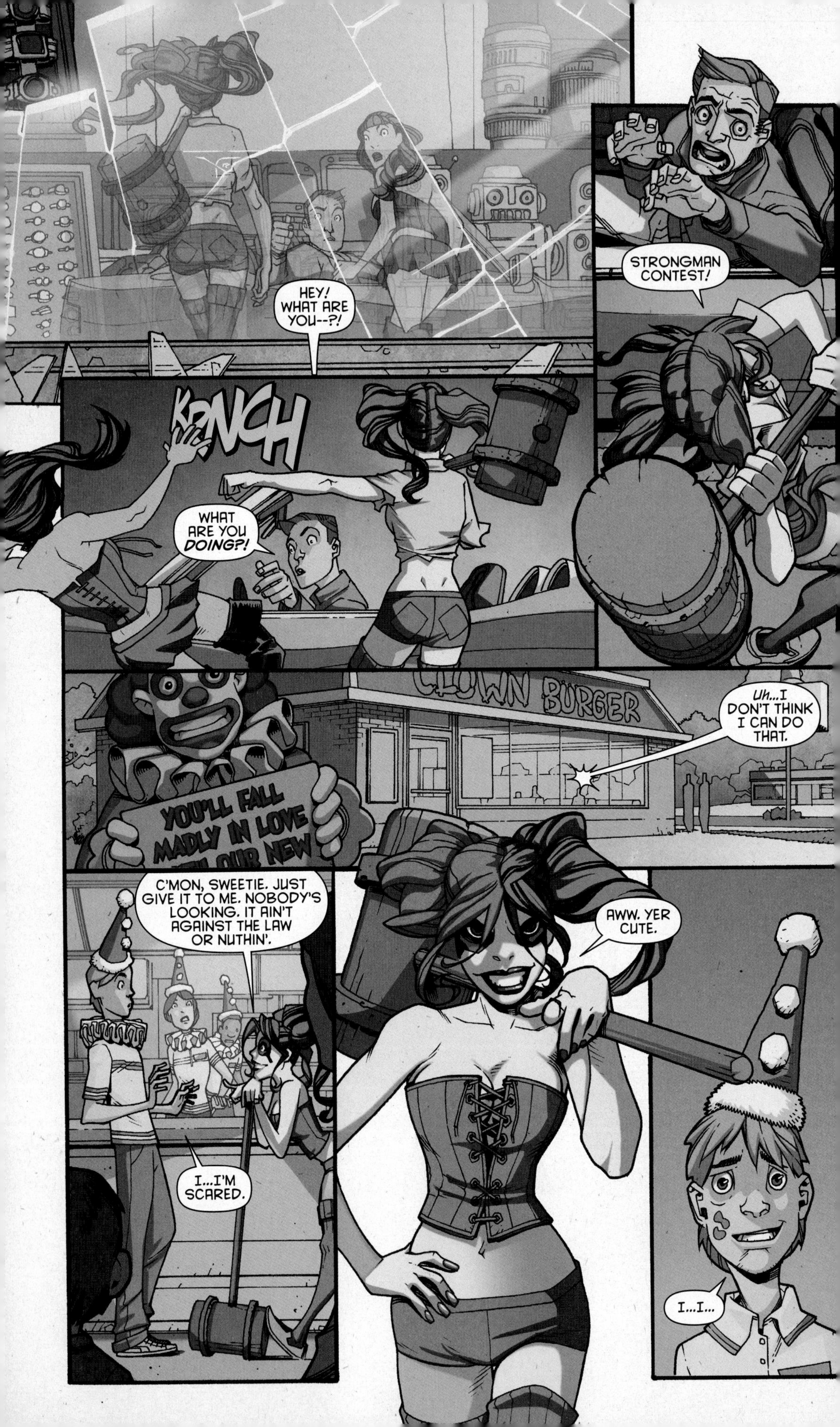

HEY! WHAT ARE YOU--?!
STRONGMAN CONTEST!
KRNCH
WHAT ARE YOU DOING?!
CLOWN BURGER
YOU'LL FALL MADLY IN LOVE
Uh...I DON'T THINK I CAN DO THAT.
C'MON, SWEETIE. JUST GIVE IT TO ME. NOBODY'S LOOKING. IT AIN'T AGAINST THE LAW OR NUTHIN'.
I...I'M SCARED.
AWW. YER CUTE.
I...I...

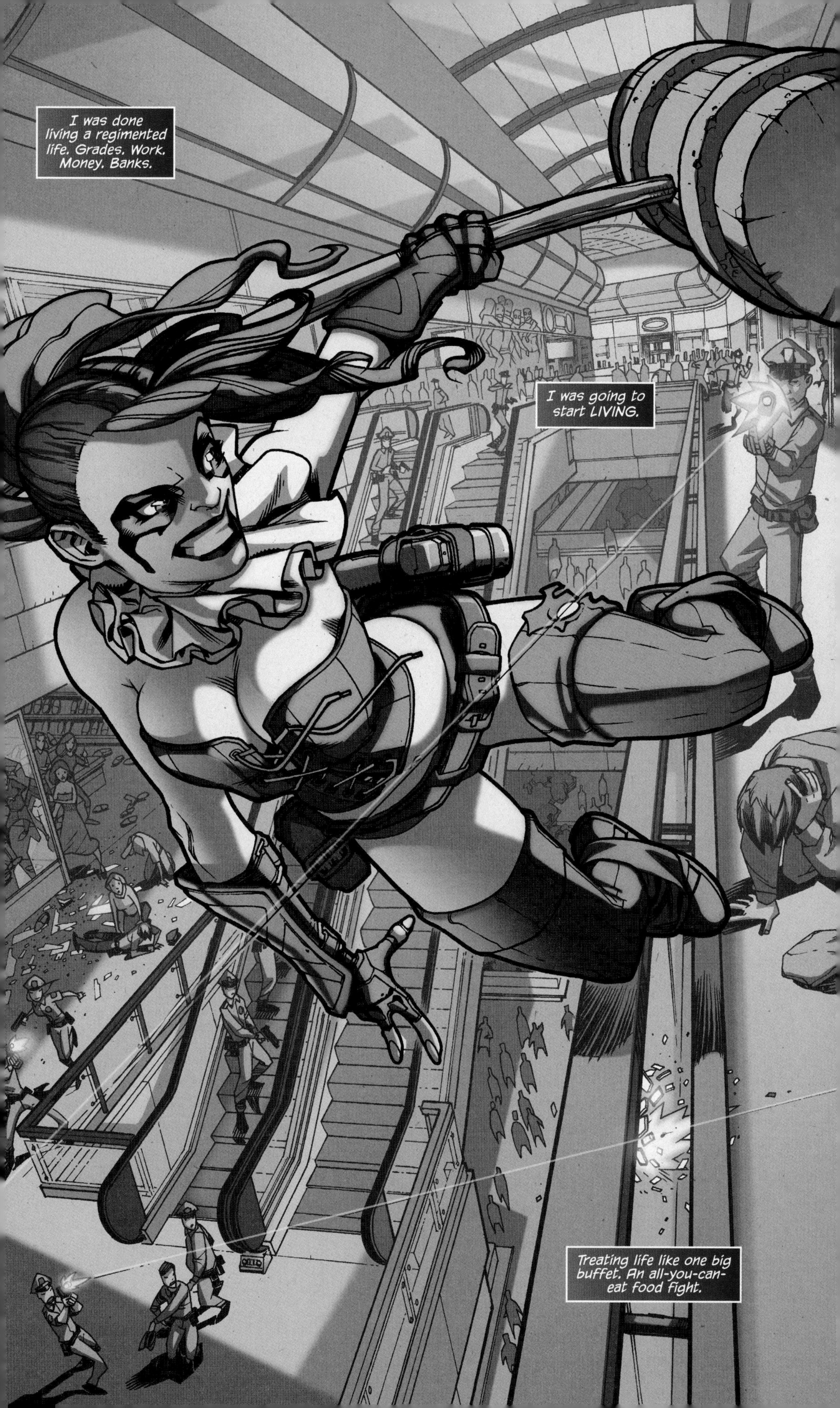
I was done living a regimented life. Grades. Work. Money. Banks.
I was going to start LIVING.
Treating life like one big buffet. An all-you-can-eat food fight.

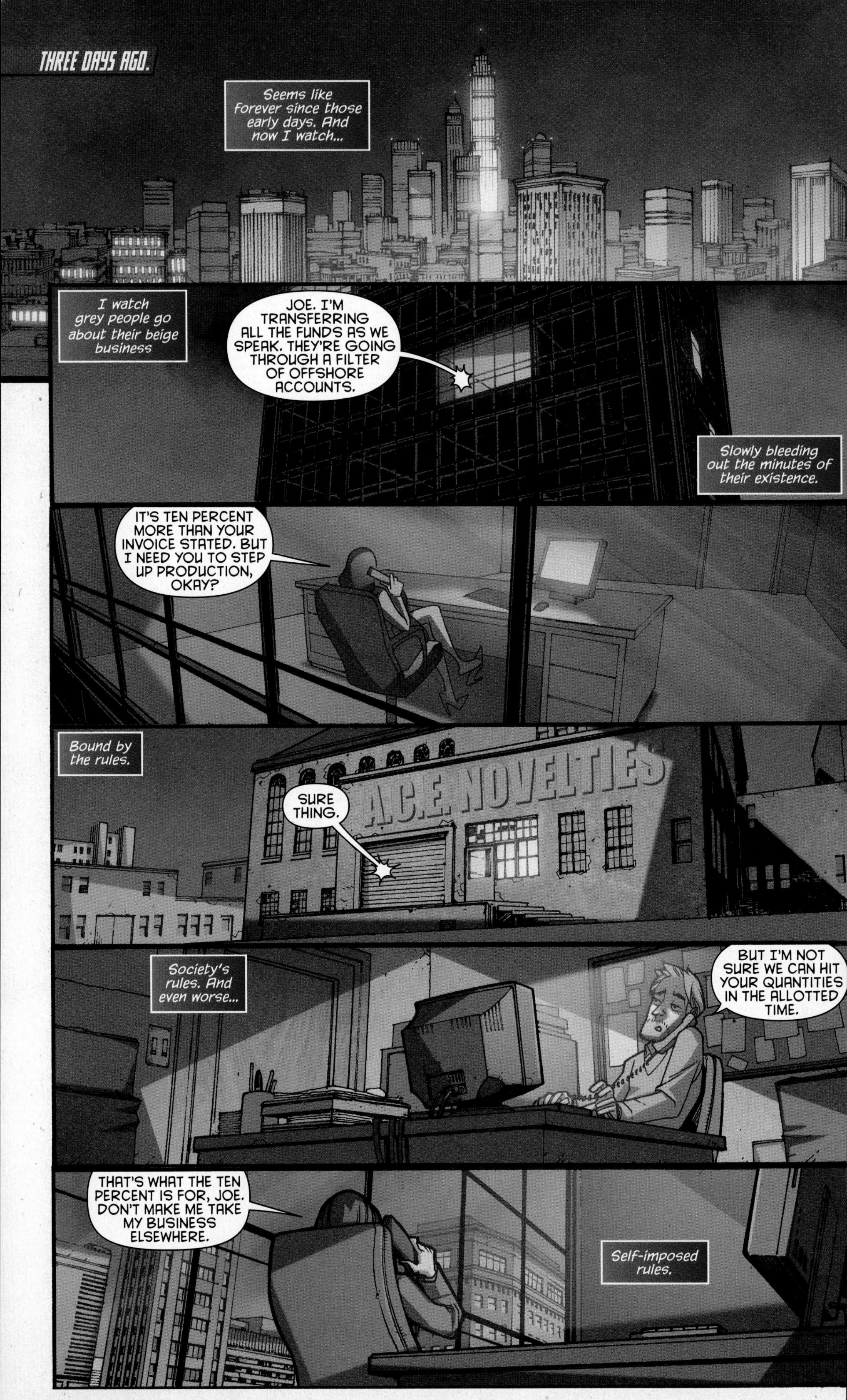
THREE DAYS AGO.
Seems like forever since those early days. And now I watch...
I watch grey people go about their beige business
JOE. I'M TRANSFERRING ALL THE FUNDS AS WE SPEAK. THEY'RE GOING THROUGH A FILTER OF OFFSHORE ACCOUNTS.
Slowly bleeding out the minutes of their existence.
IT'S TEN PERCENT MORE THAN YOUR INVOICE STATED. BUT I NEED YOU TO STEP UP PRODUCTION, OKAY?
Bound by the rules.
A.C.E. NOVELTIES
SURE THING.
Society's rules. And even worse...
BUT I'M NOT SURE WE CAN HIT YOUR QUANTITIES IN THE ALLOTTED TIME.
THAT'S WHAT THE TEN PERCENT IS FOR, JOE. DON'T MAKE ME TAKE MY BUSINESS ELSEWHERE.
Self-imposed rules.

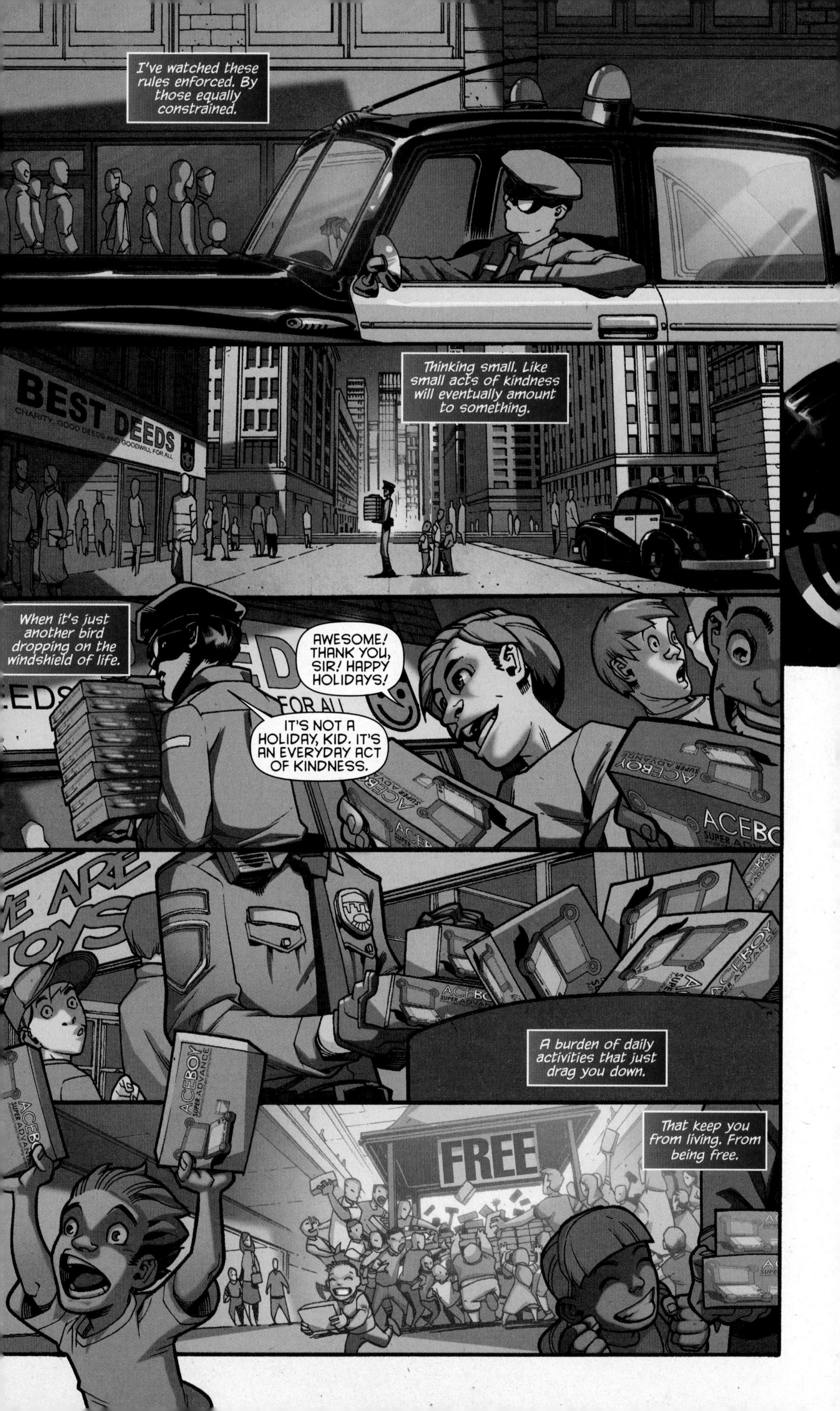
I've watched these rules enforced. By those equally constrained.
BEST DEEDS
CHARITY, GOOD DEEDS AND GOODWILL FOR ALL
Thinking small. Like small acts of kindness will eventually amount to something.
When it's just another bird dropping on the windshield of life.
AWESOME! THANK YOU, SIR! HAPPY HOLIDAYS!
IT'S NOT A HOLIDAY, KID. IT'S AN EVERYDAY ACT OF KINDNESS.
ACEBOY SUPER ADVANCE
A burden of daily activities that just drag you down.
ACEBOY SUPER ADVANCE
That keep you from living. From being free.
FREE

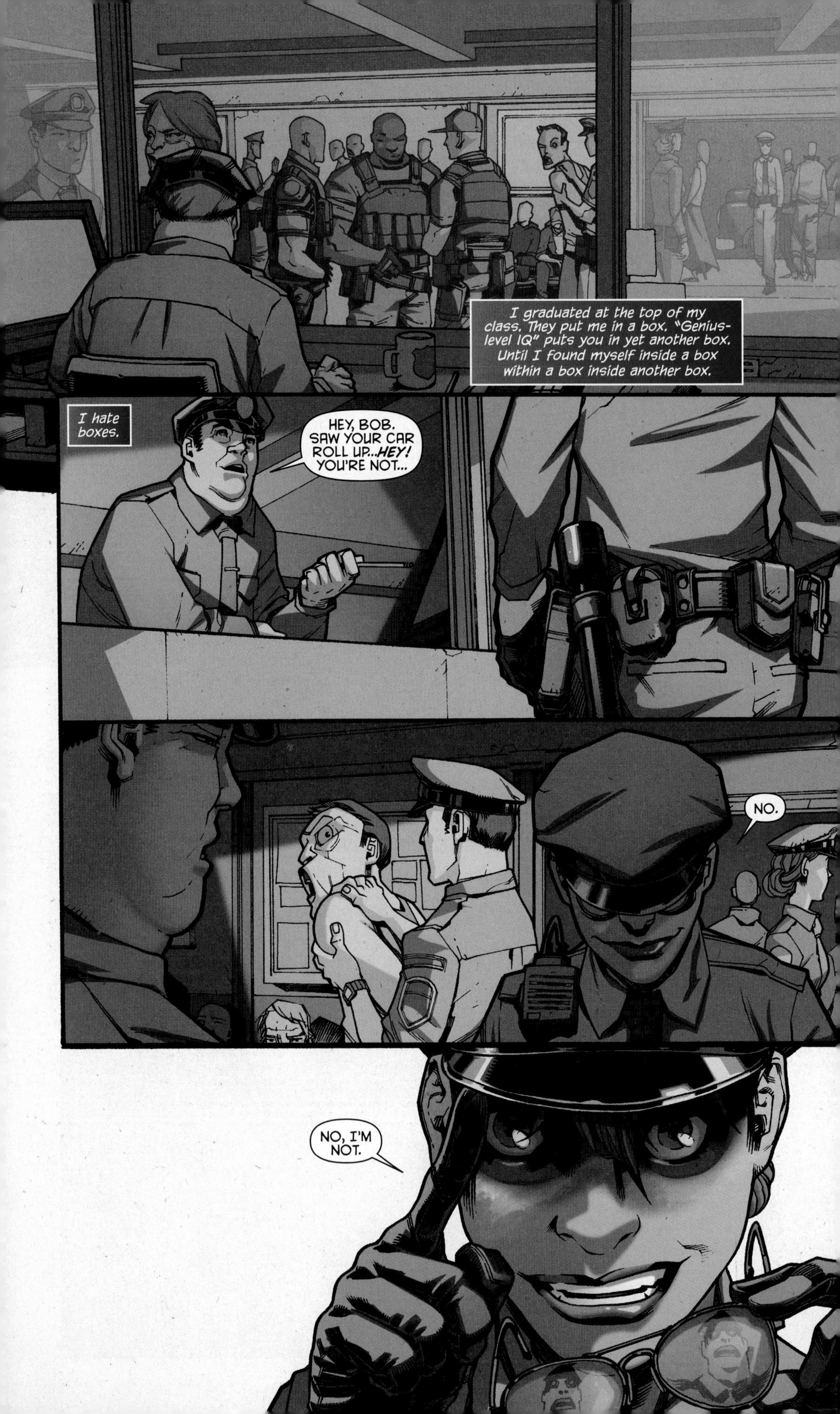
I graduated at the top of my class. They put me in a box. "Genius-level IQ" puts you in yet another box. Until I found myself inside a box within a box inside another box.
I hate boxes.
HEY, BOB. SAW YOUR CAR ROLL UP...HEY! YOU'RE NOT...
NO.
NO, I'M NOT.

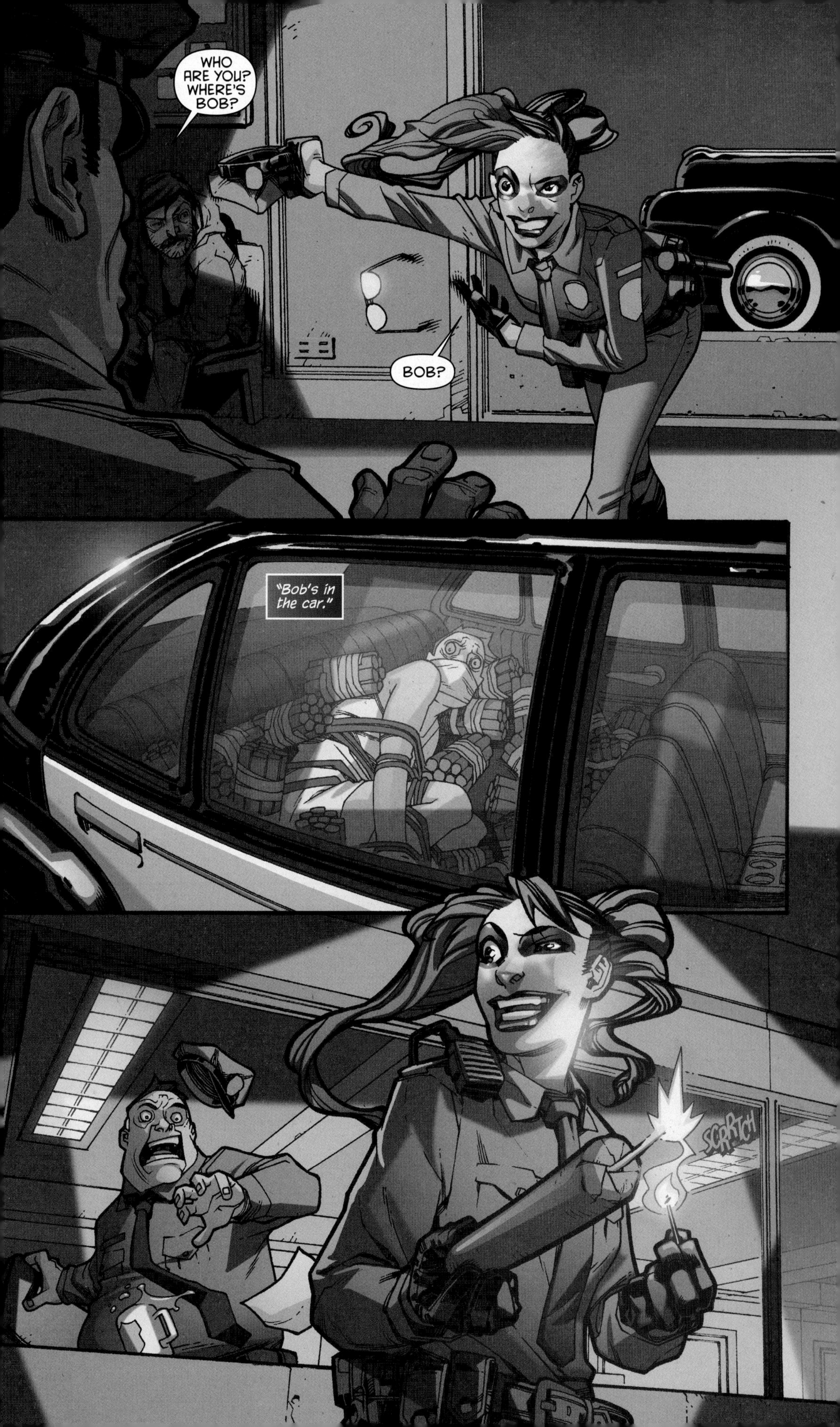
WHO ARE YOU? WHERE'S BOB?
BOB?
"Bob's in the car."
SCRRTCH

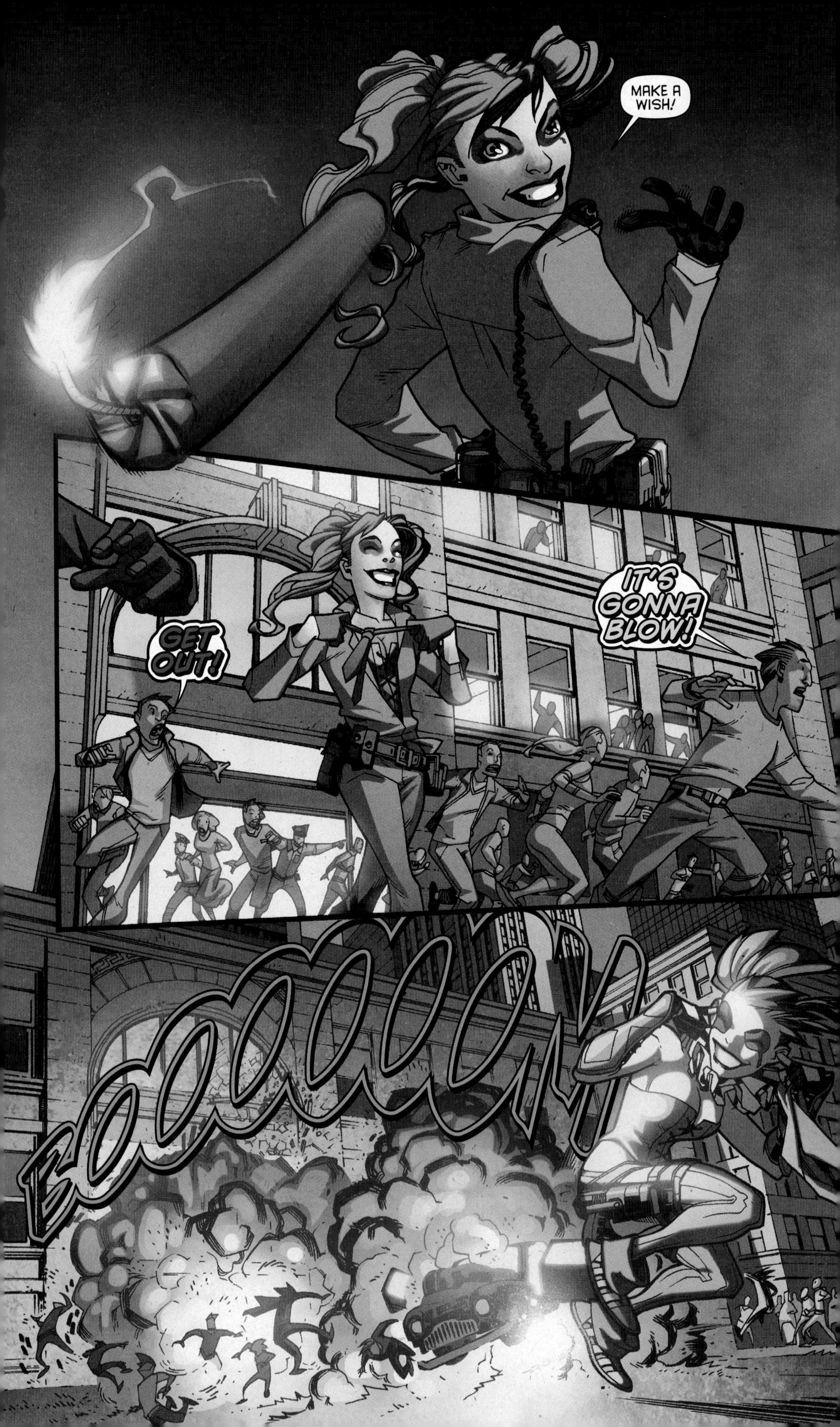
MAKE A WISH!
GET OUT!
IT'S GONNA BLOW!
BOOOOOOOM

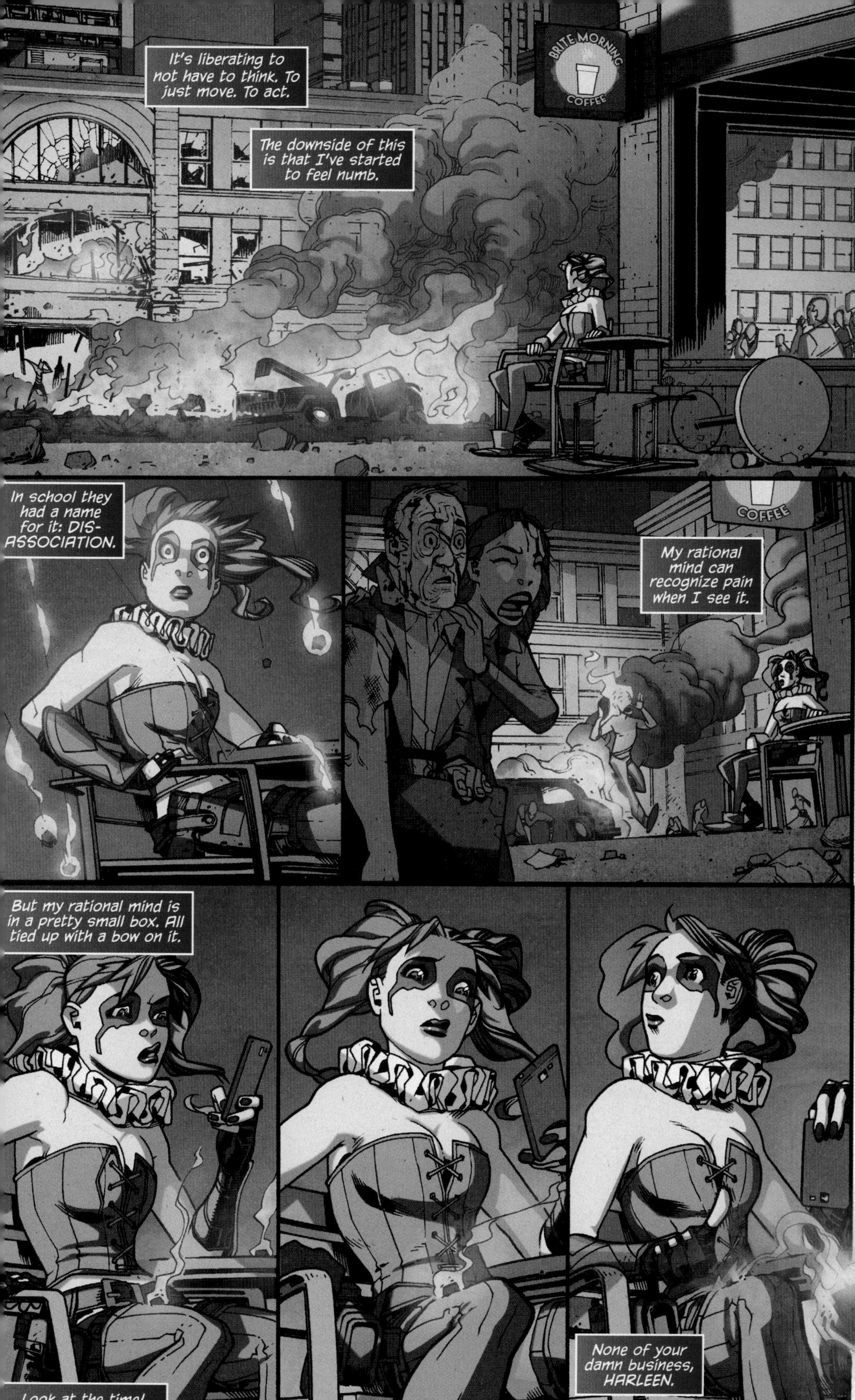

It's liberating to not have to think. To just move. To act.
The downside of this is that I've started to feel numb.
BRITE MORNING COFFEE
In school they had a name for it: DIS-ASSOCIATION.
COFFEE
My rational mind can recognize pain when I see it.
But my rational mind is in a pretty small box. All tied up with a bow on it.
Look at the time! The Secret Society's super-secret meeting is about to happen! I better get going.
And the rest of me...?
None of your damn business, HARLEEN.
Stop trying to psychoanalyze me and get back in your box.

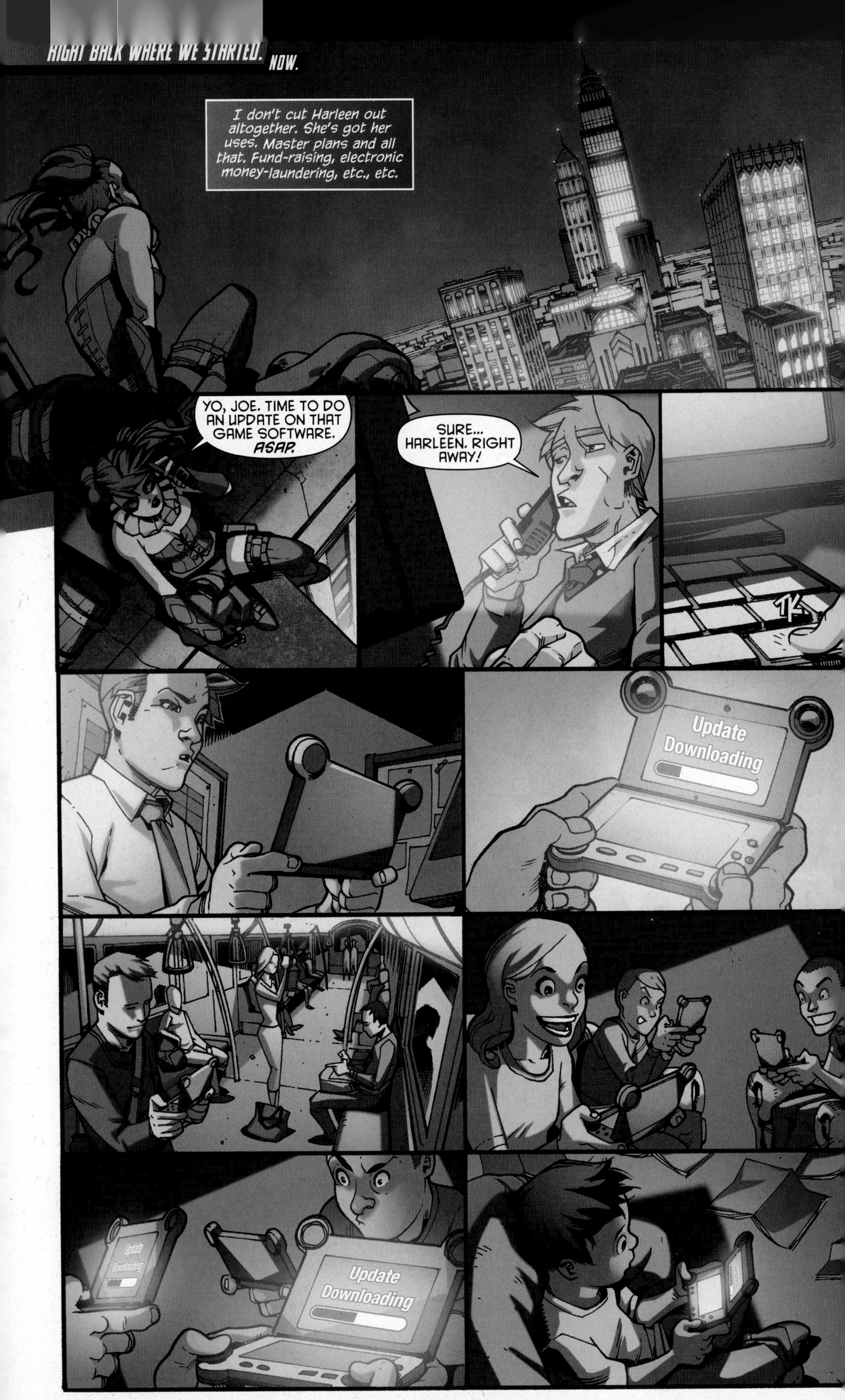
RIGHT BACK WHERE WE STARTED.
NOW.
I don't cut Harleen out altogether. She's got her uses. Master plans and all that. Fund-raising, electronic money-laundering, etc., etc.
YO, JOE. TIME TO DO AN UPDATE ON THAT GAME SOFTWARE. ASAP.
SURE... HARLEEN. RIGHT AWAY!
TK
Update Downloading
Update Downloading
Update Downloading

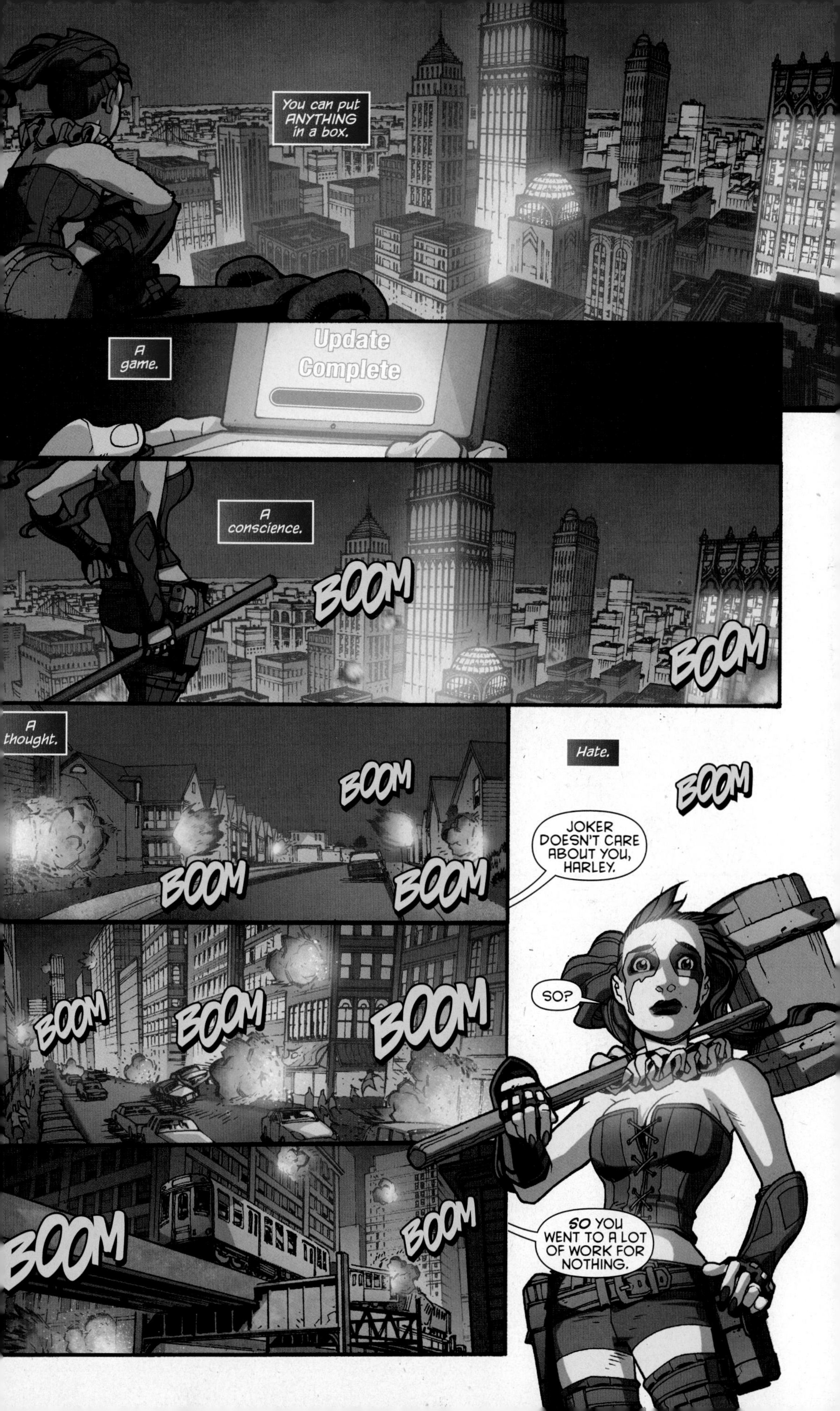
You can put ANYTHING in a box.
A game.
Update Complete
A conscience.
BOOM
BOOM
A thought.
BOOM
BOOM
BOOM
Hate.
BOOM
JOKER DOESN'T CARE ABOUT YOU, HARLEY.
SO?
BOOM
BOOM
BOOM
BOOM
BOOM
SO YOU WENT TO A LOT OF WORK FOR NOTHING.

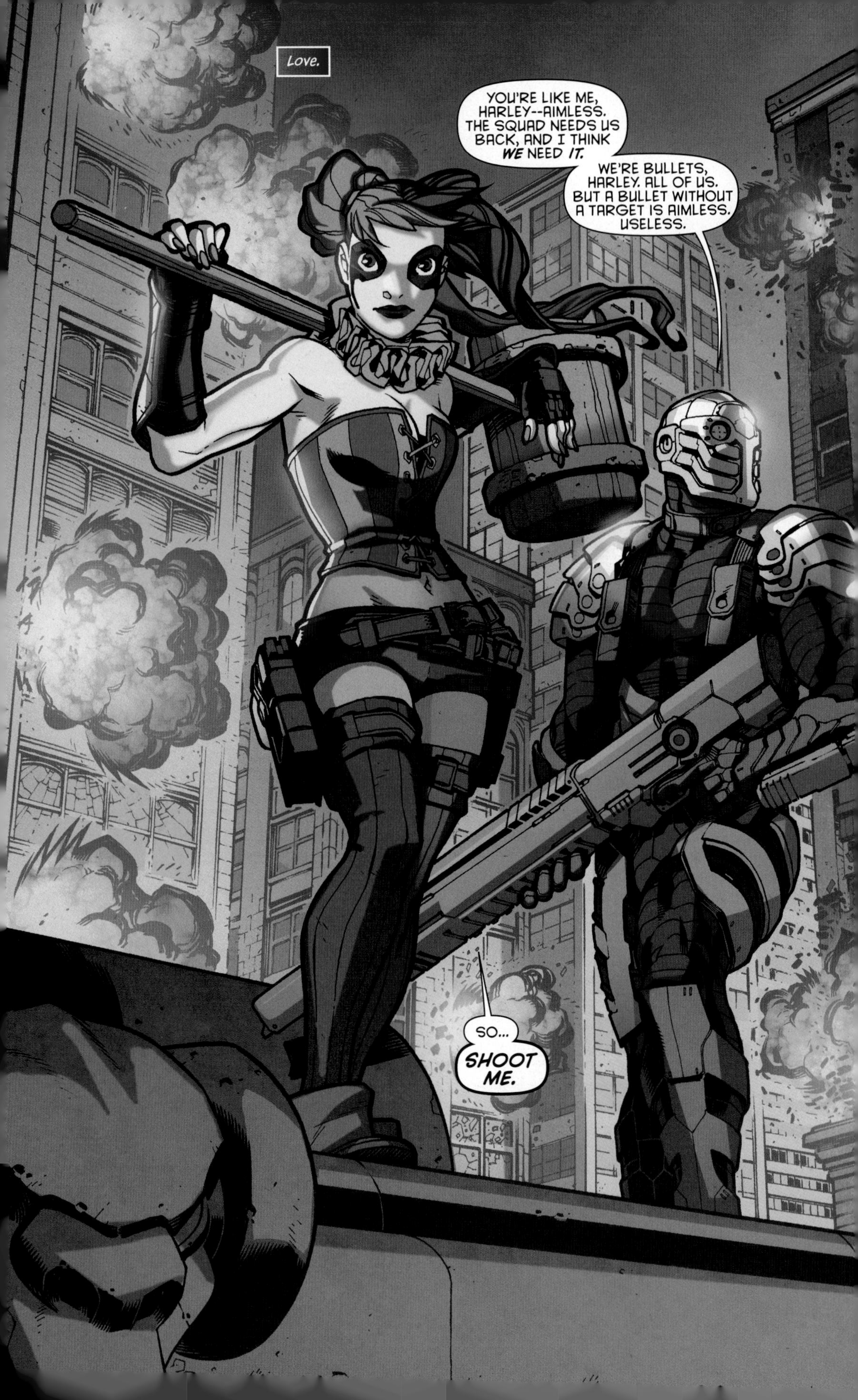
Love.
YOU'RE LIKE ME, HARLEY--AIMLESS. THE SQUAD NEEDS US BACK, AND I THINK WE NEED IT.
WE'RE BULLETS, HARLEY. ALL OF US. BUT A BULLET WITHOUT A TARGET IS AIMLESS. USELESS.
SO...
SHOOT ME.

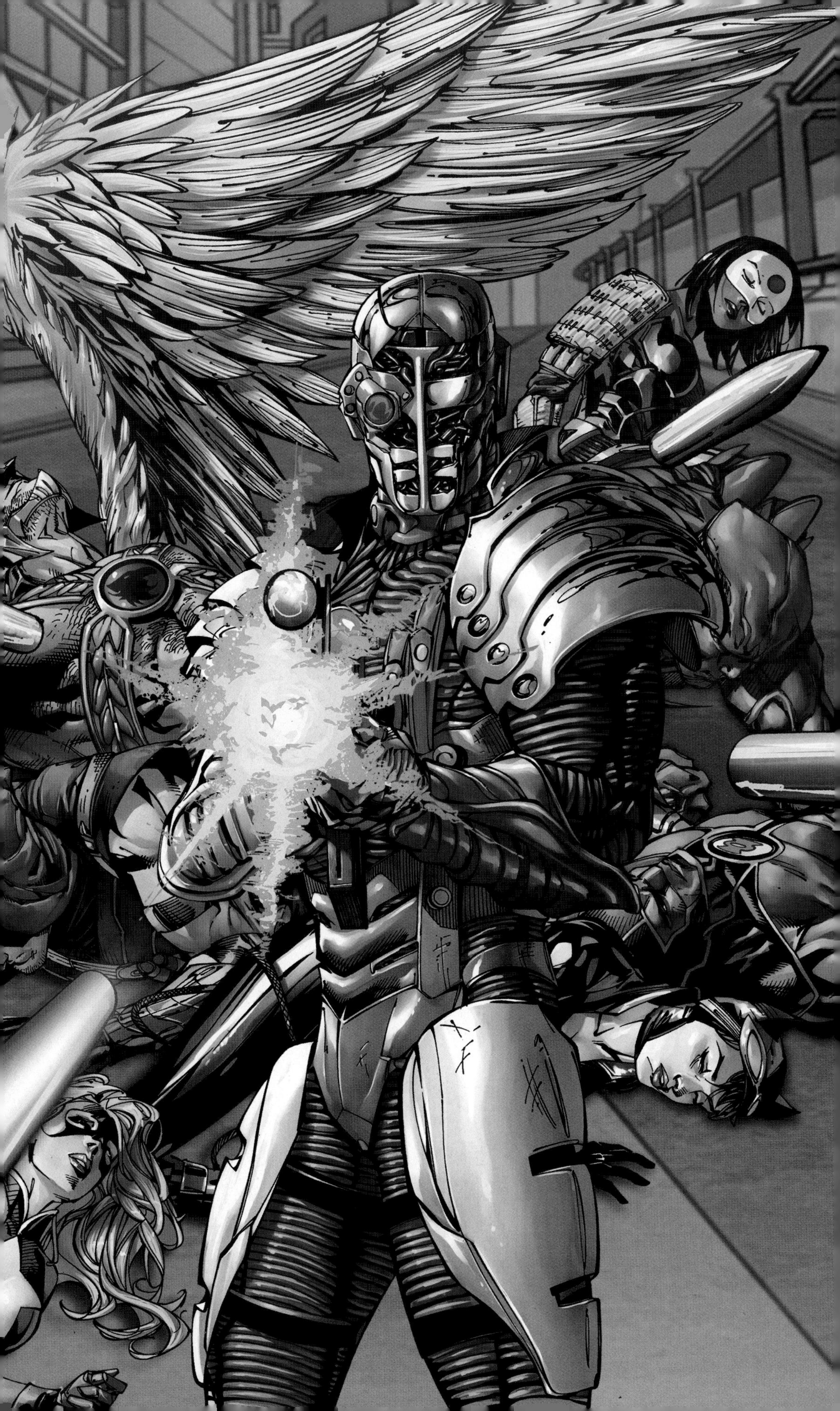

POINT AND SHOOT

MATT KINDT writer Present Sequence **SAMI BASRI & KEITH CHAMPAGNE** artists Past Sequence **CARMEN CARNERO & BIT** artists

cover by **TONY DANIEL, MATT BANNING & TOMEU MOREY**

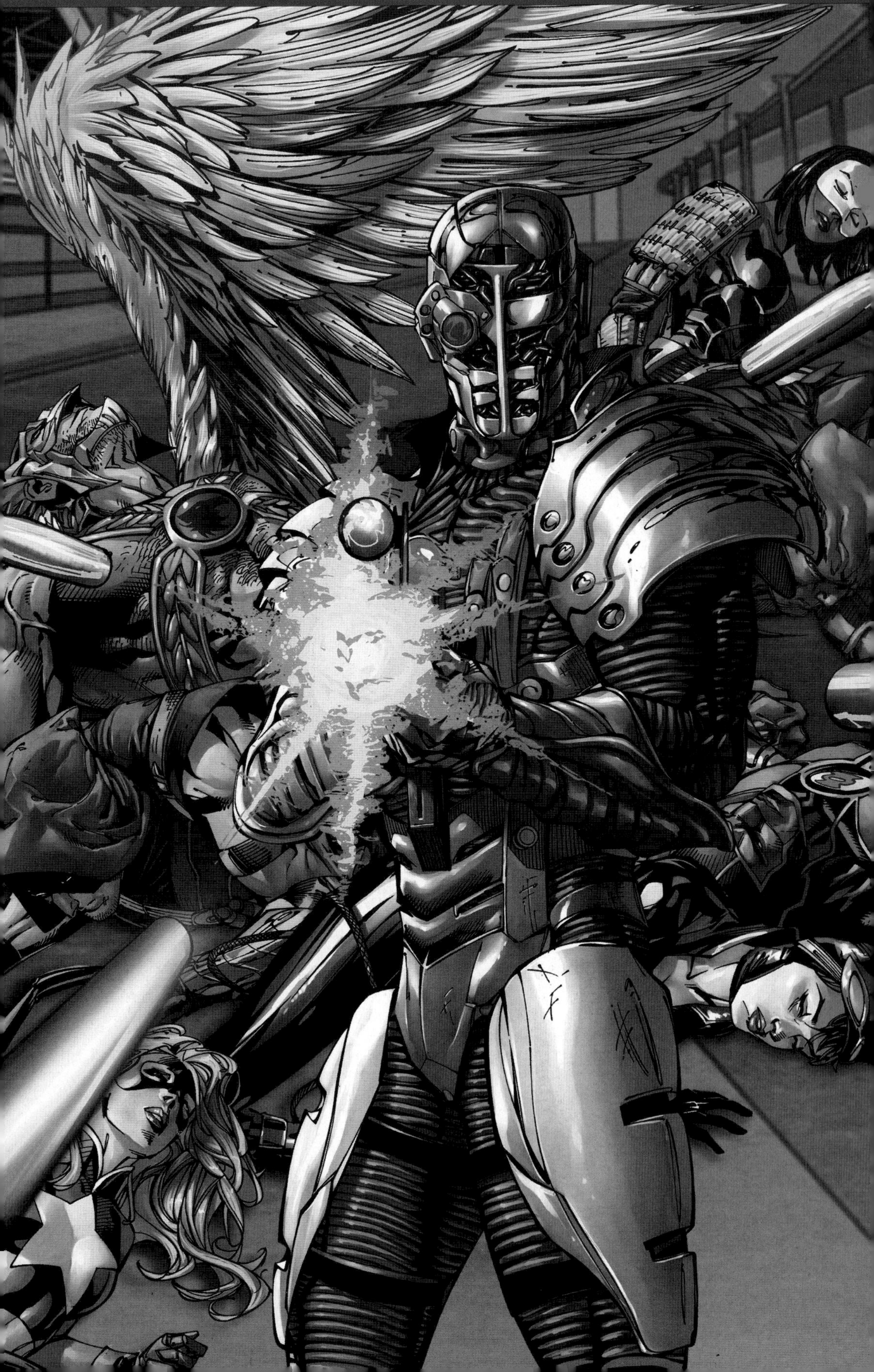

I USED TO WONDER, "WHY ME?"

BALANCE: $ 0.00

BALANCE: $ 2,000,000.00

WHY DID I LIVE? IT USED TO HAUNT ME. I USED TO THINK IT ALL HAPPENED FOR A REASON. THAT I WAS SPARED FOR A PURPOSE. BUT IN THE END...

I JUST GOT TIRED OF LOOKING. FOR AN ANSWER. FOR A REASON...THAT WASN'T THERE.

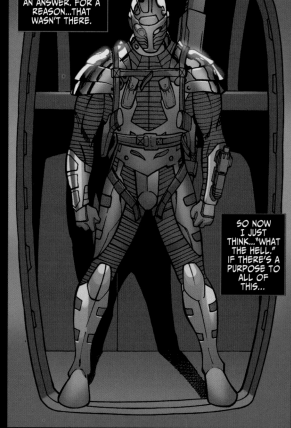

SO NOW I JUST THINK..."WHAT THE HELL." IF THERE'S A PURPOSE TO ALL OF THIS...

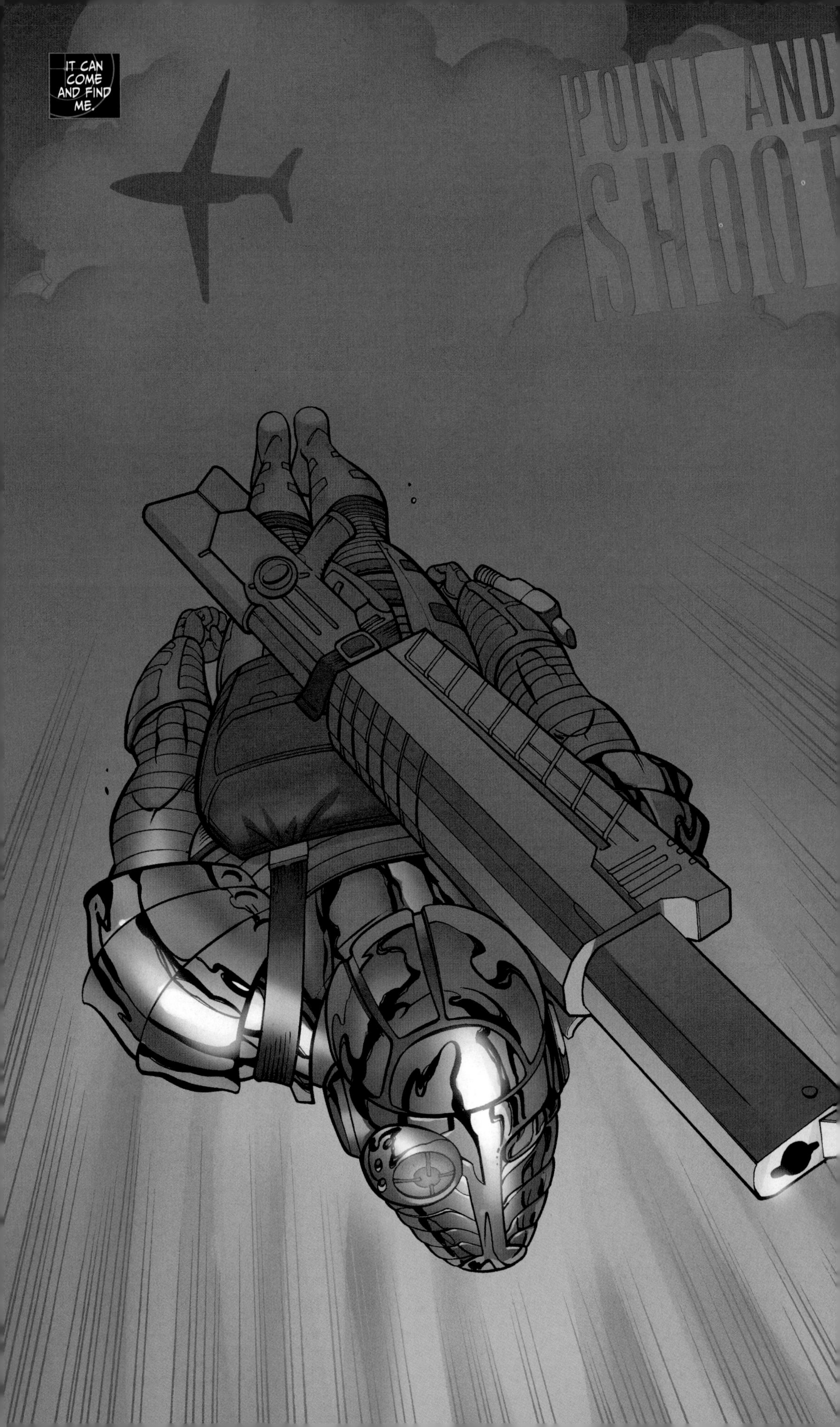
IT CAN COME AND FIND ME.
POINT AND SHOOT

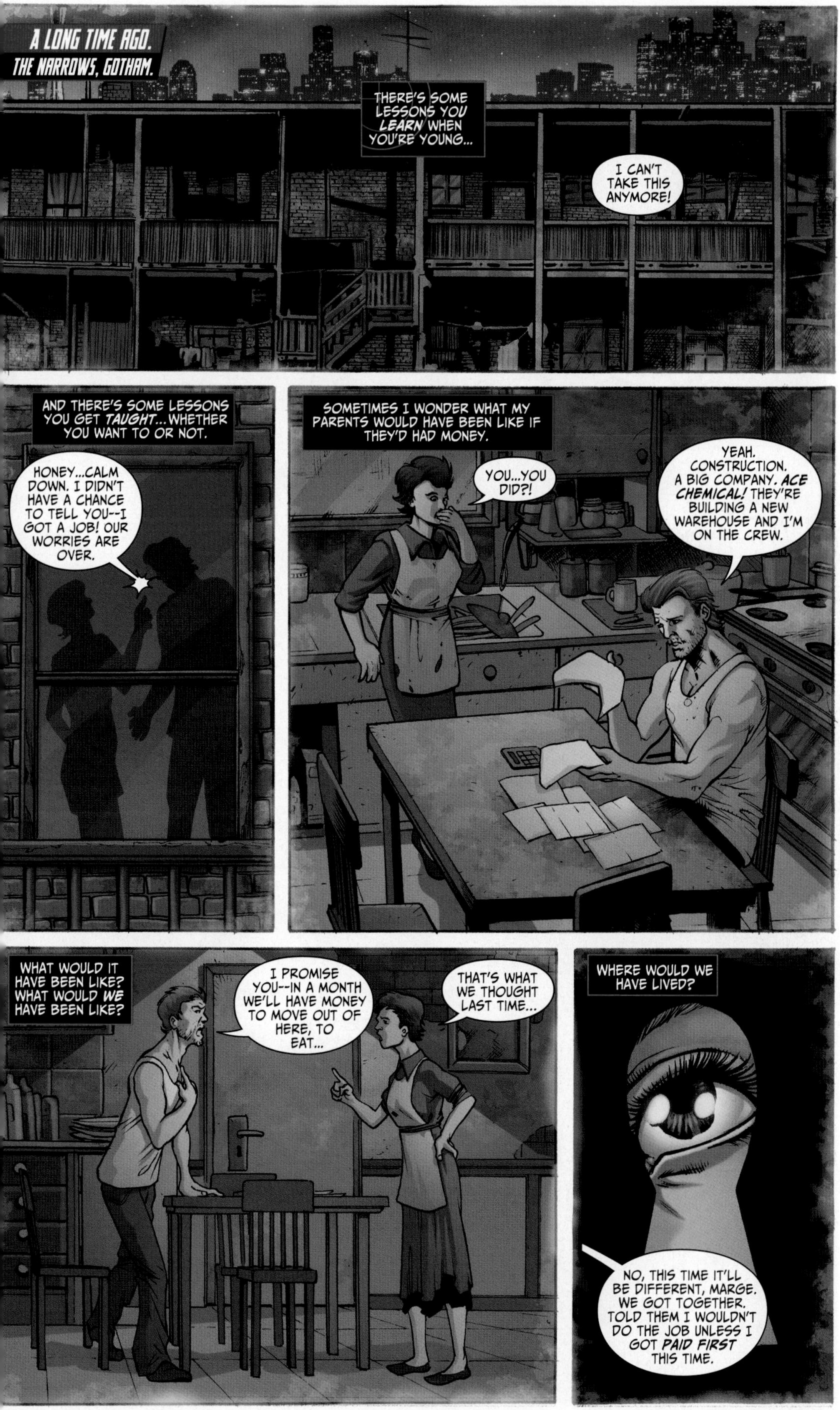
A LONG TIME AGO.
THE NARROWS, GOTHAM.
THERE'S SOME LESSONS YOU LEARN WHEN YOU'RE YOUNG...
I CAN'T TAKE THIS ANYMORE!
AND THERE'S SOME LESSONS YOU GET TAUGHT... WHETHER YOU WANT TO OR NOT.
HONEY...CALM DOWN. I DIDN'T HAVE A CHANCE TO TELL YOU--I GOT A JOB! OUR WORRIES ARE OVER.
SOMETIMES I WONDER WHAT MY PARENTS WOULD HAVE BEEN LIKE IF THEY'D HAD MONEY.
YOU...YOU DID?!
YEAH. CONSTRUCTION. A BIG COMPANY. ACE CHEMICAL! THEY'RE BUILDING A NEW WAREHOUSE AND I'M ON THE CREW.
WHAT WOULD IT HAVE BEEN LIKE? WHAT WOULD WE HAVE BEEN LIKE?
I PROMISE YOU--IN A MONTH WE'LL HAVE MONEY TO MOVE OUT OF HERE, TO EAT...
THAT'S WHAT WE THOUGHT LAST TIME...
WHERE WOULD WE HAVE LIVED?
NO, THIS TIME IT'LL BE DIFFERENT, MARGE. WE GOT TOGETHER. TOLD THEM I WOULDN'T DO THE JOB UNLESS I GOT PAID FIRST THIS TIME.

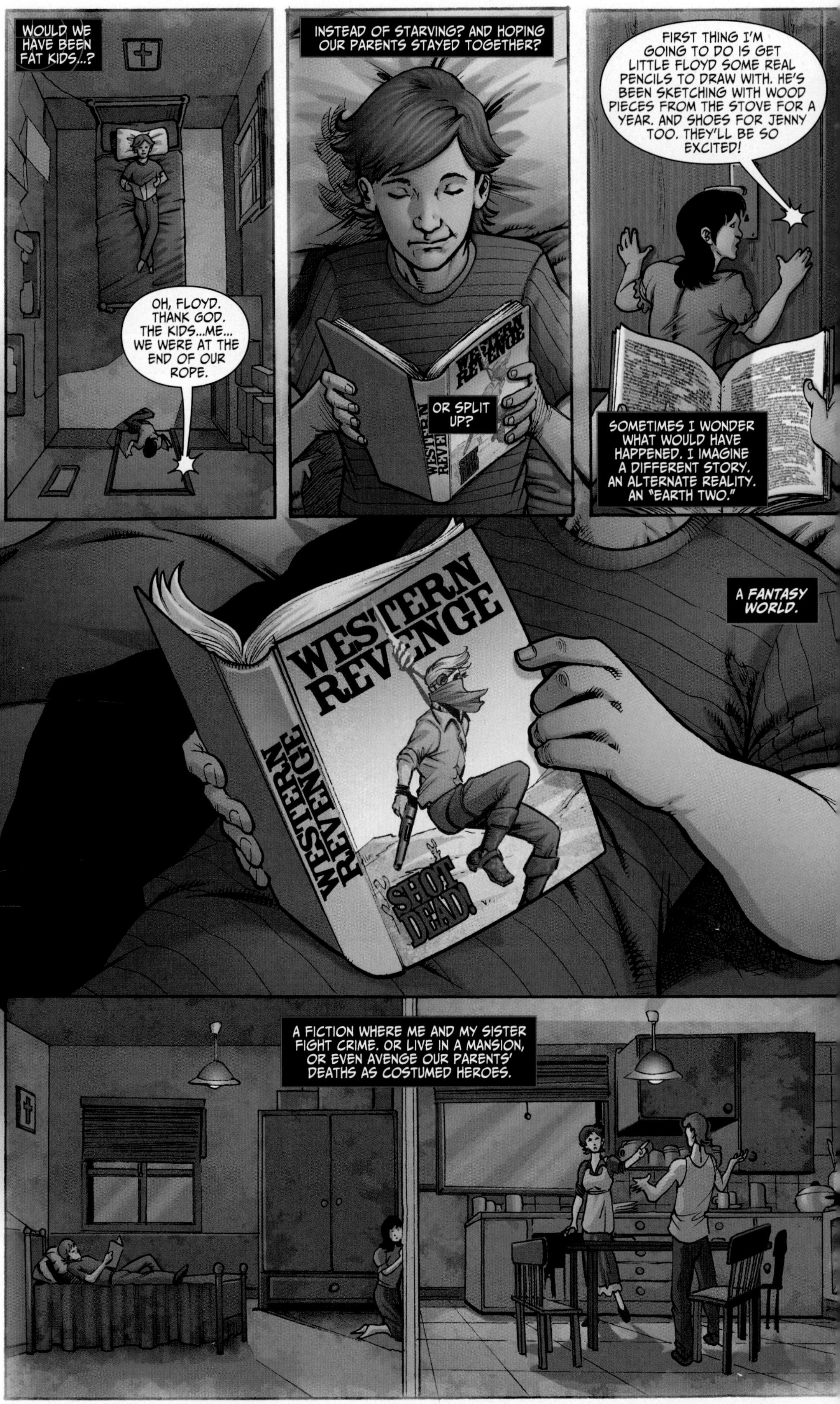
WOULD WE HAVE BEEN FAT KIDS...?
OH, FLOYD. THANK GOD. THE KIDS...ME... WE WERE AT THE END OF OUR ROPE.
INSTEAD OF STARVING? AND HOPING OUR PARENTS STAYED TOGETHER?
OR SPLIT UP?
WESTERN REVENGE
FIRST THING I'M GOING TO DO IS GET LITTLE FLOYD SOME REAL PENCILS TO DRAW WITH. HE'S BEEN SKETCHING WITH WOOD PIECES FROM THE STOVE FOR A YEAR. AND SHOES FOR JENNY TOO. THEY'LL BE SO EXCITED!
SOMETIMES I WONDER WHAT WOULD HAVE HAPPENED. I IMAGINE A DIFFERENT STORY. AN ALTERNATE REALITY. AN "EARTH TWO."
A *FANTASY WORLD.*
WESTERN REVENGE
SHOT DEAD!
A FICTION WHERE ME AND MY SISTER FIGHT CRIME. OR LIVE IN A MANSION, OR EVEN AVENGE OUR PARENTS' DEATHS AS COSTUMED HEROES.

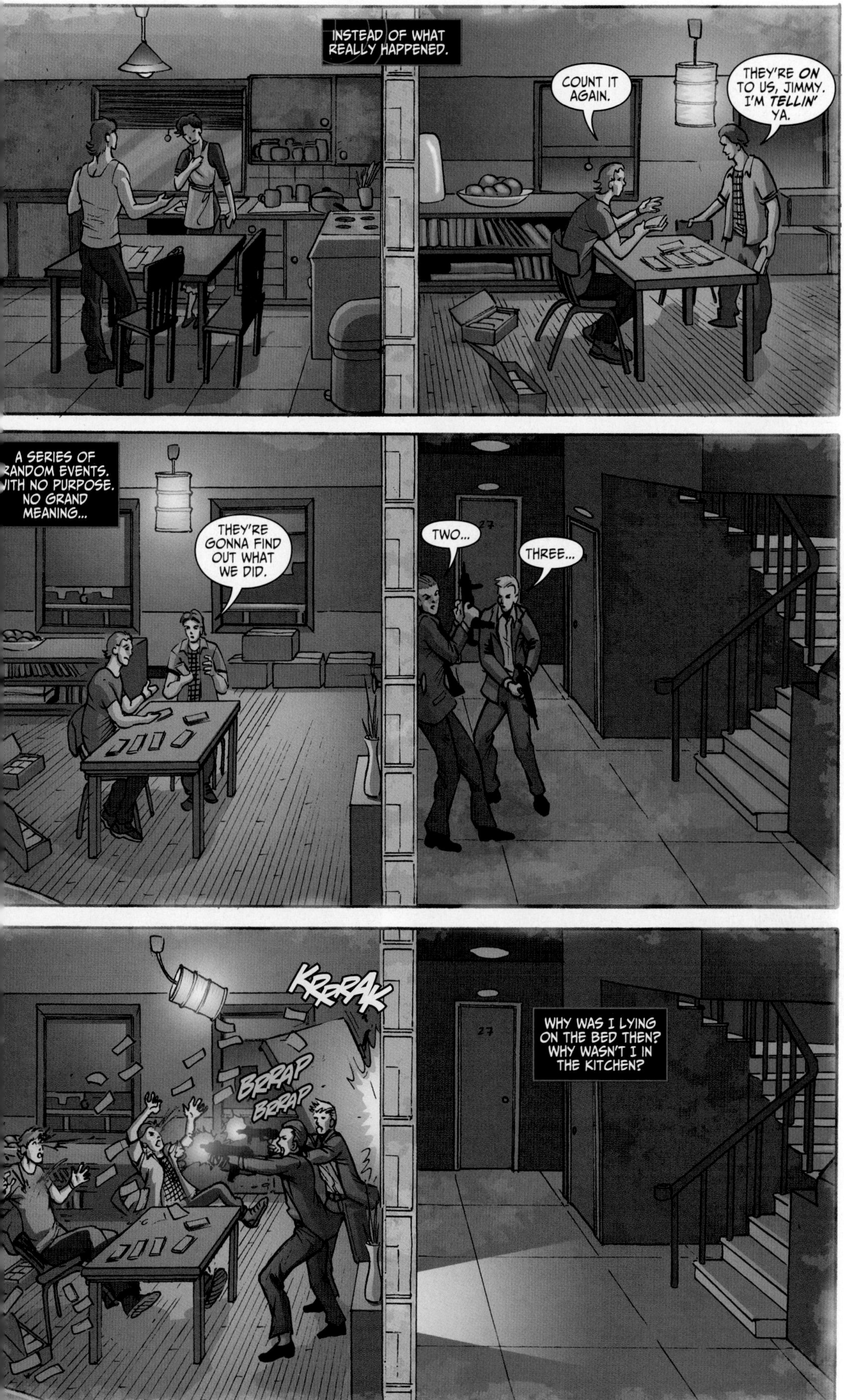
INSTEAD OF WHAT REALLY HAPPENED.
COUNT IT AGAIN.
THEY'RE ON TO US, JIMMY. I'M TELLIN' YA.
A SERIES OF RANDOM EVENTS. WITH NO PURPOSE. NO GRAND MEANING...
THEY'RE GONNA FIND OUT WHAT WE DID.
TWO...
THREE...
KRRRAK
BRRAP
BRRAP
WHY WAS I LYING ON THE BED THEN? WHY WASN'T I IN THE KITCHEN?

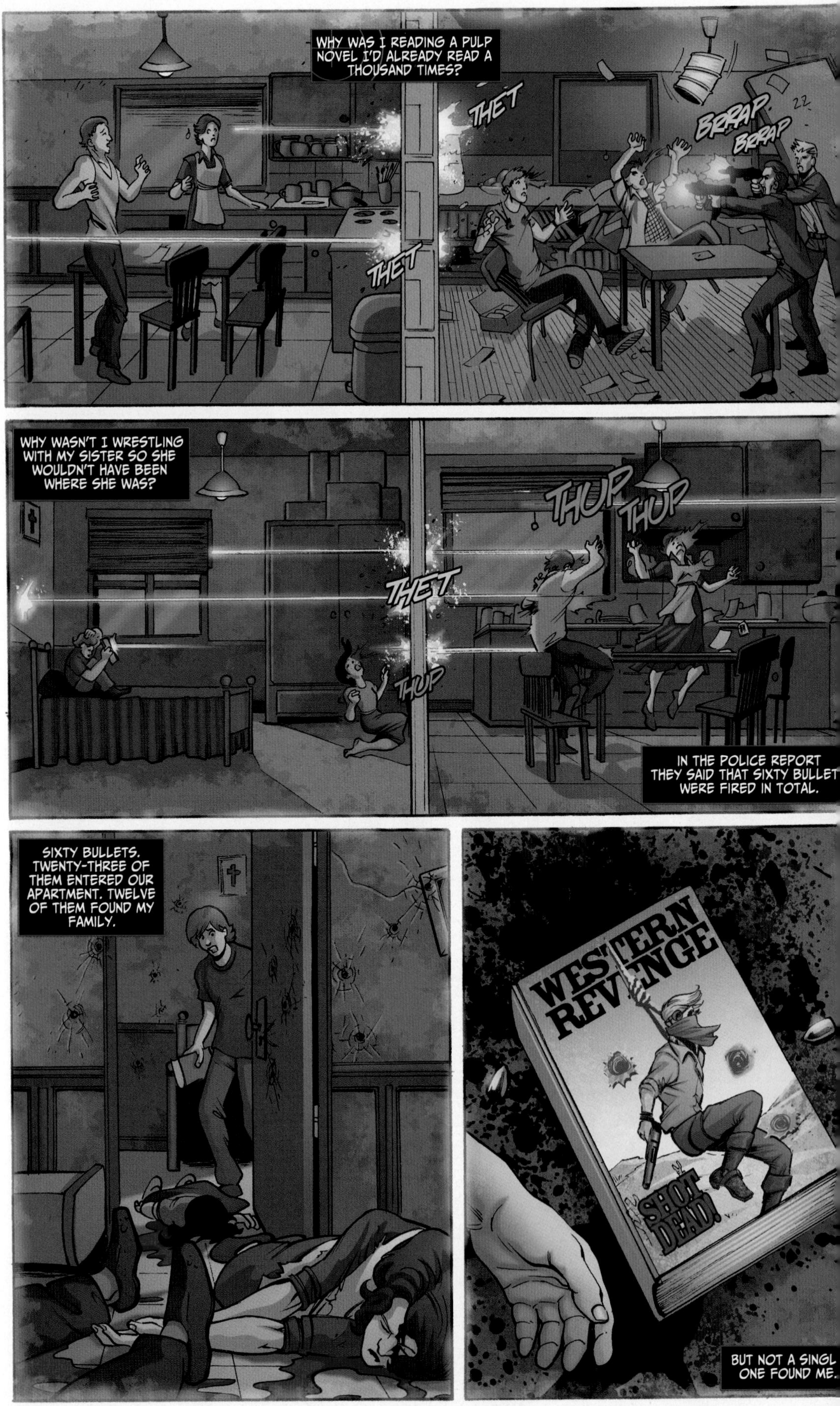
WHY WAS I READING A PULP NOVEL I'D ALREADY READ A THOUSAND TIMES?
THET
BRRAP
BRRAP
THET
WHY WASN'T I WRESTLING WITH MY SISTER SO SHE WOULDN'T HAVE BEEN WHERE SHE WAS?
THUP
THUP
THET
THUP
IN THE POLICE REPORT THEY SAID THAT SIXTY BULLET WERE FIRED IN TOTAL.
SIXTY BULLETS. TWENTY-THREE OF THEM ENTERED OUR APARTMENT. TWELVE OF THEM FOUND MY FAMILY.
WESTERN REVENGE
SHOT DEAD!
BUT NOT A SINGL ONE FOUND ME.

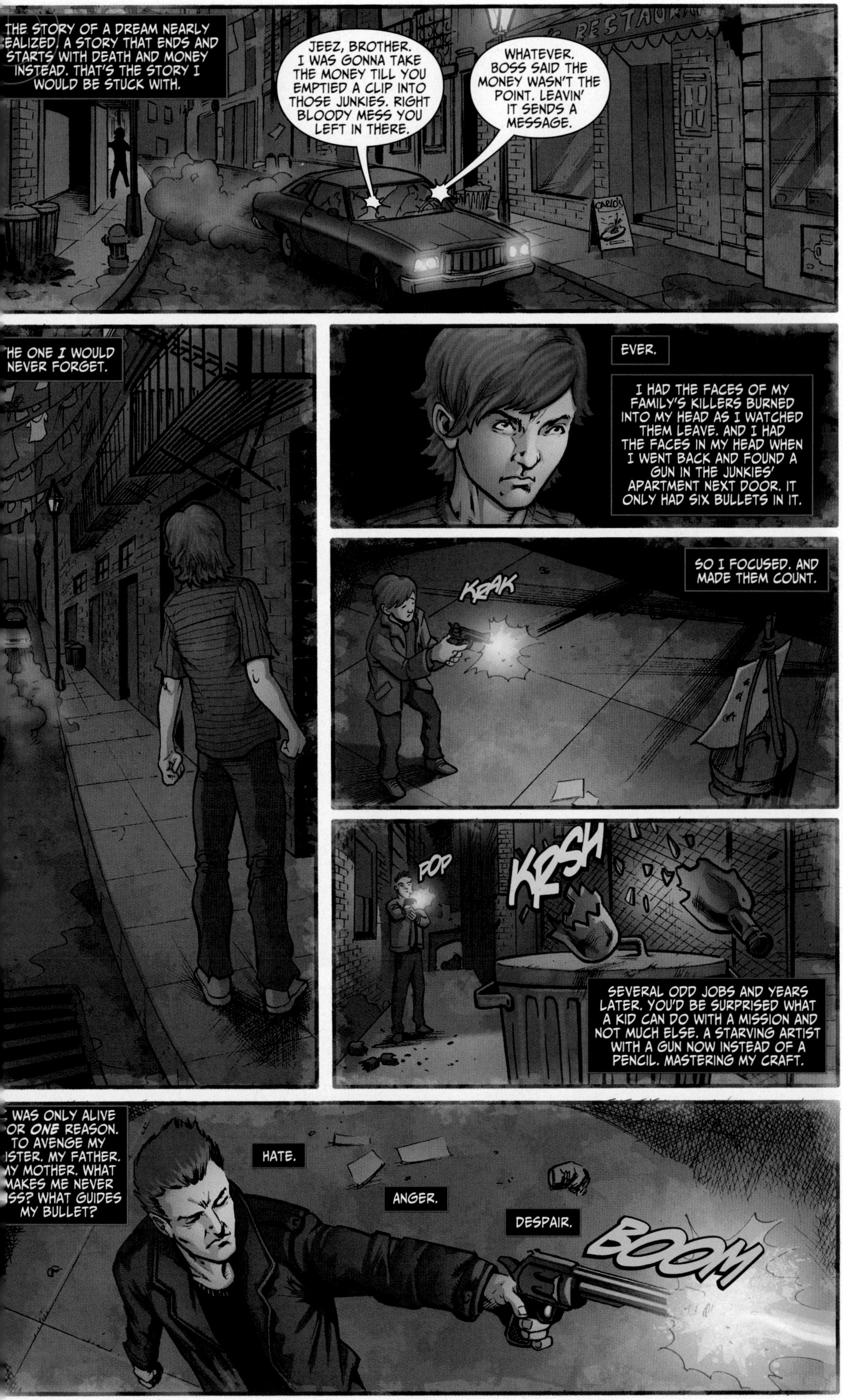
THE STORY OF A DREAM NEARLY EALIZED, A STORY THAT ENDS AND STARTS WITH DEATH AND MONEY INSTEAD. THAT'S THE STORY I WOULD BE STUCK WITH.
JEEZ, BROTHER. I WAS GONNA TAKE THE MONEY TILL YOU EMPTIED A CLIP INTO THOSE JUNKIES. RIGHT BLOODY MESS YOU LEFT IN THERE.
WHATEVER. BOSS SAID THE MONEY WASN'T THE POINT. LEAVIN' IT SENDS A MESSAGE.
CARLO'S
HE ONE *I* WOULD NEVER FORGET.
EVER.
I HAD THE FACES OF MY FAMILY'S KILLERS BURNED INTO MY HEAD AS I WATCHED THEM LEAVE. AND I HAD THE FACES IN MY HEAD WHEN I WENT BACK AND FOUND A GUN IN THE JUNKIES' APARTMENT NEXT DOOR. IT ONLY HAD SIX BULLETS IN IT.
SO I FOCUSED. AND MADE THEM COUNT.
KRAK
POP
KRSH
SEVERAL ODD JOBS AND YEARS LATER. YOU'D BE SURPRISED WHAT A KID CAN DO WITH A MISSION AND NOT MUCH ELSE. A STARVING ARTIST WITH A GUN NOW INSTEAD OF A PENCIL. MASTERING MY CRAFT.
WAS ONLY ALIVE OR *ONE* REASON. TO AVENGE MY ISTER. MY FATHER. MY MOTHER. WHAT MAKES ME NEVER SS? WHAT GUIDES MY BULLET?
HATE.
ANGER.
DESPAIR.
BOOM

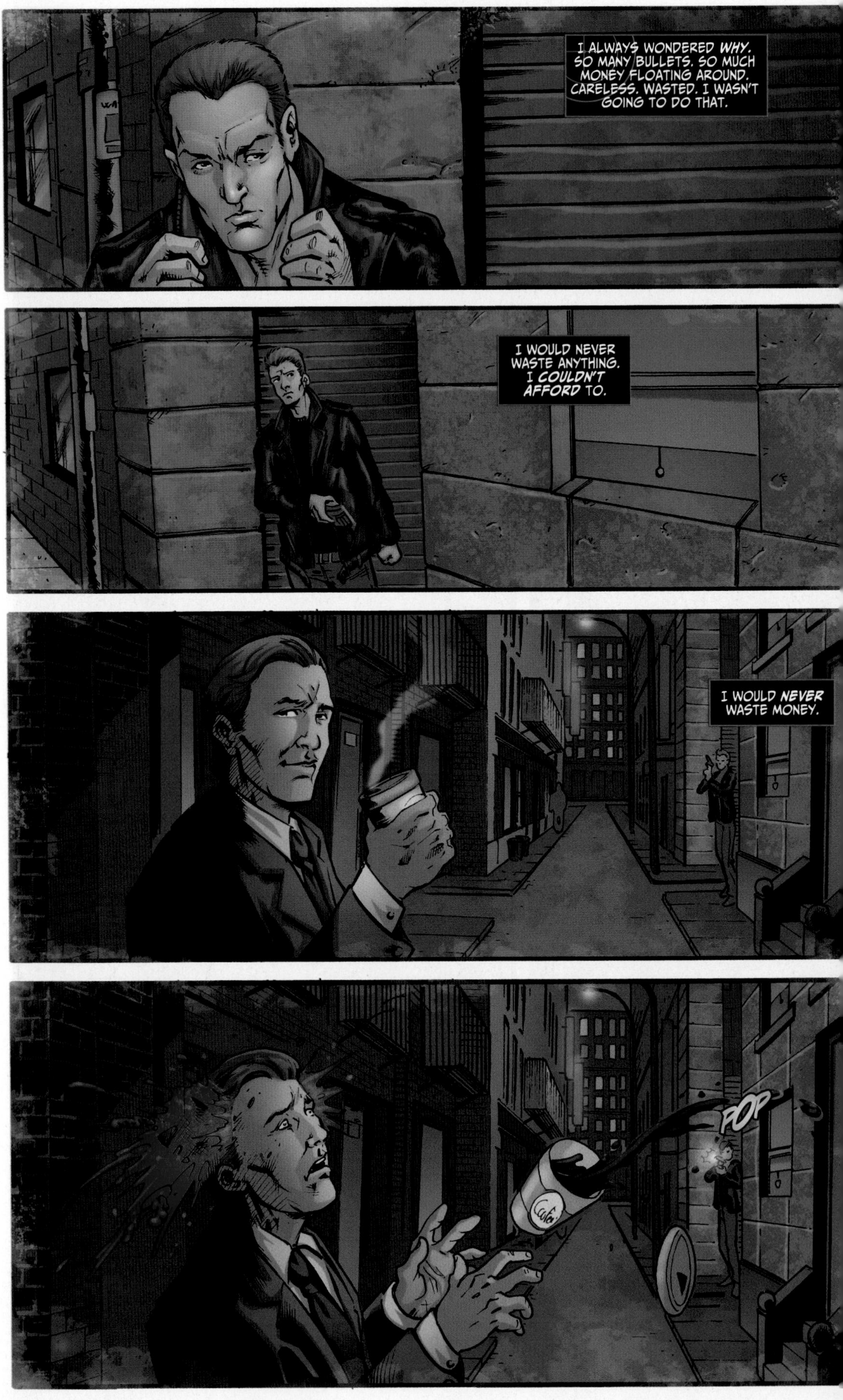
I ALWAYS WONDERED WHY. SO MANY BULLETS. SO MUCH MONEY FLOATING AROUND. CARELESS. WASTED. I WASN'T GOING TO DO THAT.
I WOULD NEVER WASTE ANYTHING. I COULDN'T AFFORD TO.
I WOULD NEVER WASTE MONEY.
POP

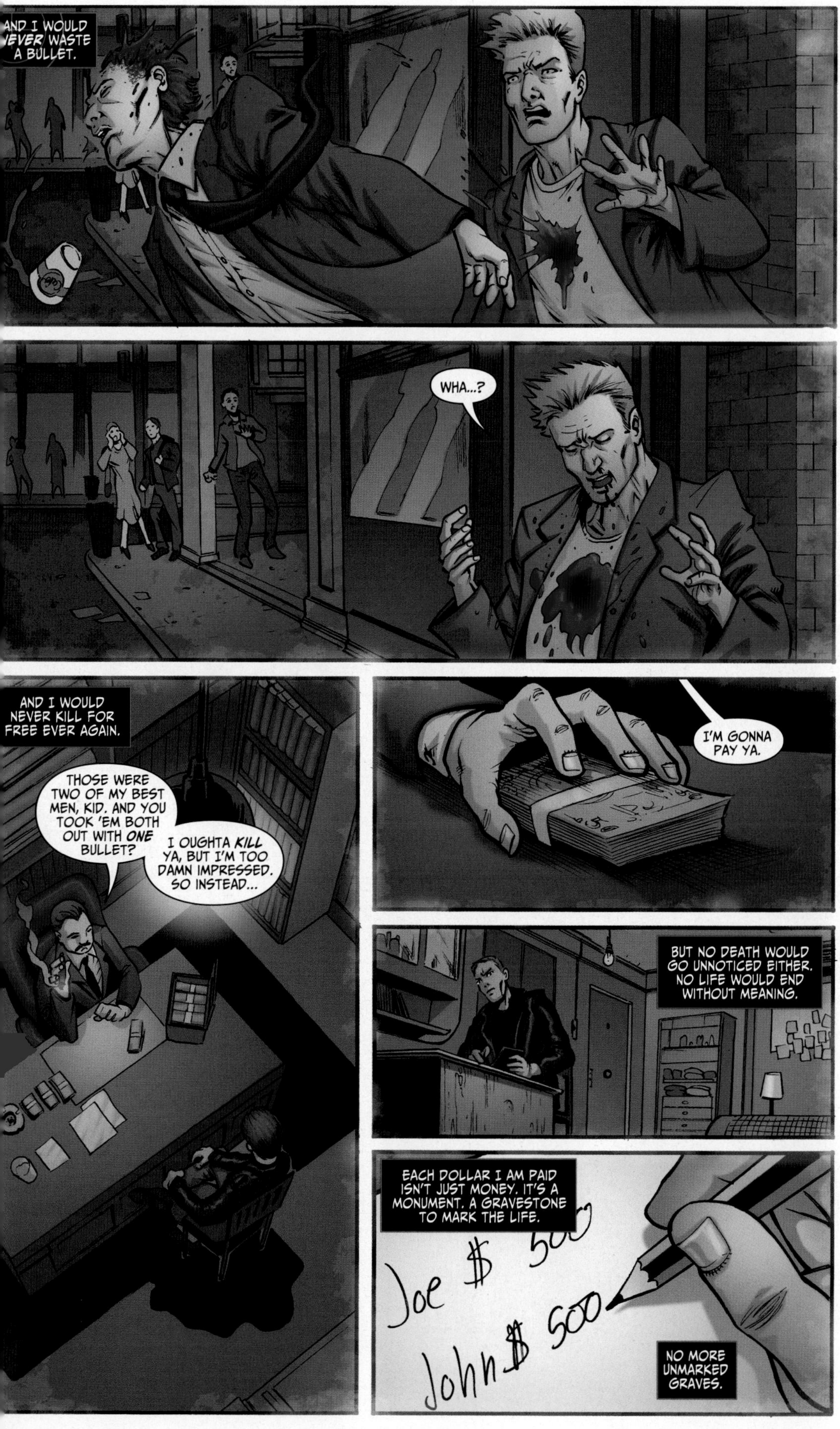
AND I WOULD NEVER WASTE A BULLET.
WHA...?
AND I WOULD NEVER KILL FOR FREE EVER AGAIN.
THOSE WERE TWO OF MY BEST MEN, KID. AND YOU TOOK 'EM BOTH OUT WITH ONE BULLET?
I OUGHTA KILL YA, BUT I'M TOO DAMN IMPRESSED. SO INSTEAD...
I'M GONNA PAY YA.
BUT NO DEATH WOULD GO UNNOTICED EITHER. NO LIFE WOULD END WITHOUT MEANING.
EACH DOLLAR I AM PAID ISN'T JUST MONEY. IT'S A MONUMENT. A GRAVESTONE TO MARK THE LIFE.
Joe $ 500
John $ 500
NO MORE UNMARKED GRAVES.

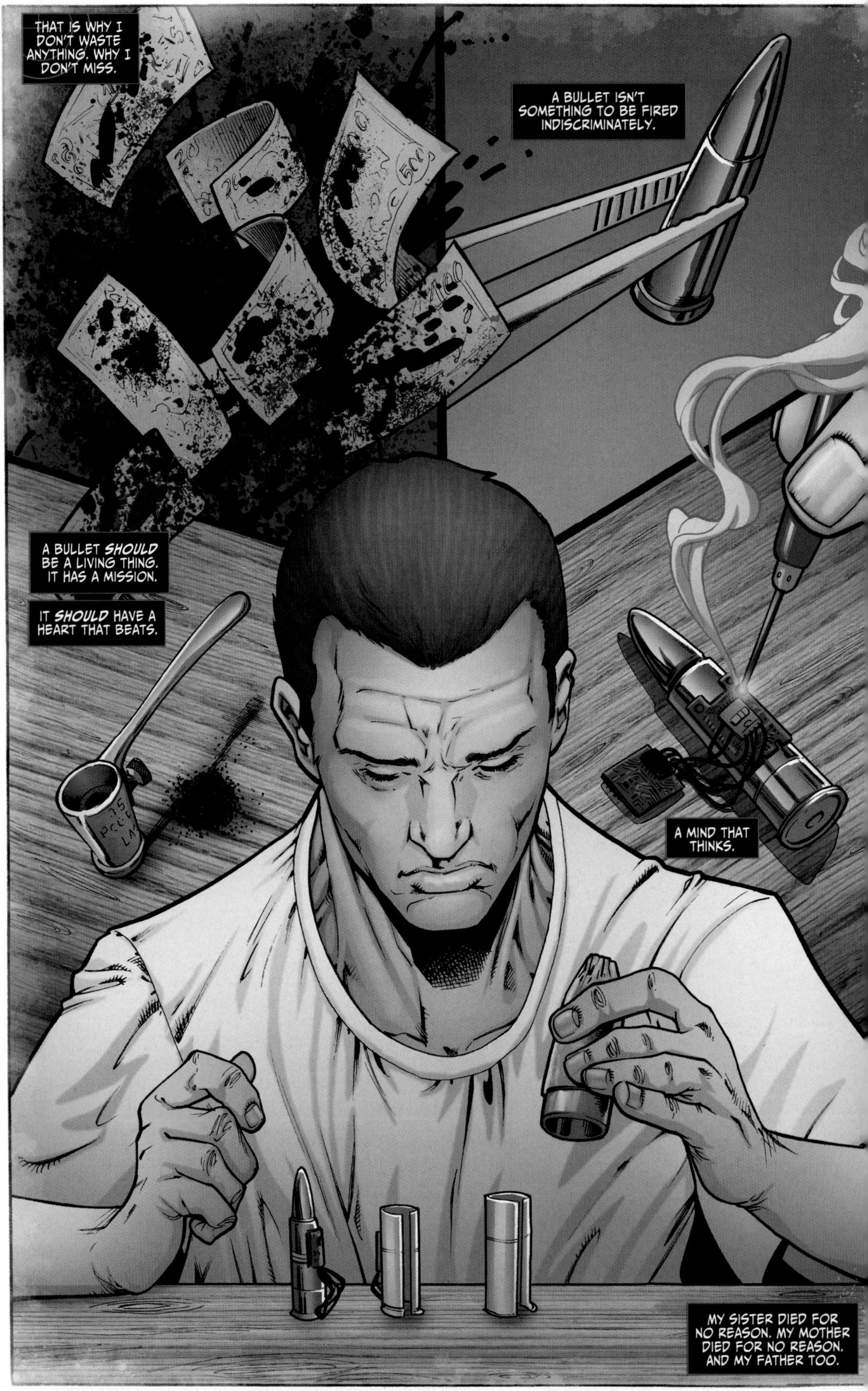
THAT IS WHY I DON'T WASTE ANYTHING. WHY I DON'T MISS.
A BULLET ISN'T SOMETHING TO BE FIRED INDISCRIMINATELY.
A BULLET SHOULD BE A LIVING THING. IT HAS A MISSION.
IT SHOULD HAVE A HEART THAT BEATS.
A MIND THAT THINKS.
MY SISTER DIED FOR NO REASON. MY MOTHER DIED FOR NO REASON. AND MY FATHER TOO.

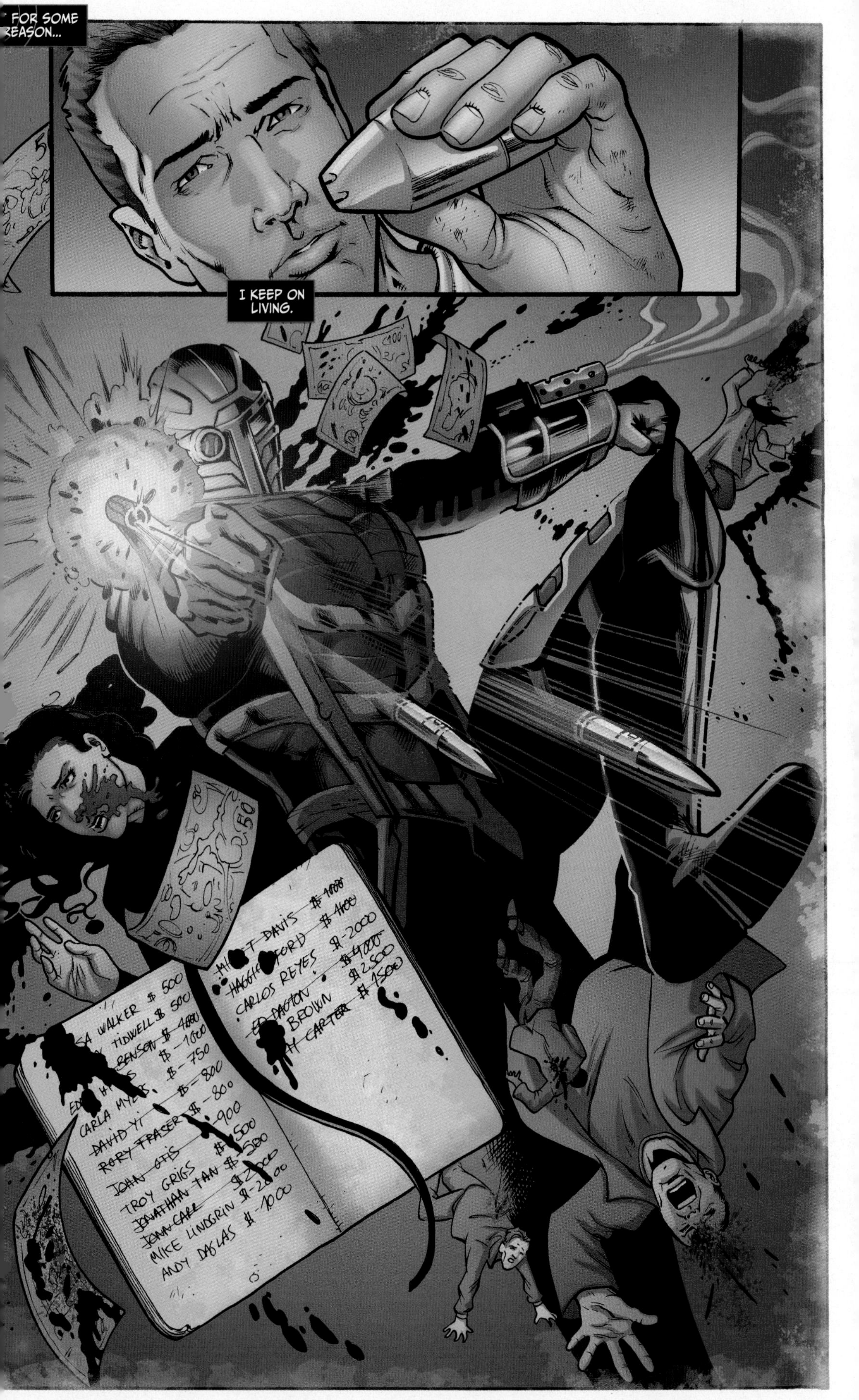
FOR SOME REASON...
I KEEP ON LIVING.
CARLOS REYES $-2000
DAVID YI
RORY FRASER
JOHN OTIS
TROY GRIGS
MIKE LINDGRIN $-2000
ANDY DAGLAS $-1000

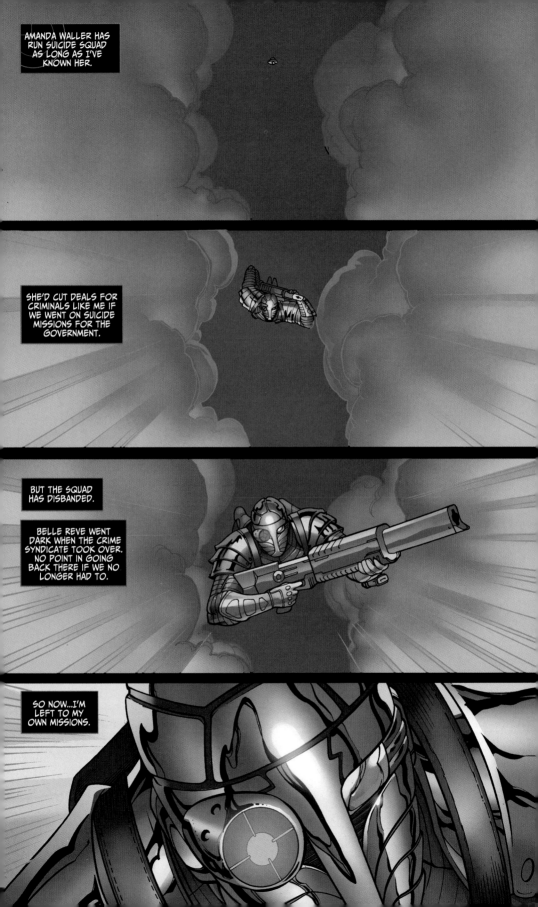

AMANDA WALLER HAS RUN SUICIDE SQUAD AS LONG AS I'VE KNOWN HER.

SHE'D CUT DEALS FOR CRIMINALS LIKE ME IF WE WENT ON SUICIDE MISSIONS FOR THE GOVERNMENT.

BUT THE SQUAD HAS DISBANDED.

BELLE REVE WENT DARK WHEN THE CRIME SYNDICATE TOOK OVER. NO POINT IN GOING BACK THERE IF WE NO LONGER HAD TO.

SO NOW...I'M LEFT TO MY OWN MISSIONS.

MY MISSIONS ARE STILL *SUICIDE.*

I JUST HAVE TO WORK A LITTLE HARDER TO *MAKE* THEM THAT WAY.

DROPPED A MILE UP FROM A DRONE. THERE'S NOT ANOTHER LIVING BEING ON EARTH WHO CAN MAKE THIS SHOT.

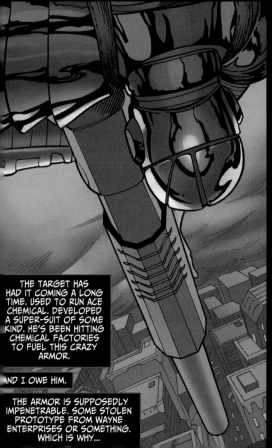

THE TARGET HAS HAD IT COMING A LONG TIME. USED TO RUN ACE CHEMICAL. DEVELOPED A SUPER-SUIT OF SOME KIND. HE'S BEEN HITTING CHEMICAL FACTORIES TO FUEL THIS CRAZY ARMOR.

...ND I OWE HIM.

THE ARMOR IS SUPPOSEDLY IMPENETRABLE. SOME STOLEN PROTOTYPE FROM WAYNE ENTERPRISES OR SOMETHING. WHICH IS WHY...

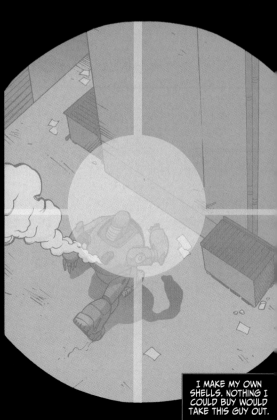

I MAKE MY OWN SHELLS. NOTHING I COULD BUY WOULD TAKE THIS GUY OUT.

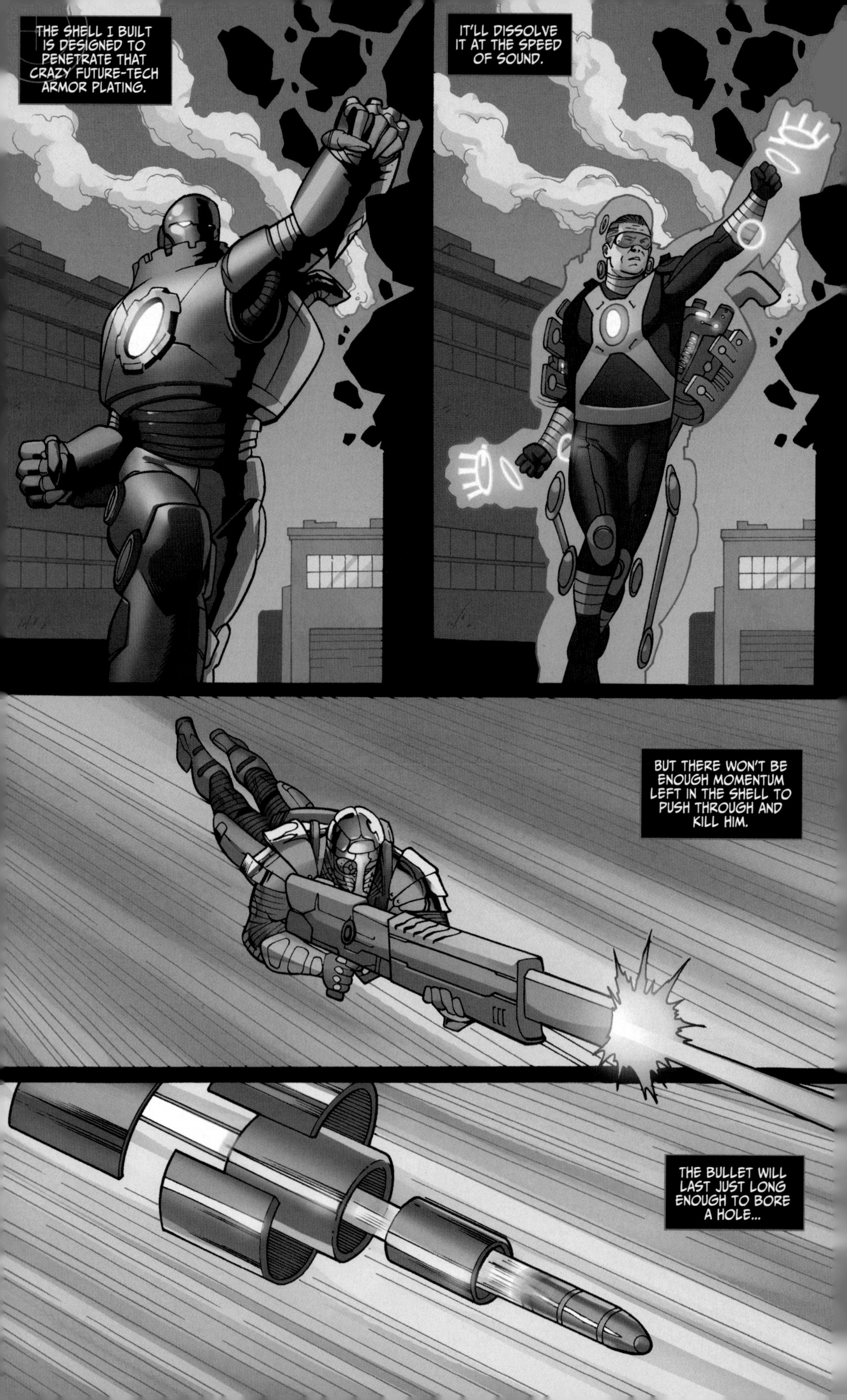
THE SHELL I BUILT IS DESIGNED TO PENETRATE THAT CRAZY FUTURE-TECH ARMOR PLATING.
IT'LL DISSOLVE IT AT THE SPEED OF SOUND.
BUT THERE WON'T BE ENOUGH MOMENTUM LEFT IN THE SHELL TO PUSH THROUGH AND KILL HIM.
THE BULLET WILL LAST JUST LONG ENOUGH TO BORE A HOLE...

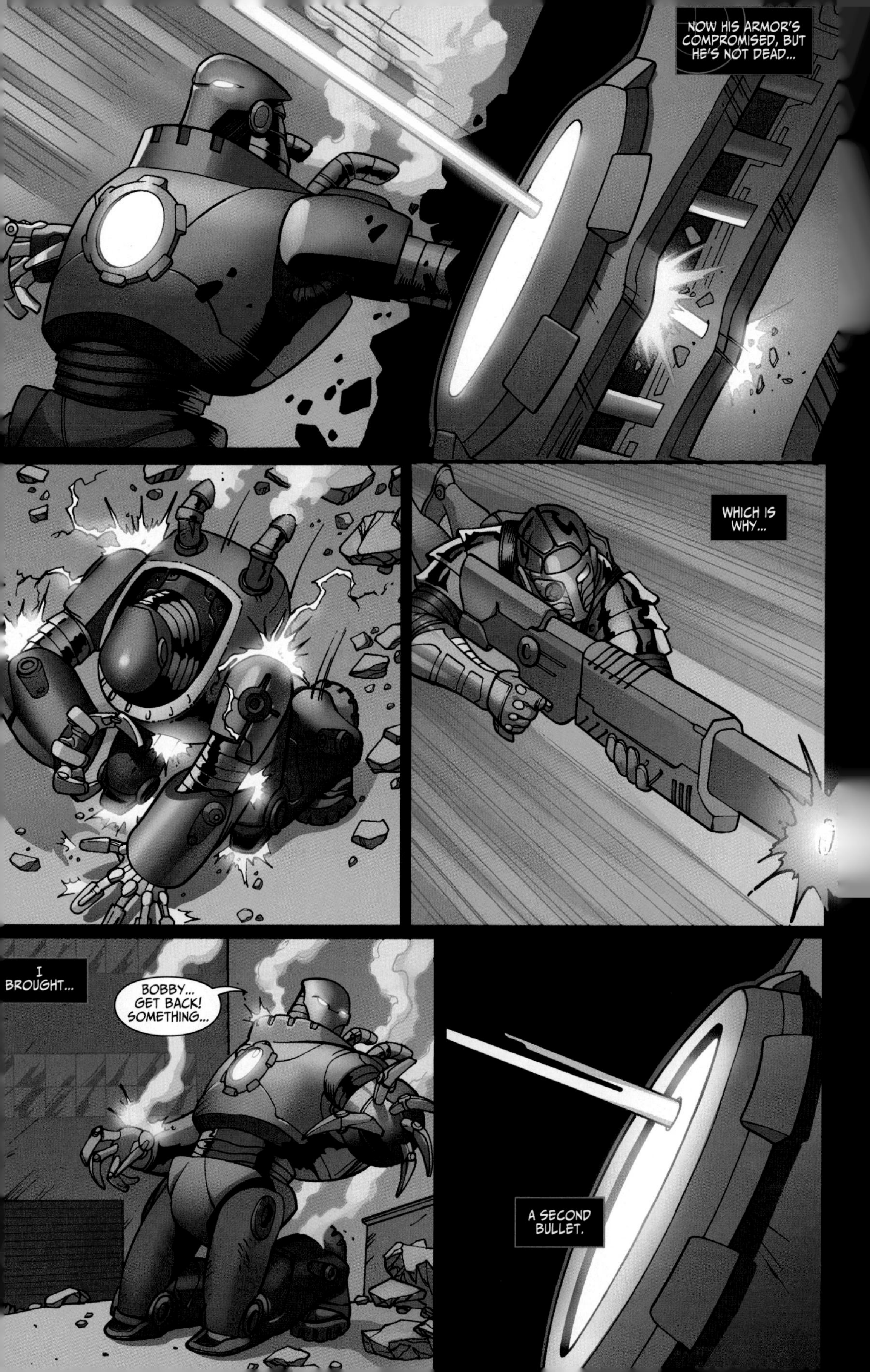
NOW HIS ARMOR'S COMPROMISED, BUT HE'S NOT DEAD...
WHICH IS WHY...
I BROUGHT...
BOBBY... GET BACK! SOMETHING...
A SECOND BULLET.

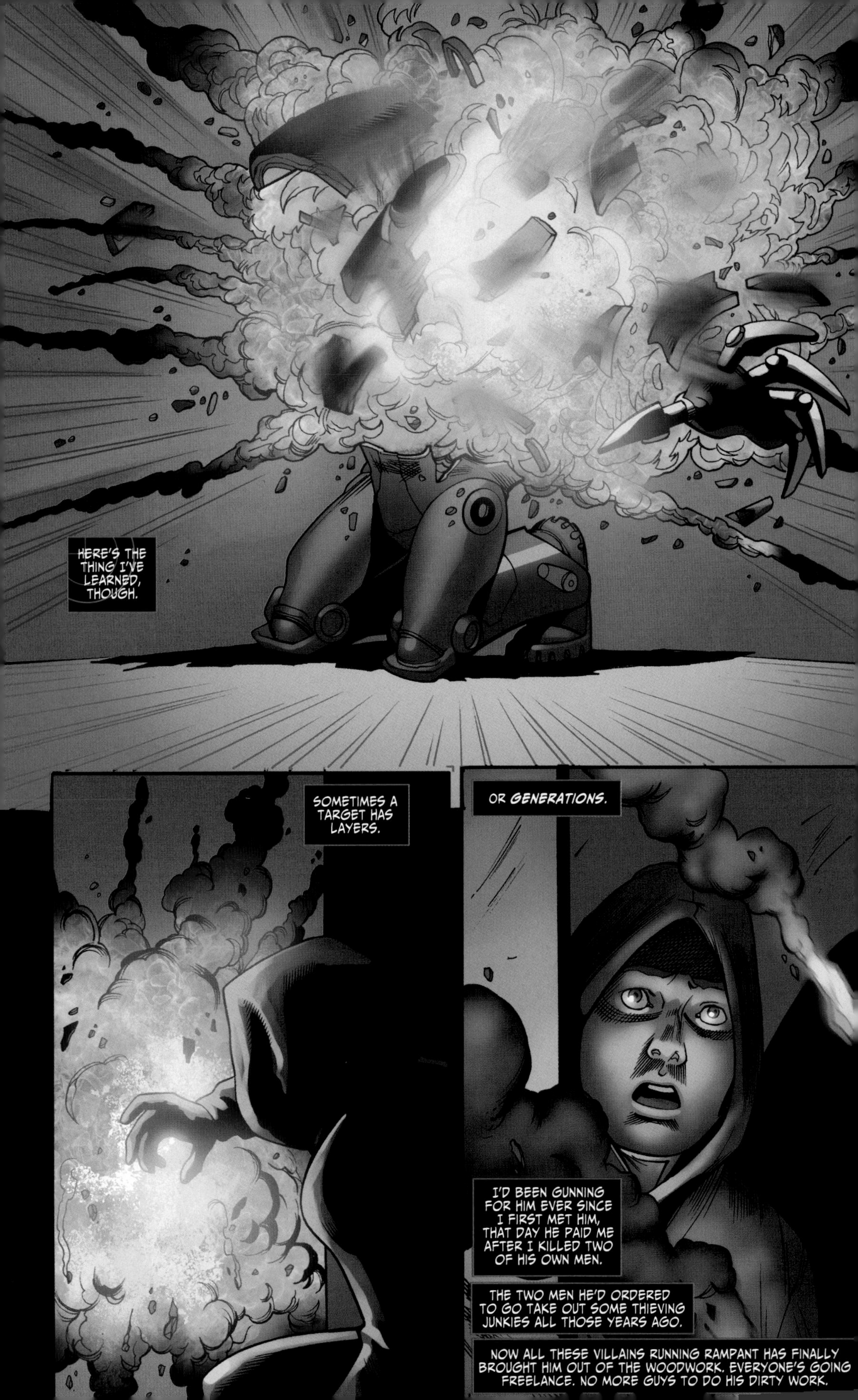
HERE'S THE THING I'VE LEARNED, THOUGH.
SOMETIMES A TARGET HAS LAYERS.
OR GENERATIONS.
I'D BEEN GUNNING FOR HIM EVER SINCE I FIRST MET HIM, THAT DAY HE PAID ME AFTER I KILLED TWO OF HIS OWN MEN.
THE TWO MEN HE'D ORDERED TO GO TAKE OUT SOME THIEVING JUNKIES ALL THOSE YEARS AGO.
NOW ALL THESE VILLAINS RUNNING RAMPANT HAS FINALLY BROUGHT HIM OUT OF THE WOODWORK. EVERYONE'S GOING FREELANCE. NO MORE GUYS TO DO HIS DIRTY WORK.

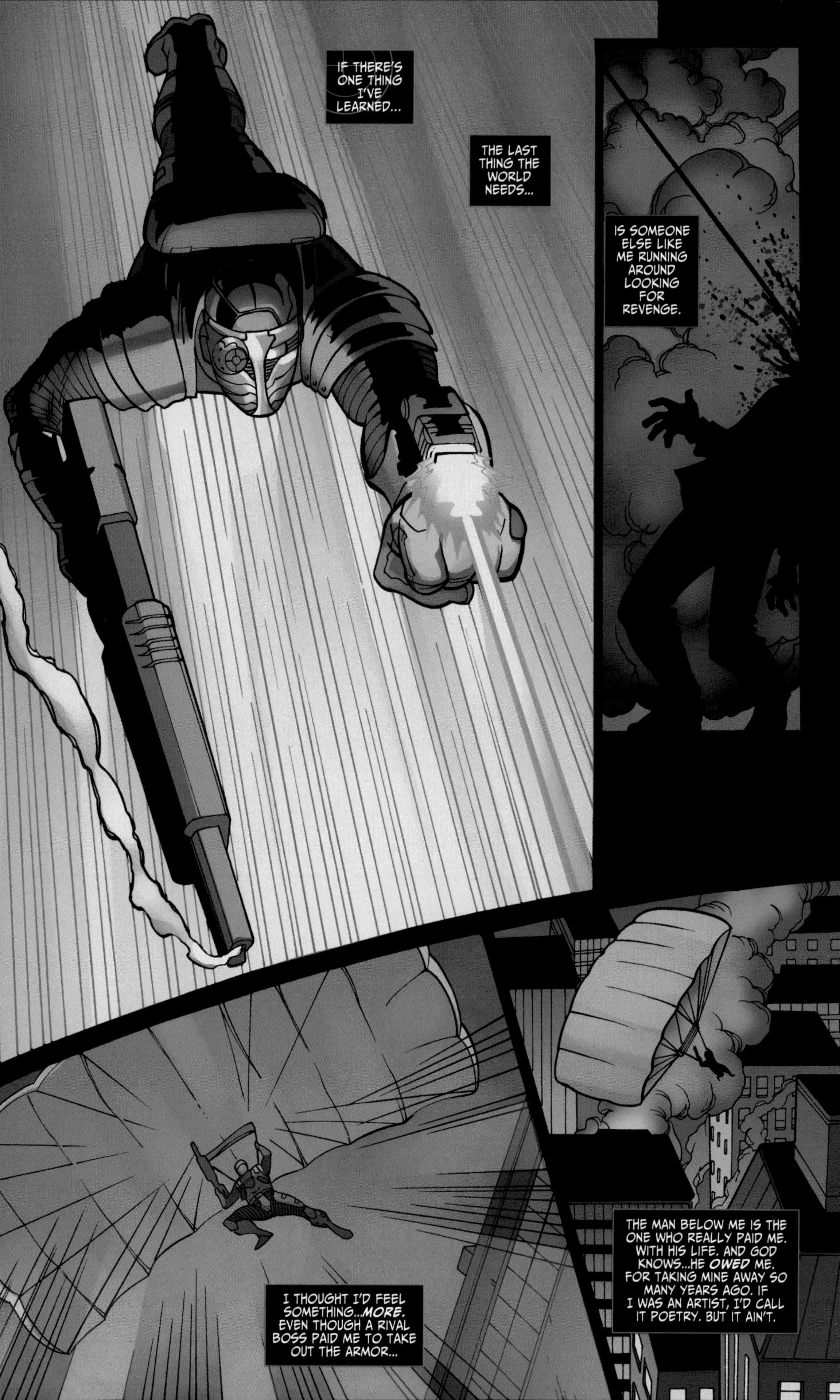
IF THERE'S ONE THING I'VE LEARNED...
THE LAST THING THE WORLD NEEDS...
IS SOMEONE ELSE LIKE ME RUNNING AROUND LOOKING FOR REVENGE.
I THOUGHT I'D FEEL SOMETHING...MORE. EVEN THOUGH A RIVAL BOSS PAID ME TO TAKE OUT THE ARMOR...
THE MAN BELOW ME IS THE ONE WHO REALLY PAID ME. WITH HIS LIFE. AND GOD KNOWS...HE OWED ME. FOR TAKING MINE AWAY SO MANY YEARS AGO. IF I WAS AN ARTIST, I'D CALL IT POETRY. BUT IT AIN'T.

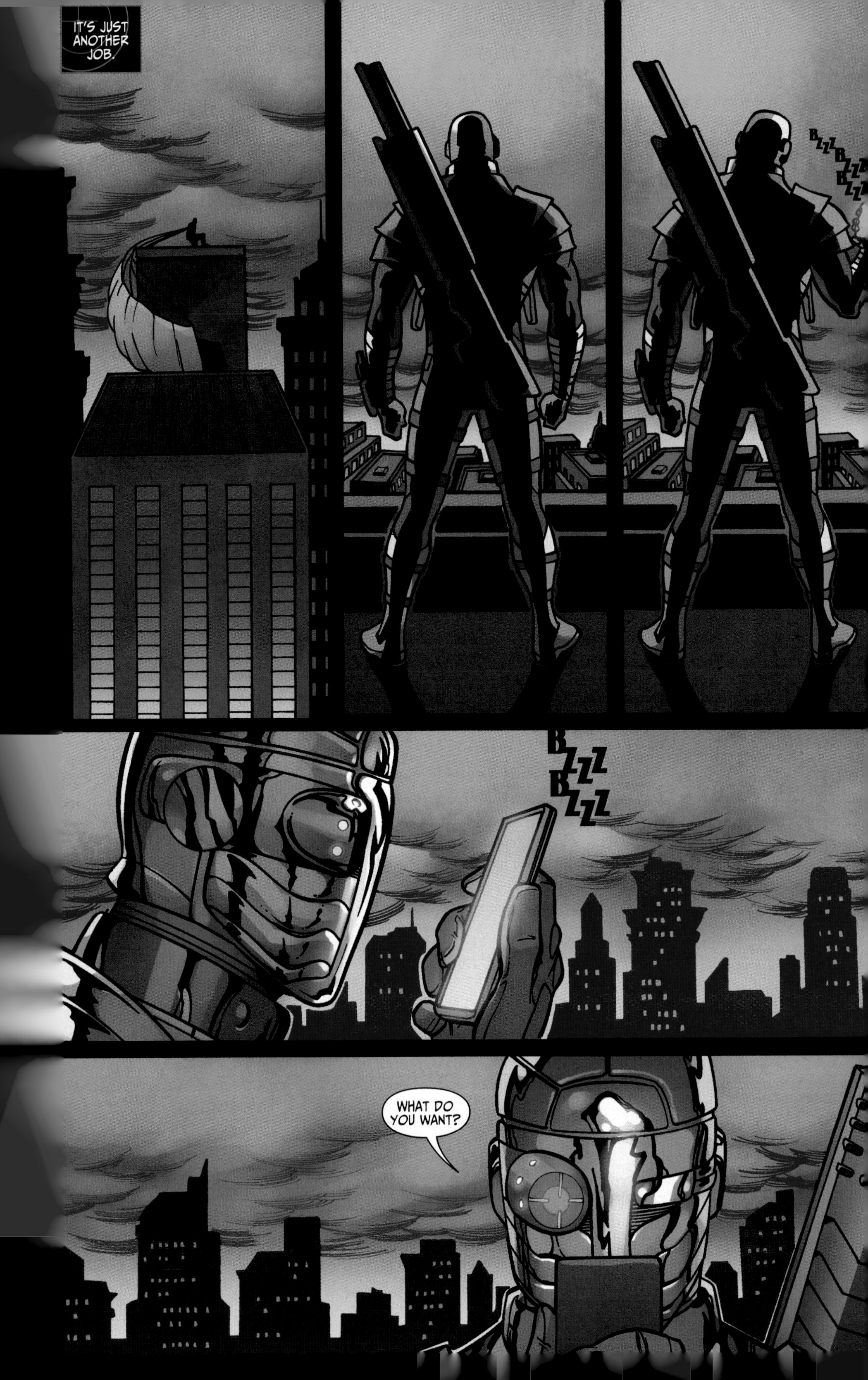
IT'S JUST ANOTHER JOB.
BZZZ BZZZ BZZZ
BZZZ BZZZ
WHAT DO YOU WANT?

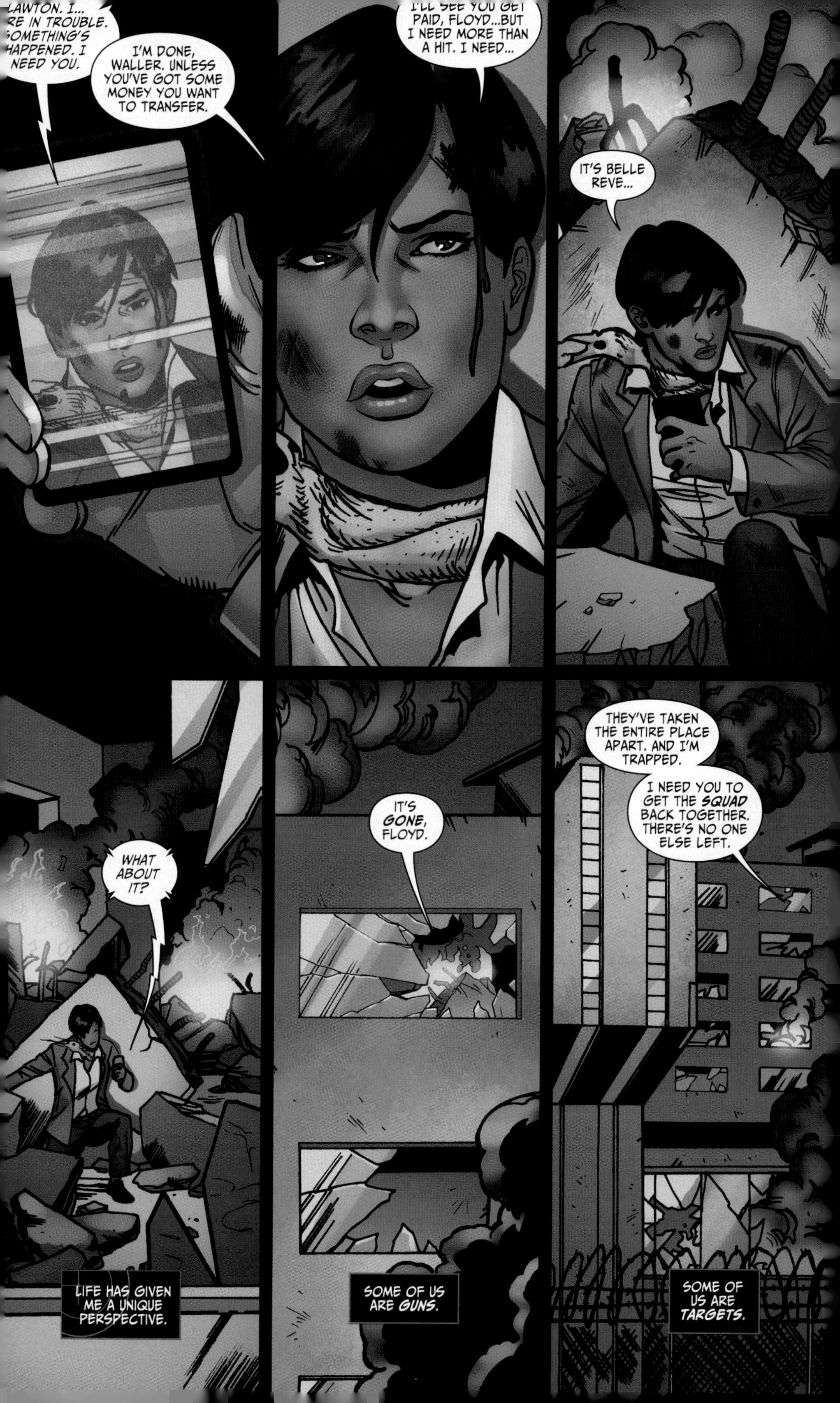
LAWTON. I... RE IN TROUBLE. SOMETHING'S HAPPENED. I NEED YOU.
I'M DONE, WALLER. UNLESS YOU'VE GOT SOME MONEY YOU WANT TO TRANSFER.
I'LL SEE YOU GET PAID, FLOYD...BUT I NEED MORE THAN A HIT. I NEED...
IT'S BELLE REVE...
WHAT ABOUT IT?
LIFE HAS GIVEN ME A UNIQUE PERSPECTIVE.
IT'S GONE, FLOYD.
SOME OF US ARE GUNS.
THEY'VE TAKEN THE ENTIRE PLACE APART. AND I'M TRAPPED.
I NEED YOU TO GET THE SQUAD BACK TOGETHER. THERE'S NO ONE ELSE LEFT.
SOME OF US ARE TARGETS.

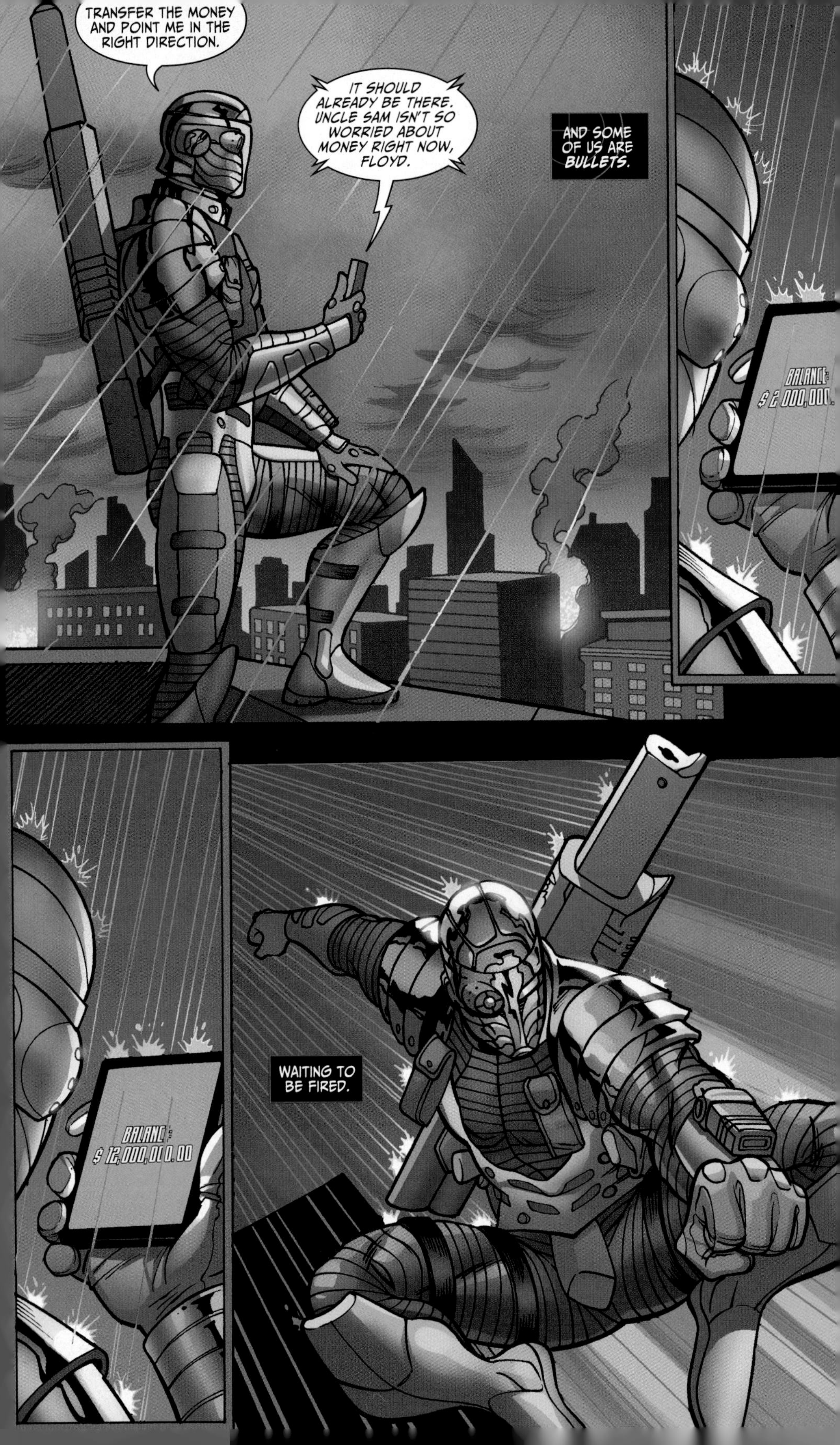
TRANSFER THE MONEY AND POINT ME IN THE RIGHT DIRECTION.
IT SHOULD ALREADY BE THERE. UNCLE SAM ISN'T SO WORRIED ABOUT MONEY RIGHT NOW, FLOYD.
AND SOME OF US ARE *BULLETS*.
BALANCE:
$ 2,000,000
BALANCE:
$ 12,000,000.00
WAITING TO BE FIRED.

SUICIDE SQUAD

STEEL DESIGNS BY PATRICK ZIRCHER

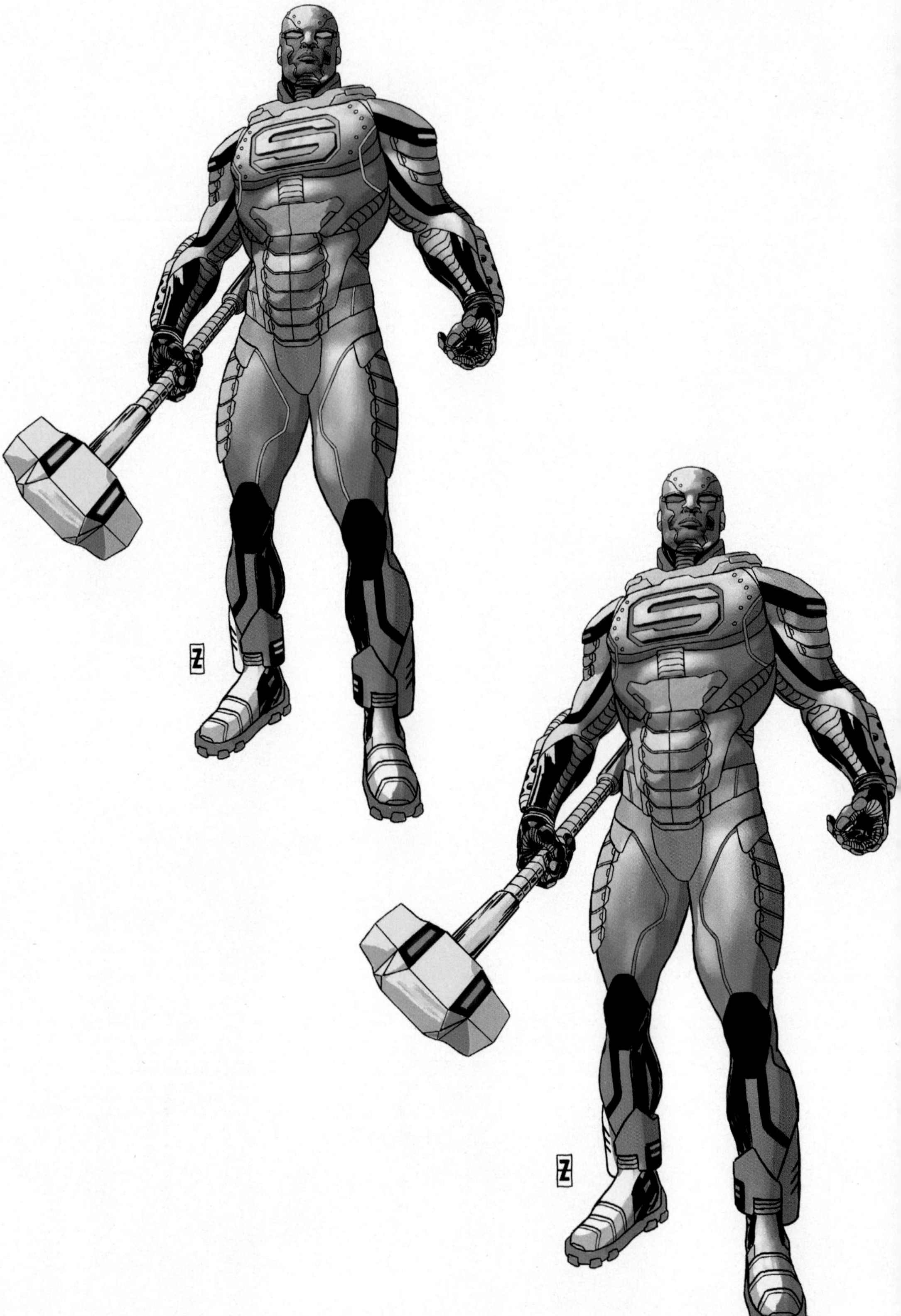

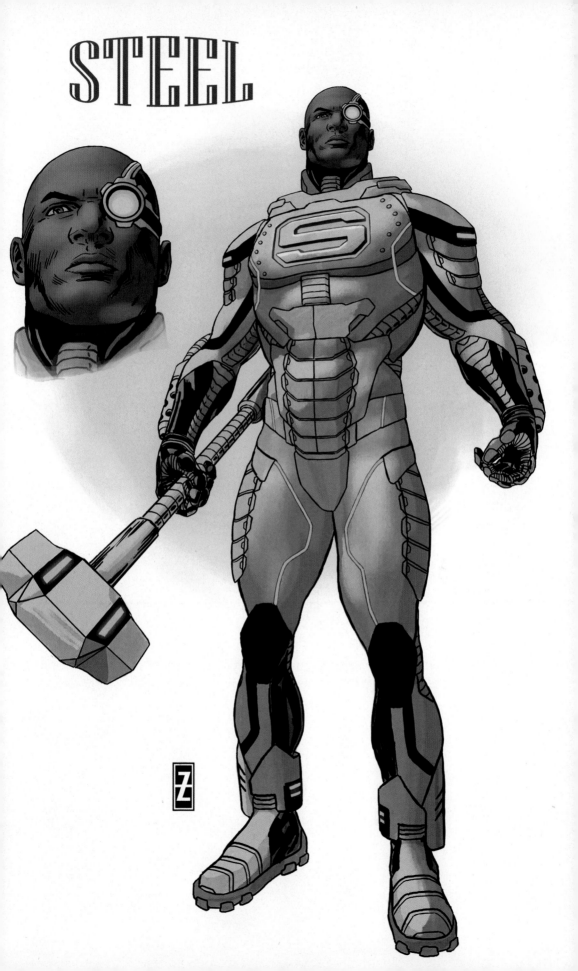

STEEL

START AT THE BEGINNING!
SUICIDE SQUAD
VOLUME 1: KICKED IN THE TEETH

DEATHSTROKE VOLUME 1: LEGACY

MEN OF WAR VOLUME 1: UNEASY COMPANY

HAWK & DOVE VOLUME 1: FIRST STRIKES

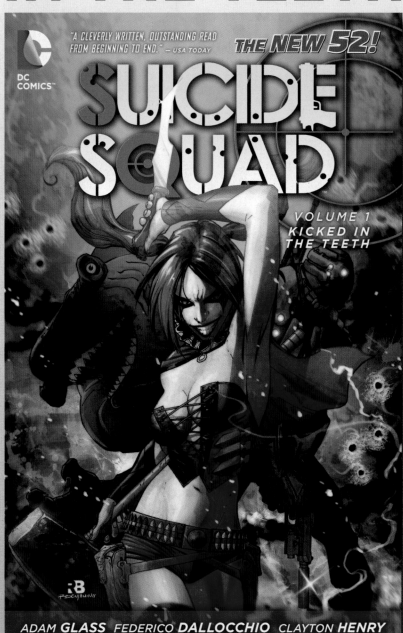

DC COMICS™

START AT THE BEGINNING

JUSTICE LEAGUE
VOLUME 1: ORIGIN

AQUAMAN
VOLUME 1:
THE TRENCH

THE SAVAGE
HAWKMAN VOLUME 1:
DARKNESS RISING

GREEN ARROW
VOLUME 1:
THE MIDAS TOUCH

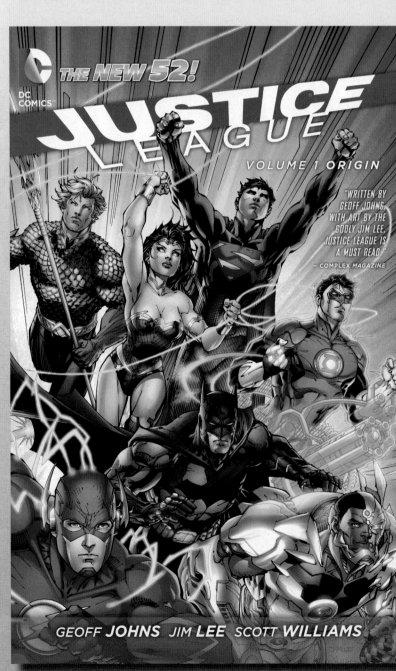

GEOFF JOHNS JIM LEE SCOTT WILLIAMS

"A stunning debut. This is definitely in the top rank of the revamp."
—THE ONION / AV CLUB

"Snyder and Capullo reach new heights of collaboration here, with Capullo making inspired storytelling choices that add additional layers to Snyder's narration and dialog."
—VANITY FAIR

START AT THE BEGINNING!

BATMAN VOLUME 1: THE COURT OF OWLS

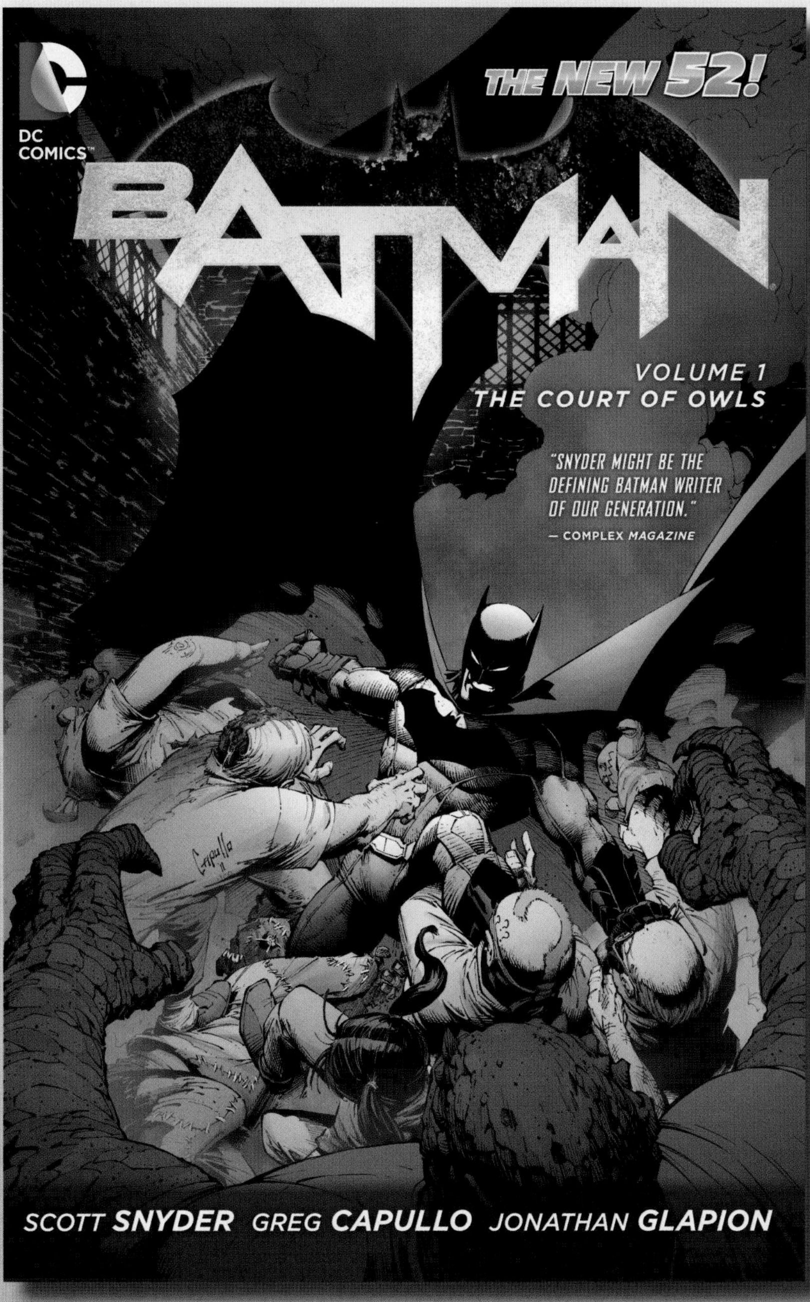
DC COMICS
THE NEW 52!
BATMAN
VOLUME 1
THE COURT OF OWLS
"SNYDER MIGHT BE THE DEFINING BATMAN WRITER OF OUR GENERATION."
— COMPLEX MAGAZINE
SCOTT SNYDER GREG CAPULLO JONATHAN GLAPION

BATMAN & ROBIN VOLUME 1: BORN TO KILL

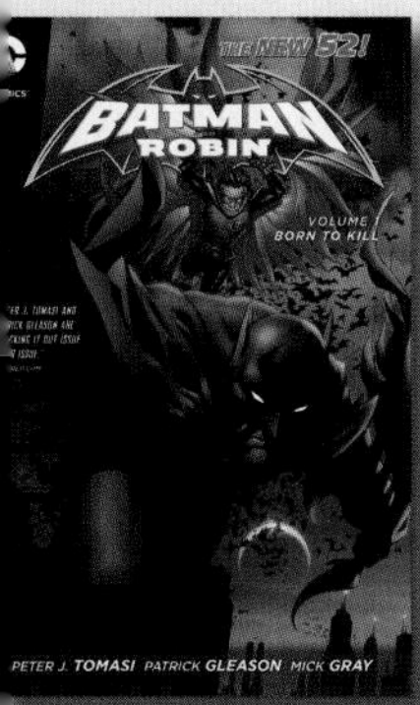
THE NEW 52!
BATMAN ROBIN
VOLUME 1
BORN TO KILL
PETER J. TOMASI PATRICK GLEASON MICK GRAY

BATMAN: DETECTIVE COMICS VOLUME 1: FACES OF DEATH

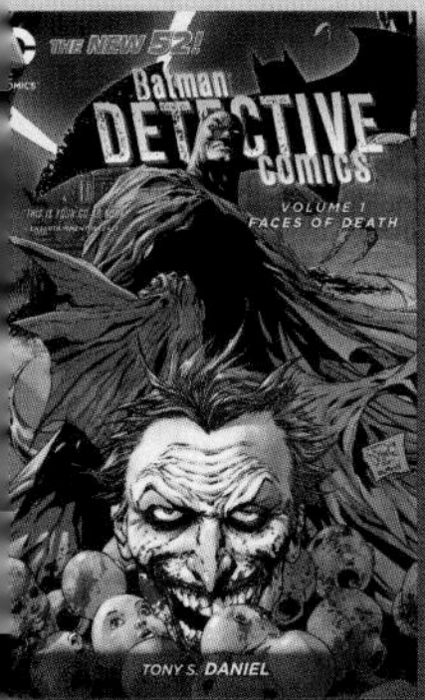
THE NEW 52!
Batman DETECTIVE Comics
VOLUME 1
FACES OF DEATH
TONY S. DANIEL

BATMAN: THE DARK KNIGHT VOLUME 1: KNIGHT TERRORS

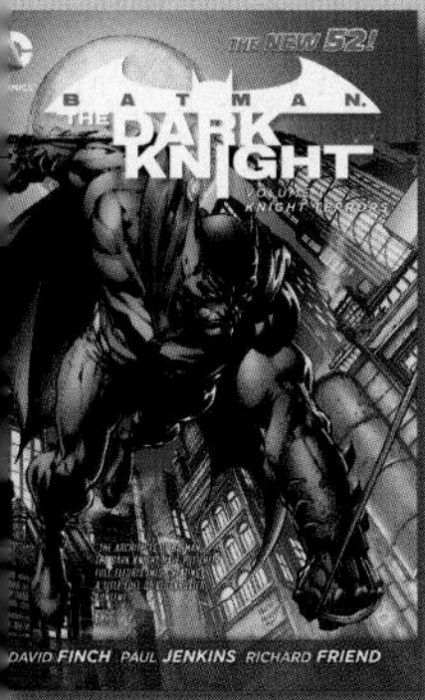
THE NEW 52!
BATMAN THE DARK KNIGHT
DAVID FINCH PAUL JENKINS RICHARD FRIEND

DC COMICS™

START AT THE BEGINNING

NIGHTWING VOLUME 1
TRAPS AND TRAPEZES

**CATWOMAN
VOLUME 1: THE GAME**

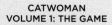

**BIRDS OF PREY
VOLUME 1: LOOKING
FOR TROUBLE**

**ALL-STAR WESTERN
VOLUME 1:
GUNS AND GOTHAM**

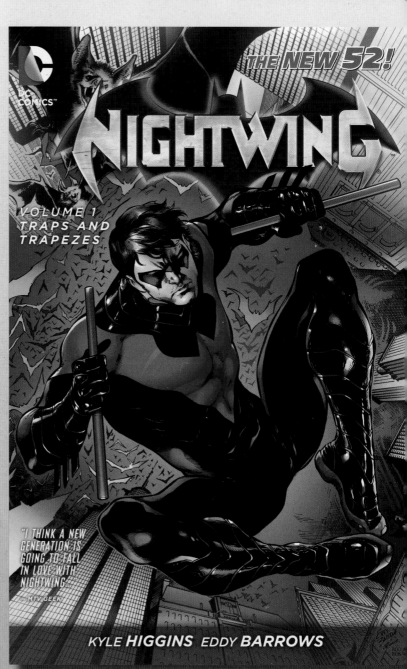